RUSHDEN & DIAMONDS

A Footballing History

Ian Addis
and
Mick Dean

DIAMETRIC PUBLICATIONS
1998

Rushden & Diamonds A Footballing History

Cover design by Robert Mercer.

ISBN 0 9533482 0 2

First published in 1998 by
Diametric Publications, 45 Grosvenor Road, Kettering, Northants NN15 6TF.

Printed & bound in the United Kingdom by Woolnough Bookbinding Ltd,
Irthlingborough, Northamptonshire NN9 5SE.

PREFACE

Rushden and Diamonds is much more than just another football club. The spectacular development at Nene Park bears testimony to chairman Max Griggs' belief, expressed shortly after the club's formation back in 1992, that the site should be *"a fun place for the benefit of the whole community"*.

However, while it is impossible to record the club's dramatic expansion without occasional reference to its off-field activities, this book is, as its title implies, essentially a footballing history concentrating on the achievements of the first team.

In charting the rapid progress of Rushden and Diamonds Football Club from its first competitive match in the Beazer Homes Midland Division in August 1992 to its final Vauxhall Conference game of the 1997-98 season we recount many of the key matches played, reflect upon the contribution made by management and players and provide a comprehensive statistical analysis of its achievements to date. All errors contained in this publication are the responsibility of the editors.

Rushden and Diamonds Football Club is already several years ahead of its ambitious schedule to bring League football to Nene Park and it is probable that the most exciting chapters are yet to be written. Whatever success the future may bring, however, it will have been made possible by the firm foundations laid in the first six years.

Ian Addis and Mick Dean
June 1998

ACKNOWLEDGEMENTS

We wish to record our thanks to everyone who has assisted in the production of this book notably Rushden and Diamonds Football Club, and in particular, Tony Jones, whose encouragement, support and loan of memorabilia were indispensable; Dave Joyce and Mark Stringer for their willingness to provide information; Ted Carroll who supplied many of the photographs and Mark Darnell for his active promotion of the project. Northamptonshire Evening Telegraph Sports Editor, Ian Davidson, reporters Steve Harrison and Derek Waugh, librarian Liz McBride and the Evening Telegraph photographic department for the use of archive material; Paul Redding and Peter Barnes, who kindly permitted the use of photographs and Robert Mercer for his imaginative cover design.

NOTES ON STATISTICS

Statistics quoted in the text refer, unless otherwise stated, to Rushden & Diamonds competitive first team games.

Matches in the following competitions are included:

Beazer Homes League. The Southern League, sponsored by Beazer Homes during Rushden & Diamonds' time in the league. From August 1996 it has been known as the Dr Martens League.

Vauxhall Conference. Founded as the Alliance Premier League in 1979, this league was sponsored by Vauxhall Motors until May 1998.

FA Cup. The Football Association Challenge Cup sponsored by Littlewoods.

FA Trophy. The Umbro Football Association Challenge Trophy. This competition is restricted to clubs playing in the Vauxhall Conference, the Isthmian, Northern Premier and Southern Leagues.

FA Vase. The Football Association Challenge Vase. This competition is for clubs playing in the leagues which feed the Isthmian, Northern Premier and Southern Leagues.

Southern League Cup. This competition is mandatory for all members of the Southern League. It was sponsored in 1992-93 by Barclays Commercial Services and since then by Dr Martens.

Spalding Challenge Cup. This competition is mandatory for all members of the Conference. The sponsor during Rushden & Diamonds' time in the Conference has been Spalding.

Hillier Senior Challenge Cup. This competition is restricted to senior clubs affiliated to the Northamptonshire Football Association.

In the statistical tables these competitions are grouped thus:

L League matches in the Beazer Homes League and/or the Vauxhall Conference.

C The FA Cup

T or ***V*** The FA Trophy and/or the FA Vase.

LC The Southern League Cup and/or the Spalding Cup.

CC The county cup, i.e. the NFA Hillier Senior Cup.

Additionally Rushden & Diamonds have competed in two other matches which are considered as first team competitive matches. The Maunsell Cup is an annual fixture played between the winners of the Hillier Senior Cup and either Northampton Town and Peterborough United. Statistics for this match are included under CC. The Southern League Championship Match is an annual match played, usually, between the league champions and the league cup winners. Statistics for this match are included under LC.

Not included in the statistics are all other matches including friendlies and charity competitions such as the Daventry Charity Cup.

Also omitted from the summaries are matches abandoned before completion and required to be replayed and matches subsequently deemed to be invalid for legal reasons, i.e. a Dr Martens Cup tie in 1995-96..

Appearances are analysed into starting and substitute appearances. Substitutes are only included in the statistics if they actually participate in the game.

During the existence of Rushden & Diamonds substitutes have been permitted as follows:

1992-93 In all matches two substitutes were allowed.

1993-94 Two substitutes were allowed in all matches except that in the FA Cup a third substitute could be named. One of the substitutes could only participate as a goalkeeper.

1994-95 The FA Cup ruling now applied to all games, i.e. three substitutes, one of whom was a goalkeeper.

1995-96 Three substitutes were allowed in all games. All three could be outfield players.

There has been no subsequent change in the legislation regarding substitutes.

Where times are quoted it should be appreciated that they are approximate.

A word of explanation about the system of promotion and relegation through the leagues may be useful, particularly as changes in sponsorship causes the names of leagues to change frequently.

The Football League (Nationwide League, Endsleigh League, Barclays League) exchanges one club with the Vauxhall Conference. The Conference relegates three and accepts one from each of the Southern (Dr Martens, Beazer Homes), Northern Premier (Unibond, HFS Loans, Multipart) and Isthmian (Ryman, ICIS, Diadora) Leagues. Clubs can move between these three leagues in agreed circumstances if the clubs relegated from the Conference cause an imbalance.

The Southern, Northern Premier and Isthmian Leagues all operate a Premier Division and a number of other divisions. Promotion to these three leagues is from "feeder" leagues. In the case of the Southern these leagues are the Midland Alliance, the United Counties (Uhlsport), the Eastern Counties (Jewson), the Hellenic (Complete Music), the Kent (Winstonlead), the Sussex County (Unijet), the Wessex (Jewson), and the Western (Screwfix Direct).

These leagues have promotion and relegation arrangements with local leagues. Promotions are usually conditional upon facilities. Often clubs are not promoted because their ground (or their finances) are not up to scratch. They can even be relegated if standards fall below those required. Which is where the story begins.

It's early season 93-94 and looking delighted with the new facilities in the north eastern corner of Nene Park is Audrey Lake. In the background is the eastern end of the ground. The small terrace and the row of poplars have now been replaced with the Airwair Stand. Just about discernible on the terrace is the portakabin which briefly housed Bernard Lake's souvenir shop. It was relocated to this area of the ground, having been situated for the first season in a glorified garden shed at the south western corner of Nene Park.

At one time serving the teas was one of the few contributions women were allowed to make to the running of the football club. Times have changed. Within the organisation at Nene Park a number of senior roles have been occupied by women. Most prominent on the football side have been the former Commercial Sales Manager Jenny Limmage and the current Business Development Manager Sheenagh Murphy.

Audrey Lake became responsible for the management of all the catering within the ground on match days. Meanwhile Bernard (right) *has an increasingly large retail arm to manage.*

INTRODUCTION

"'On either side the river lie"

Tennyson

Rushden & Diamonds Football Club was created at the end of the 1991-92 season following a merger between Rushden Town and Irthlingborough Diamonds, two clubs each with its own proud history and tradition.

Rushden Town Football Club was founded in 1889 and competed in the Midland and Northants Leagues before joining the United Counties League in 1901. Apart from a short period from 1956-61, during which the side competed in the Central Alliance, the Russians remained in the UCL until 1983, winning the Championship on ten occasions. It was a bold decision to step up into the Southern League Midland Division and for a time it appeared that the club had over-reached itself, but seven years later it gained promotion to the Southern League Premier Division. However, after finishing in fourteenth place in its first season Rushden was demoted to the Midland Division as the outdated Hayden Road ground failed to meet the required standard for the Premier Division.

Irthlingborough Diamonds Football Club was formed in 1946 and began playing competitive youth football the following year. After a lengthy association with the Rushden & District Youth and Senior Leagues, the club moved into the Kettering Amateur League in 1960 before joining the United Counties League four years later. In 1967 the Diamonds won the Division Two title and were promoted into the top section where they remained until 1992. The Championship was won on four occasions - the last of these being in 1982-83 - and foremost among other notable achievements were exciting FA Vase runs which took the club to the semi-finals in 1980-81 and 1983-84.

In 1991-92 both clubs faced an uncertain future and following lengthy discussions with local businessman Mr Max Griggs regarding possible sponsorship, a merger was agreed. Rushden & Diamonds F.C. was formed with Max Griggs as chairman and representatives from the two original clubs in senior managerial positions.

Continuity was maintained with the appointment of Roger Ashby as the new club's manager. Ashby had formerly enjoyed considerable success with Irthlingborough Diamonds and was the manager at Rushden Town prior to the amalgamation. Kenny Mist, reserve team manager at Rushden, took up similar duties with Rushden & Diamonds and coach Billy Jeffrey also came from Hayden Road.

The founding fathers pictured outside the Irthlingborough Diamonds clubhouse in April 1992. From left, Tony Jones, Max Griggs, Neil Gant and Roger Ashby.

SEASON ONE

1992 - 93

" that is young in years may be old in hours"

Francis Bacon

Back (l to r): Nigel Gore, Wayne Bellamy, Andy Kirkup, Adie Mann, Paul York, Glen Beech, Paul Brackwell, Adrian Felton.
Middle (l to r): Kenny Mist, Ollie Kearns, Mark Bushell, Darrell Page, Darren Watts, Kevin Fox, Peter Green, Mark Jameson, John Flower, Billy Jeffrey.
Front (l to r): Mick Garrett, Junior Wilson, Russell Lewis, Roger Ashby, Steve Heard, Frankie Belfon, Andy Peaks

Only relatively minor changes were necessary to make Nene Park - arguably the best facilities in the United Counties League - suitable for Beazer Homes League (as the Southern League was then called) football. In August 1992 east Northamptonshire's new club kicked off in the Midland Division in which Rushden Town had finished 8th in the previous season.

There were three changes in the composition of the Division. Champions Solihull Borough and runners-up Hednesford Town were promoted to the Premier Division and bottom-but-one Alvechurch left the League. With only three clubs deemed suitable for promotion to the League and with Hythe Town (who had beaten Rushden Town in the 1990 Vase Quarter Final) resigning from the Southern Division, the bottom Midland club, Dudley Town, was reprieved. The four clubs relegated from the Premier Division (Fisher Athletic, Gravesend & Northfleet, Poole Town and Wealdstone) all went into the Southern Division. All three new clubs came into the Midland Division.

When looking for promotion hopefuls for the 92-93 season, those three new clubs would all have to be considered contenders, having arrived in the Beazer Homes as Champions of their former leagues. Gresley Rovers stepped up from the West Midlands League. It was their second successive title - in 1991 they had been denied promotion because their ground was unsuitable. They had a formidable record: they had finished in the top four for seven consecutive seasons and had been to Wembley for the 1991 FA Vase Final. There they had come back from a 3-0 deficit to lead 4-3 with two minutes of extra time left when Guiseley snatched an equaliser. Gresley lost the replay 3-1 at Sheffield United. The other newcomers were Weston-super-Mare from the relatively strong Western League and Evesham United from the Midland Combination.

Amongst the other promotion favourites would undoubtedly be the two best supported clubs, Nuneaton Borough (6th in 91-92) and their neighbours, Tamworth (7th) and possibly another near neighbour, Bedworth United (5th). Third placed Sutton Coldfield were not expected to perform quite so well, but the clubs that attracted most national attention were the Welsh clubs, Barry Town (4th in 91-92) and Newport AFC (10th).

The Football Association of Wales was determined to set up its own national league and attempted to cajole or coerce the Welsh clubs competing in English leagues to leave those leagues. Newport, in particular, were determined not to comply. They had been founded in 1989 to replace Newport County with only one aim - to regain a place for the town in the Football League. That would be impossible if they joined the League of Wales. They began a long, and eventually successful, legal fight against the Welsh FA. In the meantime, though, they were not allowed to play in Wales and negotiated a tenancy at Gloucester City's Meadow Park, forty-five miles away from home. Barry Town moved in at Worcester City's St. George's Lane ground, ninety-five miles distant. To *"emphasise their Welshness"* the club adopted the Welsh spelling of the town, Barri.

Rushden Town had ended the 1991-92 season by winning the South Midlands Floodlight Cup, defeating Leighton Town 4-2 after extra time at Hayden Road on May 12th.

The side that evening was: Darren Watts, Andy Peaks, Junior Wilson, Colin Waite, Darrell Page, Steven Heard, Andy Kirkup, Mick Garrett, Peter Green (sub Barrington Leslie 87), Frankie Belfon, Paul York. Subs not used: Mark Jameson and Billy Jeffrey.

The side that represented Irthlingborough Diamonds in their final game, a 2-2 draw with Eynesbury Rovers at Nene Park, was: Paul Myers, Paul Redding, Simon Munns, John Sellers, Stuart Abrahart, Kevin Payne, Simon Kibler, Matt Thompson, Shaun Wills, Ben Lord, Steve Downing. Subs used: Chris Munns, Paul Smith (both substitutes were sons of former Rushden Town players). Abrahart got the opening Diamonds goal and it fell to Isham man Shaun Wills to score the last Irthlingborough Diamonds goal. The last men to score against Irthlingborough were Billy Horn, once a Doughboy, and Neil Pope who subsequently played in the Conference for Kettering Town.

THE INAUGURAL BOARD OF DIRECTORS
From left: RW Langley, M Darnell, N Gant, WM Griggs, AC Jones, C Smith, S Griggs

Manager Roger Ashby had greatly strengthened his squad during the summer and although injuries incurred in pre-season friendlies restricted his choice, several of his new signings appeared in the club's inaugural Beazer Homes Midland Division fixture against Bilston Town at re-vamped Nene Park on Saturday August 22nd 1992.

Even so, the line-up on that afternoon was largely that which had represented Rushden Town in its farewell game back in May. Indeed of the Rushden side which had defeated Leighton Town, all joined the new club and all but Mick Garrett and Billy Jeffrey appeared in first team games for Rushden & Diamonds. In contrast none of the Irthlingborough Diamonds players who appeared in that club's final match made a first team appearance for the new club.

Goalkeeper Kevin Shoemake, a late signing from Redbridge Forest, necessary because of Kevin Fox's long-term injury, was joined by fellow newcomers centre-half John Flower, who had begun his career at Corby Town before moving into League football with Sheffield United and the ill-fated Aldershot, former Northampton Spencer pair Mark Bushell and a rehabilitated Adie Mann, and veteran striker Ollie Kearns. Thirty-six years old Kearns, a close season signing from Worcester City, had scored 11 Beazer Homes Premier Division goals during a brief spell at Hayden Road towards the end of the abortive 1990-91 campaign. Disappointingly, Russell Lewis, the former Northampton and Kettering central defender, did not make a competitive appearance for the club.

Rushden & Diamonds (0) 2		**Bilston Town (0) 2**	
1	Kevin Shoemake	1	Kevan Williams
2	Mark Bushell	2	Steve Frisby
3	Junior Wilson	3	Kenny Mower
4	John Flower	4	Mike Hart
5	Darrell Page	5	Mark Bowater
6	Steve Heard	6	Jim Skidmore
7	Dave Johnson	7	Andy Chappell
8	Adie Mann	8	Gary Jones
9	Ollie Kearns	9	Michael Gayle
10	Frankie Belfon	10	John Baker
11	Paul York	11	Howard Revan
12	Peter Green	12	Danny Williams
14	Mark Jameson	14	Mark Stanton

Referee: B Curson (Leicester)

Goals: Kearns (53, **1-0**); Baker (63, **1-1**); Belfon (80, **2-1**); Gayle (90, **2-2**)
Booked: Wilson

It is a measure of the interest generated in the new club that the opening league fixture attracted a crowd of 315 (Bilston's visit to Rushden the previous season had enticed 155 spectators through the Hayden Road turnstile), though outside east Northamptonshire the birth of the new club passed almost unremarked. A Wolverhampton newspaper merely stated, "*Bilston travel to Willingboro on Saturday for their first BML game against Rushden & Diamond.*"

The game itself proved a huge disappointment, the first half being utterly devoid of interest with neither side managing a single shot on target. There was some improvement eight minutes into the second period when Ollie Kearns *(left, in action in this game)* neatly converted Frankie Belfon's cross to achieve the distinction of scoring the club's first goal. Bilston levelled ten minutes later through John Baker. Belfon restored the lead, but the Diamonds were denied a morale boosting victory when the visitors snatched a last minute equaliser through Michael Gayle.

Bilston could probably be fairly described as a typical Midland Division side. Their best known player was the former Walsall full back Ken Mower. John Baker, the first man to score against Rushden & Diamonds, began as an apprentice at Oxford United before moving into the Southern League with Banbury and Redditch. Neither Diamonds substitute was used but Danny Williams became the first substitute used in an R&D game when he replaced Andy Chappell in the 61st minute. Junior Wilson was the first to be shown a yellow card.

Mark Jameson replaced Steve Heard for the next match, away at Redditch United. The game followed an identical pattern to its predecessor, the Diamonds twice leading before conceding a goal in the ninetieth minute to surrender two points.

Conscious of his side's attacking shortcomings, Roger Ashby beat off competition from Boston United and Dagenham & Redbridge to sign former Cobbler, Glenville Donegal from the defunct Maidstone United, but he was ineligible for the Diamonds first FA Cup tie, a preliminary round game against Desborough Town.

Frankie Belfon attacks the Desborough goal.

The Diamonds progressed into the next round but it was something of a struggle. Despite going behind to a Frankie Belfon goal after thirty minutes, the United Counties League side put up stern resistance. The arrival of Glen Beech, who replaced Mark Jameson after sixty-five minutes, brought a marked improvement. The former Kettering Town and Boston United playmaker, signed from Stamford during the close season, had missed the opening games through injury but quickly established his authority in midfield sparking the home attack into life. It was from his deflected shot that Adie Mann scored an 86th minute goal to make the game safe.

Donegal made his debut in the August Bank holiday fixture at Grantham but the Diamonds had to rely upon an own goal, cancelling out Grantham's seventeenth minute opener (scored by Dale Watkins), to earn a third successive league draw.

The first Beazer Homes victory was secured on the following Saturday when visitors Bridgnorth Town were defeated 2-1. Frankie Belfon and Glenville Donegal scored the Diamonds goals, but the side's unimpressive start was reflected in the size of the crowd - down to 215, exactly 100 fewer than witnessed the opening game a fortnight earlier. Bridgnorth were hardly overawed by the occasion, the attendance figure being exactly the same as their previous home match.

A goalless draw at Hinckley Town extended the unbeaten run to six games but Diamonds dropped to 13th in the table, six points behind the leaders Newport. Second and third were Gresley and Nuneaton. The unbeaten record was almost shattered in the next game when lowly Long Buckby came close to ending the Diamonds' first FA Cup campaign. Only a goal line clearance by Mark Bushell prevented the United Counties League side taking an early lead. However, the Diamonds were spared a half time tongue-lashing by manager Ashby when Glenville Donegal crashed home Dave Johnson's cross via the underside of the bar in injury time. The second half proved goalless and the Diamonds were through. The meagre crowd at Station Road that afternoon, 105, remains the lowest attendance for a Rushden & Diamonds first team game.

The trip to Weston-super-Mare was the first to feature an overnight stop. It also saw Colin Waite make his debut in a splendid team performance, Dave Johnson adding to an earlier own goal to secure a 2-0 victory.

Mark Bushell

There was no such joy in the next match, the FA Cup Second Qualifying Round against Hednesford Town. The Beazer Premier Division club, who included Brendan Hackett in their side, won 4-1, Adie Mann netting the consolation goal. Locally the Diamonds' exit was overshadowed by neighbours Raunds Town's victory at Northwich Victoria of the Vauxhall Conference.

Hednesford went on to beat Shepshed but lost at home in the 4th Qualifying Round to a Dagenham & Redbridge side whose line-up contained Garry Butterworth and Mickey Nuttell. Not only did this match provide links to the future but there was also a reminder of Irthlingborough's past. At right back for Hednesford was Richus White who had, eleven years previously, played for Willenhall Town when the old Diamonds lost in the FA Vase semi-final.

John Coe and Andy Kirkup had made their debuts at Hednesford and both appeared in the next fixture, the first FA Vase game. Anstey Nomads of the Leicestershire Senior League provided the opposition. Leading 3-0 after 78 minutes, victory seemed assured for the Diamonds, but after slack marking had gifted the visitors an opener and Paul York headed into his own goal, only desperate defending prevented the under-dogs from snatching an unlikely draw.

Just three days later roles were reversed as the Diamonds faced Atherstone United of the Beazer Premier Division in their first Southern League Cup tie, the competition being sponsored that season by Barclays Commercial Services. The

Adders were defeated 4-0, with goals by Donegal (2), Kirkup and Kearns to provide Rushden & Diamonds with their first victory over higher grade opposition. An Ollie Kearns double in the next game at Bridgnorth earned a 2-2 draw, extending the unbeaten league run to seven matches. Kearns might have had two more in the 5-0 NFA Hillier Senior Cup victory over Brackley Town (who managed the magnificent total of three points in the United Counties League that season), but spurned the opportunity to add to his early goal by failing to convert the first penalty awarded to the club.

Junior Wilson

The first defeat of the season finally occurred on Saturday October 17th when a spectacular strike by Yate Town winger, Richard Smith, proved the only goal of a dull encounter. The result pushed the Diamonds down to fifteenth place prompting Evening Telegraph correspondent, Neil Stacey, to enquire, *"Where do Rushden & Diamonds go from here?"*

The answer was, "*to Premier Division Atherstone for the second leg of their League Cup tie.*" Goals from Kearns, Flower and Donegal achieved a 3-2 score-line, extending the aggregate lead to 7-2.

Fans of bottom markers Forest Green Rovers were decidedly unimpressed by this famous victory and only 109, the lowest attendance ever recorded for a Rushden & Diamonds league match (though nowhere near the lowest recorded (62) at Forest Green that season), saw the Diamonds triumph 4-1, Ollie Kearns netting another double. How many of the 109 (or indeed the 62) would have wagered a fiver that Forest Green would be promoted to the Conference before the turn of the century?

The week's double success heralded something of a false dawn as the side struggled to a goalless draw at home to Redditch in the next game before Halesowen Harriers earned a replay in their FA Vase First Round tie at Nene Park, drawing 3-3. Darrell Page has good reason to recall this encounter against Halesowen's lesser known club as he achieved the dubious distinction of being the first Rushden & Diamonds player to be sent off. Andy Peaks has better reason to remember the replay as his opening goal in the 2-0 victory was the first and only goal he scored for Rushden & Diamonds.

Kevin Shoemake

November brought the first away defeat, 0-2 at Sutton Coldfield Town, but there was further progress in the League Cup at the expense of one of Irthlingborough's old rivals, Buckingham Town. Adie Mann hit the club's first hat-trick in the 6-2 win, and then title contenders Barri were held to a 1-1 draw at Nene Park. Barrington Leslie, making his league debut, scored the Diamonds goal on a grey afternoon that saw Kevin Shoemake dismissed for handling outside the penalty area, striker Glenville Donegal proving an able replacement between the sticks. Leslie might well have been performing in a sunnier clime had he accepted an offer from top Maltese side Rabat Ajax after impressing during Rushden Town's tour of the island back in May.

Victory over Grantham Town elevated the Diamonds to ninth place but local interest had waned since the heady days of August and only 201 spectators, the lowest ever home league attendance, watched the 4-1 success. Grantham's goal, a 31st minute effort which put them briefly back in contention at 1-2 was the first Nene Park goal scored by Dale Watkins.

Honours were even in the FA Vase Second Round meeting with Gresley Rovers, the first of five during the season, but the replay was lost 1-3. The attendance at the Moat Ground was 717, the biggest crowd that had watched the club so far. Rovers progressed to the semi-final stage of the competition before losing to the eventual winners, Bridlington Town.

A last minute penalty enabled Andy Kirkup to register the first League hat-trick as second placed Evesham United were given a five goal drubbing. Goalkeeper Darren Watts replaced the suspended Shoemake for his Rushden & Diamonds debut but it would be nearly five years before he made his second appearance. His opposite number, Chris Taylor, was destined to make future appearances at Nene Park for Vauxhall Conference sides, Bromsgrove Rovers and Kettering Town (and perhaps Stevenage Borough). Successive victories over Dudley Town and Newport AFC preceded an intriguing third meeting with leaders Gresley Rovers. It proved a sad Saturday as Dave Johnson received marching orders after 48 minutes, Adie Mann followed eight minutes later and the nine man side went down to a 1-2 defeat. Quite how impressive Mann's performance was is open to debate but it is nevertheless true that when he left Nene Park, Gresley was his destination.

The Boxing Day fixture with Leicester United was a victim of the seasonal weather, but two days later Andy Kirkup enjoyed belated Christmas celebrations hitting all three goals in the 3-1 victory over struggling King's Lynn to become the first Rushden & Diamonds player to score two league hat-tricks.

1993 began with the disappointment of the New Year's Day visit of Racing Warwick being postponed because of the frosty Nene Park surface. However the following day a Glen Beech goal defeated Bilston Town at a Queen Street ground arguably in much more dangerous condition.

Colin Waite in action against Weston.

Stewarts & Lloyds were comfortably beaten 4-0 in the Hillier Senior Cup as Kevin Fox, Richard Bailey and Simon Richmond all made debuts against the Corby side, watched by just 113 spectators, the lowest ever home first team crowd. Richmond enjoyed the shortest career of a Rushden & Diamonds player on record, his only appearance, as substitute, lasting a mere nine minutes.

Stourbridge were the next to leave Nene Park empty handed, Colin Waite netting twice in the 5-2 victory. The visitors' second goal was scored by the Division's leading scorer (he finished the season with 46 goals), Evran Wright, a name with which Diamonds fans would certainly become familiar in the next few seasons.

A fourth meeting with Gresley Rovers brought success at last as the Diamonds moved into the Fourth Round of the League Cup by virtue of a 2-1 home win. However, perhaps the more significant event during the second week of January was the signing of twenty-one years old Dale Watkins from Grantham Town. The flying striker, once clocked at eleven seconds over 100 metres, made a two minute appearance as substitute in the 1-1 away draw at title contenders Nuneaton Borough. A hat-trick in his first full game, the 6-0 win against Hinckley Town, followed by a double in the 3-2 victory over Bedworth United gave early notice of his goalscoring potential.

Success against Bedworth took Roger Ashby's side to the top of the league, a position occupied for just one week. Following a crushing 1-4 defeat at Tamworth, the only Midland Division game in which the club conceded four goals, both Gresley and Barri moved back above the Diamonds. An Evran Wright hat-trick ended League Cup hopes as Stourbridge won a replay 4-2 to progress into the semi-finals. There they defeated Halesowen Town and eventually won the Cup beating the holders, Dover Athletic, in a two-legged final.

Kevin Fox made his first league appearance in the 3-2 victory over Dudley Town that restored Rushden & Diamonds to the top spot, Dale Watkins adding two more goals to his rapidly growing tally, and the side reached the final of the Hillier Senior Cup after a 3-0 success at Long Buckby. Yate were avenged 3-0 and successive victories over Weston-super-Mare, Newport AFC, Racing Warwick and Forest Green Rovers made promotion a distinct possibility.

Fittingly, the club began a multi-million pound development programme to improve facilities at Nene Park. The northern side of the ground was fenced off following demolition of the covered terracing and the site prepared to house a new 1000 seat stand,' *incorporating turnstiles, refreshment room and toilet facilities*', in readiness for the 1993-94 season.

Glenville Donegal

Hopes of starting the new campaign in the Premier Division were dealt a severe blow when the side lost its next two league games. The suspended John Flower was absent for the trip to St George's Lane, Worcester, temporary home of exiled Barri, whose winning goal came just five minutes from time. The highest Nene Park crowd of the season, 887, saw visitors Nuneaton Borough produce a fine display of attacking football to earn a convincing 2-0 victory. Central defender, John Coe, an able deputy for the missing Flower and voted Dolben Insurance 'Man of the Match' in both games never re-appeared in a Diamonds shirt.

These two defeats required that both Gresley Rovers and Nuneaton Borough drop a significant number of points in their remaining games if the Diamonds were to obtain one of the two promotion places. A home victory over bottom club Racing Warwick revived supporters' hopes, but missed chances and inspired goalkeeping displays contributed to a goal-less draw with Tamworth and a shock defeat at Leicester United.

On the afternoon that the Grand National was declared void after a spectacular cock-up, Rushden & Diamonds suddenly raced back into promotion contention with a spectacular 3-0 victory at rivals Bedworth. Substitute Andy Kirkup - replacing Barrington Leslie after an early injury had ended his Rushden & Diamonds career - scored twice against a defence marshalled by Jim Rodwell. A rumour before the match suggested that Kirkup might be on his way out of Nene Park. It wasn't the last time there was such a rumour and it certainly wasn't the last time that such a rumour proved to be false. A week later another 3-0 victory, Nene Park revenge over a Leicester United side that included future Corby & Kettering striker Anton Thomas, kept hopes alive, not that either Irthlingborough or Rushden was overcome by promotion fervour - the attendance for this match falling to 281, a drop of 91 from the previous League fixture.

And so to the Walks on an Easter Monday of great dampness. The King's Lynn secretary regarded relegation as such a serious threat that he interrogated KCBC's roving reporter on the facilities of the clubs in the United Counties League First Division as they were considering applying for admission to the UCL rather than being placed in the Eastern Counties League. The answers did not seem to lighten his mood. A John Flower header shortly before the final whistle enabled the Diamonds to scrape three points and deepen the Linnets' gloom.

As rivals Gresley began to falter, taking just two points from four games, interest was heightened in the home game with Sutton Coldfield on Saturday April 17th. Goals from Kirkup and Donegal brought a 2-0 victory, but while leaders Nuneaton lost to Barri, Gresley returned to winning ways at Racing Warwick. Both Gresley and Barri won in midweek while the Diamonds could only draw at Stourbridge despite leading twice. Evran Wright equalised from the penalty spot twenty minutes from the end. Glenville Donegal's fourth minute opener proved to be his last goal for the club whilst he and Darrell Page were becoming the first players to make 50 appearances for Rushden & Diamonds.

The Diamonds last gasp 2-1 victory at Evesham and Gresley's home defeat by Leicester United on Saturday April 24th kept promotion hopes alive as the season entered its final week. The Rovers recovered quickly beating Barri on the Monday but the position was still wide open. Defeats for Gresley against Hinckley in midweek and at Nene Park on Saturday would give the Diamonds the second promotion place - provided Barri lost one of their two remaining games. With the club's fate resting in other people's feet, Roger Ashby took his side to Rockingham Road on the Tuesday evening for the Hillier Senior Cup Final against Kettering Town. A gathering of 873 watched the first meeting between the clubs; they witnessed the Poppies, inspired by midfielder Richard Hill, win the game 2-1.

There was further disappointment for the Diamonds the following evening. Stourbridge beat Barri but Gresley secured the three points necessary to clinch promotion, beating Hinckley by the odd goal of three.

With just pride at stake Rushden & Diamonds recorded a well-deserved victory in their final game defeating Gresley 3-1 with goals from Ollie Kearns, Adie Mann and John Flower. The result ensured that the side finished in third place, but the quality of the performance suggested that the side could go two better in 1993-94.

Beazer Homes League Midland Division 1992-1993

			Home					Away					
		P	W	D	L	F	A	W	D	L	F	A	Pts
1	Nuneaton Borough (6)	42	12	4	5	53	23	17	1	3	49	22	**92**
2	Gresley Rovers (-)	42	15	1	5	49	28	12	5	4	45	27	**87**
3	Rushden & Diamonds (8)	42	15	4	2	51	17	10	6	5	34	24	**85**
4	Barri (4)	42	13	1	7	40	25	13	4	4	42	24	**83**
5	Newport AFC (10)	42	11	4	6	34	27	12	4	5	39	31	**77**
6	Bedworth United (5)	42	10	4	7	31	29	12	4	5	41	26	**74**
7	Stourbridge (9)	42	10	5	6	45	35	7	4	10	48	44	**60**
8	Sutton Coldfield Town (3)	42	12	2	7	46	36	5	7	9	36	42	**60**
9	Redditch United (20)	42	9	3	9	42	39	9	3	9	33	40	**60**
10	Tamworth (7)	42	10	5	6	40	24	6	6	9	25	27	**59**
11	Weston-super-Mare (-)	42	11	4	6	54	40	6	3	12	25	46	**58**
12	Leicester United (16)	42	11	4	6	41	26	5	5	11	26	41	**57**
13	Grantham Town (13)	42	10	4	7	35	32	6	5	10	25	41	**57**
14	Bilston Town (12)	42	11	5	5	47	30	4	5	12	27	39	**55**
15	Evesham United (-)	42	5	7	9	36	41	10	1	10	31	42	**53**
16	Bridgnorth Town (17)	42	7	6	8	28	31	8	1	12	33	37	**52**
17	Dudley Town (22)	42	9	2	10	32	34	5	6	10	28	41	**50**
18	Yate Town (11)	42	11	2	8	34	30	4	3	14	29	51	**50**
19	Forest Green Rovers (19)	42	7	3	11	36	45	5	3	13	25	52	**42**
20	Hinckley Town (15)	42	6	6	9	31	36	3	5	13	25	53	**38**
21	King's Lynn (14)	42	6	4	11	30	42	4	2	15	15	48	**36**
22	Racing Warwick (18)	42	2	5	14	17	34	1	2	18	23	54	**16**

Figures in brackets are 1991-92 positions.

- There were only three changes in the composition of the Midland Division for 1993-94. Nuneaton Borough and Gresley Rovers were promoted to the Beazer Homes Premier Division. Only one club, VS Rugby, was relegated into the Midland Division.

- Barri decided to return to Barry. They reverted to their old name, Barry Town, presumably to emphasise something other than their Welshness, and played in the Abacus Welsh League. They won promotion to the League of Wales at the first attempt.

- Only three clubs from the feeder leagues were considered suitable for promotion. Tonbridge joined the Southern Division and into the Midland came the Western League champions, Clevedon Town, and the Midland Combination's top side, Armitage.

- As three clubs resigned from the league - Andover, Barri, Dartford - neither King's Lynn nor Racing Warwick were relegated.

1992-1993 Results

Beazer Homes League Midland Division

Aug	22	Bilston Town	H	2	2	Kearns, Belfon	315
Aug	25	Redditch United	A	2	2	Belfon, Jameson	158
Aug	31	Grantham Town	A	1	1	own goal	345
Sep	5	Bridgnorth Town	H	2	1	Belfon, Donegal	215
Sep	9	Hinckley Town	A	0	0		120
Sep	19	Weston-super-Mare	A	2	0	own goal, Johnson	345
Oct	10	Bridgnorth Town	A	2	2	Kearns 2	137
Oct	17	Yate Town	H	0	1		239
Oct	24	Forest Green Rovers	A	4	1	Wilson, Kearns 2, Belfon	109
Oct	27	Redditch United	H	0	0		227
Nov	7	Sutton Coldfield Town	A	0	2		189
Nov	14	Barri	H	1	1	Leslie	213
Nov	17	Grantham Town	H	4	1	Donegal 2, York, Leslie	201
Nov	28	Evesham United	H	5	0	Kirkup 3, Leslie, Donegal	247
Dec	5	Dudley Town	A	2	1	Mann, Flower	147
Dec	12	Newport AFC	H	1	0	Kirkup	354
Dec	19	Gresley Rovers	A	1	2	Donegal	533
Dec	28	King's Lynn	H	3	1	Kirkup 3	277
Jan	2	Bilston Town	A	1	0	Beech	147
Jan	9	Stourbridge	H	5	2	Waite 2, Donegal, Coe, Kearns	247
Jan	16	Nuneaton Borough	A	1	1	Beech	856
Jan	19	Hinckley Town	H	6	0	Leslie, Watkins 3, Mann, Donegal	204
Jan	23	Bedworth United	H	3	2	Waite 2, Watkins	304
Jan	30	Tamworth	A	1	4	Johnson	601
Feb	6	Dudley Town	H	3	2	Watkins 2, Donegal	242
Feb	13	Yate Town	A	3	0	Waite, Leslie, Mann	239
Feb	20	Weston-super-Mare	H	3	0	Donegal, Kirkup, Wilson	279
Feb	24	Newport AFC	A	3	1	Mann 2, Kearns	275
Feb	27	Racing Warwick	A	2	1	Watkins 2	128
Mar	6	Forest Green Rovers	H	2	1	Donegal, York	326
Mar	13	Barri	A	1	2	Mann	177
Mar	18	Nuneaton Borough	H	0	2		887
Mar	23	Racing Warwick	H	3	0	Watkins, Kearns, Beech	254
Mar	27	Tamworth	H	0	0		372
Mar	30	Leicester United	A	0	1		162
Apr	3	Bedworth United	A	3	0	Kirkup 2, Watkins	196
Apr	10	Leicester United	H	3	0	Beech, Watkins, Mann	281
Apr	12	King's Lynn	A	1	0	Flower	242
Apr	17	Sutton Coldfield Town	H	2	0	Kirkup, Donegal	344
Apr	22	Stourbridge	A	2	2	Donegal, Kirkup	315
Apr	24	Evesham United	A	2	1	Kearns, Watkins	218
May	1	Gresley Rovers	H	3	1	Kearns, Mann, Flower	647

1992-1993 Results

FA Cup

Aug	29 PQ	Desborough Town	H	2	0	Belfon, Mann	301
Sep	12 1Q	Long Buckby	A	1	0	Donegal	105
Sep	26 2Q	Hednesford Town	A	1	4	Mann	683

FA Vase

Oct	3 P	Anstey Nomads	H	3	2	York, Mann, Donegal	242
Oct	31 1	Halesowen Harriers	H	3	3	Donegal 2, Flower	248
Nov	3 1R	Halesowen Harriers	A	2	0	Peaks, Donegal	123
Nov	21 2	Gresley Rovers	H	2	2	Donegal, Kirkup	423
Nov	24 2R	Gresley Rovers	A	1	3	Kirkup	717

Barclays Commercial Services Cup

Oct	6 1.1	Atherstone United	H	4	0	Donegal 2, Kirkup, Kearns	162
Oct	20 1.2	Atherstone United	A	3	2	Kearns, Flower, Donegal	120
Nov	10 2	Buckingham Town	H	6	2	Mann 3, York, Belfon, Donegal	204
Jan	12 3	Gresley Rovers	H	2	1	Donegal, Kearns	243
Jan	26 4	Stourbridge	A	2	2	Donegal, Mann	203
Feb	2 4R	Stourbridge	H	2	4	Mann, Watkins	242

NFA Hillier Senior Cup

Oct	13 1	Brackley Town	H	5	0	Kirkup, Kearns, Donegal 2, Beech	128
Jan	6 2	Stewarts & Lloyds	H	4	0	Kearns 2, Belfon, Leslie	113
Feb	9 SF	Long Buckby	A	3	0	Beech 2, Waite	165
Apr	27 F	Kettering Town	A	1	2	Kirkup	873

- The FA Cup was won by Arsenal who beat Sheffield Wednesday 2-1 in a Wembley replay after the final had been drawn 1-1. Three non-League sides reached the Third Round proper: Marine lost 1-3 at Crewe Alexandra, Marlow lost 1-5 at Tottenham Hotspur and north London's other big club, Arsenal, won 3-1 at Yeovil Town thanks to an Ian Wright hat-trick. Six non-League sides beat Football League opposition: Altrincham (Chester City), Bath City (Cardiff City), Macclesfield Town (Chesterfield), Marine (Halifax Town), Stafford Rangers (Lincoln City) and Yeovil Town (Torquay United & Hereford United).

- In the FA Vase final, Bridlington Town of the HFS Loans (Northern Premier) League beat Tiverton Town of the Western League 1-0. Playing for Tiverton was Jason Smith who signed for Rushden & Diamonds in the summer of 1995 but did not play any competitive games.

- In the BCS sponsored Southern League Cup, Rushden & Diamonds' conquerors, Stourbridge, beat Dover Athletic in the final, winning 2-0 at Stourbridge and restricting Dover to 1-2 in the second leg. Stourbridge beat two other Premier Division sides, Halesowen and Hednesford, on the way to their triumph.

1992-1993 Teams
Beazer Homes League Midland Division

		Bailey	Beech	Belfon	Bushell	Coe	Donegal	Flower	Fox	Green	Heard	Jameson	Johnson	Kearns	Kirkup	Leslie	Mann	Page	Peaks	Shoemake	Waite	Watkins	Watts	Wilson	York
Bilston	H			10	2			4			6		7	9			8	5		1				3	11
Redditch	A			10	2			4		sb		6	7	9			8	5		1				3	11
Grantham	A		6	10	2		9	4		sb			7				8	5		1				3	11
Bridgnorth	H		6	10	8		9	5		sb	sb						7	4	2	1				3	11
Hinckley	A		6	10	2		9						7				8	4	3	1	5				11
Weston	A		6	10	2		9	4					7				8	5	3	1	sb			sb	11
Bridgnorth	A				2	6	9	4						10	7		8	5		1				3	11
Yate Town	H			sb	2		9	4						10	7		8	5	6	1				3	11
Forest Grn	A			9	2			4						10	7		8	5	6	1	sb			3	11
Redditch	H			sb	2		9	4						10	7		8	5	6	1				3	11
Sutton	A			10	6		9	4					3				8	5	2	1	7			sb	11
Barri	H			10	2		9	4					3			7	8		6	1	5				11
Grantham	H			10	2		9	4							sb	7	8		6	1	5			3	11
Evesham	H				2		9	4					3	sb	7	10	8		6		5		1		11
Dudley	A				2		9	4					3		7	10	8	6		1	5				11
Newport	H				2		9	4					3		7	10	8	6		1	5				11
Gresley	A				2		9	4					3		7	10	8	6		1	5			sb	11
King's Lynn	H				2		9	4					3	sb	7	10	8	6		1	5			sb	11
Bilston	A		8		2	4	9							10	7	sb		6		1	5			3	11
Stourbridge	H	sb	8			4	9	sb						10	7	2		6		1	5			3	11
Nuneaton	A		8				9	4					3	10		7		6	2	1	5	sb			11
Hinckley	H		11				9	4					3	sb		7	8	6	2	1	5	10			
Bedworth	H		11			6	9	4					3		7	2	8			1	5	10			
Tamworth	A		11			4	9						3		7	2	8	6		1	5	10			
Dudley	H		11				9	4	1				3	sb	7	8		6	2		5	10		sb	
Yate	A		11				9	4	1				3	sb	7	10	8	6	2		5			sb	
Weston	H		11				9	4	1				3	sb	7		8	6	2		5			10	
Newport	A		11					4	1				3	9	7		8	6	2		5	sb		10	
R Warwick	A		11					4	1				3	9			8	6	2		5	10		7	
Forest Grn	H		11				9	4	1				3	sb	7		8	6	2		5			10	sb
Barri	A		7			4	9		1				3	sb			8	6	2		5	10		sb	11
Nuneaton	H		7			4	9		1				3		sb		8	6	2		5	10			11
R Warwick	H		7					4	1				3	9		sb	8	6	2		5	10			11
Tamworth	H		7				sb	4	1				3	9		sb	8	6	2		5	10			11
Leicester	A		7				9	4	1				3			sb	8	6	2		5	10			11
Bedworth	A		7				9	4	1				3		sb	8		6	2		5	10			11
Leicester	H		8				9	4	1				3		7		sb	6	2		5	10		sb	11
King's Lynn	A		8		5		9	4	1				3	sb	7		sb	6	2			10		11	
Sutton	H		8				9	4	1				3	sb	7		sb	6	2		5	10			11
Stourbridge	A		8				9	4	1				3	sb	7			6	2		5	10		sb	11
Evesham	A		8		11		sb	4	1				3	9	7		sb	6	2		5	10			
Gresley	H		5					4	1				3	9	7		8	6	2			10			11

1992-1993 Teams   Cup Competitions

		Bailey	Beech	Belfon	Bushell	Coe	Donegal	Flower	Fox	Green	Jameson	Johnson	Kearns	Kirkup	Leslie	Mann	Page	Peaks	Richmond	Shoemake	Waite	Watkins	Wilson	York
FA Cup																								
Desborough Town	H		sb	10	2			4		sb	6	7	9			8	5			1			3	11
Long Buckby	A		7	10	2		9					3				8	5	6		1	4			11
Hednesford Town	A		6	9		5	10	4				3		sb		7	sb	2		1	8			11
FA Vase																								
Anstey Nomads	H		sb	10	2	6	9	4				3		7		8	5			1				11
Halesowen Harriers	H			sb			9	4				3	10	7		8	5	2		1	6		sb	11
Halesowen Harriers	A		sb	10			9	4				3		7		8	5	2		1	6			11
Gresley Rovers	H			10	2		9	4				3		sb	7	8		6		1	5			11
Gresley Rovers	A				2		9	4				3	10	sb	7	8		6		1	5			11
Barclays CS Cup																								
Atherstone United	H				2	6	9	4					10	7		8	5			1			3	11
Atherstone United	A				2		9	4					10	7			5	6		1	8		3	11
Buckingham Town	H			10	2		9	4				3		7	sb	8		6		1	5		sb	11
Gresley Rovers	H		8				9	4					10	7	2	sb	6			1	5		3	11
Stourbridge	A		11				9	4				3		7	2	8	6	sb		1	5	10		
Stourbridge	H		11			4	9					3	sb	7	2	8	6	sb		1	5	10		
Hillier Cup																								
Brackley Town	H		sb		2	6	9	4					10	7		8	5			1			3	11
Stewarts & Lloyds	H	11	8	sb		4	9		1				10	7	2		6		sb		5		3	
Long Buckby	A		8				9	4	1			3		7	11	10	6	2			5			
Kettering Town	A		8				9	4	1			3	sb	7		sb	6	2			5	10	11	

Luminaries of the founding clubs, Dave Joyce (left) was appointed Secretary and Bernard Lake was appointed Commercial Manager of Rushden & Diamonds.

Appearances 1992-1993

	Start						Substitute						Total					
	L	C	V	LC	CC	Tot	L	C	V	LC	CC	Tot	L	C	V	LC	CC	Tot
Richard BAILEY					1	**1**	1					**1**	1				1	**2**
Glen BEECH	28	2		3	3	**36**		1	2		1	**4**	28	3	2	3	4	**40**
Frankie BELFON	10	3	3	1		**17**	2		1		1	**4**	12	3	4	1	1	**21**
Mark BUSHELL	21	2	3	3	1	**30**						**0**	21	2	3	3	1	**30**
John COE	7	1	1	2	2	**13**						**0**	7	1	1	2	2	**13**
Glenville DONEGAL	33	2	5	6	4	**50**	2					**2**	35	2	5	6	4	**52**
John FLOWER	36	2	5	5	3	**51**	1					**1**	37	2	5	5	3	**52**
Kevin FOX	18				3	**21**						**0**	18				3	**21**
Peter GREEN						**0**	3	1				**4**	3	1				**4**
Steven HEARD	1					**1**	1					**1**	2					**2**
Mark JAMESON	1	1				**2**						**0**	1	1				**2**
Dave JOHNSON	34	3	5	3	2	**47**						**0**	34	3	5	3	2	**47**
Ollie KEARNS	15	1	2	3	2	**23**	11			1	1	**13**	26	1	2	4	3	**36**
Andy KIRKUP	24		3	6	4	**37**	3	1	2			**6**	27	1	5	6	4	**43**
Barrington LESLIE	15		2	3	2	**22**	4			1		**5**	19		2	4	2	**27**
Adie MANN	32	3	5	4	2	**46**	4			1	1	**6**	36	3	5	5	3	**52**
Darrell PAGE	38	2	3	5	4	**52**		1				**1**	38	3	3	5	4	**53**
Andy PEAKS	30	2	4	2	2	**40**				2		**2**	30	2	4	4	2	**42**
Simon RICHMOND						**0**					1	**1**					1	**1**
Kevin SHOEMAKE	23	3	5	6	1	**38**						**0**	23	3	5	6	1	**38**
Colin WAITE	31	2	4	5	3	**45**	2				1	**3**	33	2	4	5	4	**48**
Dale WATKINS	17			2	1	**20**	2					**2**	19			2	1	**22**
Darren WATTS	1					**1**						**0**	1					**1**
Junior WILSON	16	1		3	3	**23**	9		1	1		**11**	25	1	1	4	3	**34**
Paul YORK	31	3	5	4	1	**44**	1					**1**	32	3	5	4	1	**45**
MAXIMUM	42	3	5	6	4	60							42	3	5	6	4	60

Goalscorers

	L	C	V	LC	CC	Total
Glenville DONEGAL	12	1	5	6	2	26
Andy KIRKUP	12		2	1	2	17
Ollie KEARNS	10			3	3	16
Adie MANN	8	2	1	5		16
Dale WATKINS	12			1		13
Glen BEECH	4				3	7
Frankie BELFON	4	1		1	1	7
Barrington LESLIE	5				1	6
Colin WAITE	5				1	6
John FLOWER	3		1	1		5
Paul YORK	2		1	1		4
Dave JOHNSON	2					2
Junior WILSON	2					2
John COE	1					1
Mark JAMESON	1					1
Andy PEAKS			1			1
own goal	2					2
TOTAL	85	4	11	19	13	132

1992-93 Playing Record

HOME	P	W	D	L	F	A	Pts
League	21	15	4	2	51	17	49
FA Cup	1	1	0	0	2	0	
FA Vase	3	1	2	0	8	7	
League Cup	4	3	0	1	14	7	
County Cup	2	2	0	0	9	0	
TOTAL	31	22	6	3	84	31	
AWAY							
League	21	10	6	5	34	24	36
FA Cup	2	1	0	1	2	4	
FA Vase	2	1	0	1	3	3	
League Cup	2	1	1	0	5	4	
County Cup	2	1	0	1	4	2	
TOTAL	29	14	7	8	48	37	
TOTAL							
League	42	25	10	7	85	41	85
FA Cup	3	2	0	1	4	4	
FA Vase	5	2	2	1	11	10	
League Cup	6	4	1	1	19	11	
County Cup	4	3	0	1	13	2	
TOTAL	**60**	**36**	**13**	**11**	**132**	**68**	

Attendance Summary

HOME	Total	Ave	High		Low	
League	6675	318	887	Nuneaton	201	Grantham
FA Cup	301	301	301	Desborough	301	Desborough
FA Vase	913	304	423	Gresley	242	Anstey
League Cup	851	213	243	Gresley	162	Atherstone
County Cup	241	121	128	Brackley	113	S&L
TOTAL	8981	290	887	Nuneaton	113	S&L
AWAY						
League	5639	269	856	Nuneaton	109	Forest Green
FA Cup	788	394	683	Hednesford	105	Long Buckby
FA Vase	840	420	717	Gresley	123	Halesowen Hr
League Cup	323	162	203	Stourbridge	120	Atherstone
County Cup	1038	519	873	Kettering	165	Long Buckby
TOTAL	8628	298	873	Kettering	105	Long Buckby
TOTAL						
League	12314	293	887	Nuneaton H	109	Forest Green A
FA Cup	1089	363	683	Hednesford A	105	Long Buckby A
FA Vase	1753	351	717	Gresley A	123	Halesowen Hr A
League Cup	1174	196	243	Gresley H	120	Atherstone A
County Cup	1279	320	873	Kettering A	113	S&L H
TOTAL	**17609**	**293**	**887**	Nuneaton H	**105**	Long Buckby A

The 1992-93 season has just ended and major drainage work on the Nene Park pitch has just commenced. Looking towards the A6 this photograph was taken from the Irthlingborough Diamonds stand. Within a few days it was demolished to make way for the construction of the Diamond Centre.

The Nene Park pitch is now part of the responsibilities of Head Groundsman Ray Bailey (left) and assistant John Underwood. Bedford born Bailey played first class cricket for Northamptonshire and league football for Gillingham, as well as Bedford Town when they were one of the top sides in the Southern League. His most memorable cricketing achievement was when he and Brian Crump bowled unchanged through both Glamorgan innings at Cardiff in 1967, the only occasion this has ever happened in a County Championship match.

Ready to dig the footings (above) *for the North Stand in February 1992, the contractors were faced with these three applicants for a job on site, from left, Tobey Graham, Max Griggs and Dave Joyce.*

SEASON TWO

1993 - 94

"" It takes two to make a marriage a success "

Herbert Louis Samuel

Back (l to r): Glen Beech, Dougie Keast, Tim Wooding, Kevin Fox, John Flower, Lee Crane, Paul York, Dave Johnson, Billy Jeffrey, Pete Brown.
Front (l to r): Alan Kurila, Dale Watkins, Richard Bailey, Paul Coe, Roger Ashby, Adie Mann, Mickey Nuttell, Andy Peaks, Darren Hillier.

Rushden & Diamonds had finished their first season still as a Midland Division club both in terms of status and image. It was certainly the public's perception that little had changed. True there were grand plans for ground development. But they seemed more grand than plans, and as for the artists' impressions of the future stadium, well, it's an indisputable fact that artists' impressions never remotely resemble the result.

There was no real doubt that Rushden & Diamonds had been the third best team in the Midland Division. Nuneaton Borough had provided a footballing lesson at Nene Park in March and Gresley Rovers had won the matches that mattered. The club had hardly attracted any additional support. An average gate of 318 for a side chasing promotion for most of the season was not unduly impressive and was only lifted over the 300 mark by large away contingents from Nuneaton and Gresley. Bedworth, Evesham, Newport and Tamworth all attracted better gates.

By the start of the new season, the cynics were no longer doubting that anything would ever happen; they were now wondering what was the point of building the 1000 seat North Stand which could never possibly be filled. But it wasn't just the North Stand that was different for the start of the second season. The whole ground had been transformed.

On the south side, the Irthlingborough Diamonds stand, dressing rooms, clubhouse *et al.* had been razed to the ground and the shell of what was to become the South Stand and the Diamond Centre was taking shape. At the west end of the ground a number of portakabins provided offices and dressing rooms. No more would those who'd watched an evening match from the covered terrace twist an ankle as they stumbled off that single shadowy row of slabs while making their way towards the exit. A re-laid pitch and new floodlights made the ground even further removed from that which Irthlingborough Diamonds had inaugurated in 1969. It was only at the east end of the ground that there was still something, the fifty poplar trees, recognisable as the old Nene Park.

Inevitably there were changes in playing personnel. Manager Ashby had been particularly disappointed with his strikers and he released Glenville Donegal who emigrated to Australia, Frankie Belfon who joined Northampton Spencer and Ollie Kearns, later destined to revisit Nene Park with Racing Club Warwick. The man selected to partner Dale Watkins up front was Mickey Nuttell. The 25 year old native of Boston was signed from Dagenham & Redbridge where he had scored 9 goals (one more than Dagenham team-mate Garry Butterworth) in 31 Conference appearances the previous season. Nuttell had started with Peterborough United before turning out for Cheltenham, Wycombe, Boston United and Kettering Town where he made just one appearance during the Poppies' ill-fated Mark English regime.

The other big close season signing was also from Dagenham and Redbridge, midfielder Paul Richardson. His Football League career with Derby County had been cruelly cut short by serious illness and his successful return to the non-league game owed much to a lengthy period of rehabilitation at Rockingham Road during

Paul Richardson

the late eighties. He subsequently was a member of the Barnet side that won promotion from the Conference and at 32 would bring plenty of experience to the middle of Diamonds line-up.

Defender Alan Kurila from Burton Albion completed the list of incomers. An older brother of former Rushden Town and Irthlingborough Diamonds striker, Mick, and son of the former Cobblers wing-half John, he brought additional experience and versatility to the squad.

Utility player Junior Wilson left during the summer and Mark Bushell, John Coe and Colin Waite had all played their last game for Rushden & Diamonds. Bushell, following Steve Heard to Raunds, and Waite left early in the 93-94 season whilst Coe spent most of the year on loan to Rothwell Town.

The final pre-season friendly, a 1-1 draw against Northampton Town's full Third Division line-up, attracted over 1,000 spectators to Nene Park (thus filling the North Stand - the only available spectator accommodation - for the first time), many no doubt curious to witness the remarkable transformation at first hand. They also witnessed a Diamonds goal scored by Mickey Nuttell, an event that was to happen with great regularity during the coming season.

It was Nuttell who opened the Midland Division campaign by netting against visitors Clevedon Town, the newly promoted Western League champions. A crowd of 641, over twice the number that had watched the previous season's curtain raiser against Bilston Town, saw the Diamonds achieve a comfortable 2-0 victory, Dale Watkins netting the second shortly after half time. The Diamonds team was: Fox, Kurila, Johnson, Flower, Richardson, Page, Kirkup, Mann, Nuttell, Watkins, York. Subs not used: Peaks and Bailey.

A 1-1 result at Tamworth in the next game, an 87th minute header from the prolific Nuttell salvaging a draw after the home side had taken the lead on the hour was probably a good result even though it provided a timely reminder of the excessive number of points dropped in drawn games at a similar stage of the 1992-93 campaign. Manager Ashby played an extra defender, Andy Peaks, instead of Andy Kirkup but the idea of playing a more defensive formation in away matches was abandoned twenty minutes before the end of this game.

Nuttell continued in his rich vein of form, netting the only goal in the F A Cup Preliminary Round game at Rocester, and then adding two more as the Diamonds gave visitors Bedworth United a goal start before winning 3-1.

Victory at Stourbridge, Paul Richardson netting his first goal for the club, was followed by a trip to Grantham. Diamonds were one of four clubs required to play in the preliminary round of the Southern League Cup, known from this season as the Dr Martens Cup. A 3-1 victory, with one of the goals scored by Dale Watkins on his return to his former club, was marred by an injury to keeper Kevin Fox that kept him out of the side for a month.

Adie Mann

FA Cup progress at the expense of Sutton Coldfield was followed by the 6-0 thrashing of King's Lynn in which Adie Mann scored a hat-trick and new signing Shaun Diver came off the bench to score a well-taken goal. That emphatic victory took the Diamonds to the top of the league in front of a new Nene Park record crowd for a home League match, 901. Four days later, Diver, the former Steelman, repeated the feat at Bridgnorth in his second appearance as substitute, adding to Mann's opener. There followed a home victory in the second leg of the Dr Martens Cup over Grantham. Fittingly Diamonds became the first club to win a tie in this competition as the other Preliminary Round tie went to extra time and penalties.

The Second Qualifying Round of the FA Cup on September 25th revived memories of past encounters in the United Counties League for followers of the founding clubs as it brought league leaders Rothwell Town to Nene Park. It proved an intriguing contest against a Bones side that was to retain the UCL Championship and gain promotion to the Beazer Homes League. A Mickey Nuttell header gave Roger Ashby's side a 1-0 interval lead but the dismissal of Darrell Page - the first R&D player to be sent off twice - for a 'professional' foul on Shaun McPolin five minutes after the break reduced the Diamonds to ten men. Glyn Davies converted the penalty to force a replay which attracted the biggest crowd to Cecil Street since Irthlingborough Diamonds had defeated Rothwell 2-1 to seal the UCL Championship back in 1971. 929 spectators watched the Beazer Midland League side move into the next round, courtesy of two goals from Dale Watkins in an impressive display.

The side returned to league action at Dudley on October 2nd, Mickey Nuttell's two goals taking his season's tally into double figures and securing a point in a dour 2-2 draw. Left back Dave Johnson was sorely missed and Valley Sports Rugby leapfrogged back into top spot. Cup involvement meant that momentum was lost and it was a further four weeks before the Diamonds could renew their title challenge.

In the Third Qualifying Round of the FA Cup Premier Division Burton Albion were comprehensively beaten 4-0 in front of an official attendance of 1,201, the first four figure crowd for a competitive match. Darren Hillier made his debut for R&D whilst Albion selected George Foster, recently sacked as Mansfield's manager, with the intention of strengthening their defence. Goals from Nuttell, Mann, Richardson and Watkins suggested that the plan didn't quite work.

Albion were due to return to Nene Park the following Saturday for Rushden & Diamonds' first ever FA Trophy tie. Before that there was a Senior Cup Quarter Final against Cogenhoe in which the Cooks, including former Russian Steve Forbes and former and future R&D keeper Darren Watts, succumbed only in extra time.

For the Trophy game, Diamonds made one change, fielding a more defensive line-up by replacing Adie Mann with Darrell Page. Albion made three changes, Foster having taken the manager's job at Telford United, and in a complete contrast to the previous week, the visitors won with the only goal of the game. It ended Diamonds' unbeaten run of fifteen games but was regarded by many as a 'blessing in disguise'. The club was rapidly accumulating a backlog of league fixtures and there were justifiable concerns that the prime objective, promotion, could be jeopardised by continued involvement in cup competitions.

Darrell Page

A 2-0 aggregate victory over Bedworth United took the side into the Second Round of the Dr Martens Cup but the two games sandwiched one of the most memorable matches of the 1993-94 campaign.

The visit of Conference side Bromsgrove Rovers for the FA Cup Fourth Qualifying Round tie attracted 1,521 spectators to Nene Park. The Diamonds more than matched their lofty opponents for the first 45 minutes. The half-time whistle was imminent and the game goalless, when the incident occurred which probably shaped the outcome of an enthralling encounter. John Flower, in commanding form at the heart of the Diamonds defence, clashed with Bromsgrove midfielder, Paul Webb, on the halfway line. The challenge was interpreted as violent conduct

John Flower

by referee Martin, who promptly issued a red card. The Conference side - which included future Diamond Steve Stott - quickly capitalised upon the big man's absence from the defensive line-up, floating the resulting free kick deep into the opposing penalty area. Still disorganised, and with keeper Kevin Shoemake some distance from his line, the Diamonds failed to clear, the ball falling to Paul Wardle who hooked it home from close range to put his side 1-0 ahead. There was an element of controversy about the second goal, too, the ball having appeared to go out of play for a throw in during the build up to Recky Carter's diving header in the 73rd minute. The dangerous Andy Kirkup reduced the arrears within three minutes but hopes of a Diamonds equaliser virtually disappeared shortly after when the lively winger departed through injury following an accidental clash with visiting keeper Scott Cooksey. Rovers' substitute, Colin Radburn, added another goal to give the final scoreline a flattering look but the Diamonds had provided spectacular notice of their ability to compete against the best in non-league football.

Thoughts of what might have been caused rueful smiles amongst fans as they followed Rovers' Cup progress. Drawn away to the Cobblers in the First Round proper, Bromsgrove won at the County Ground, defeated Yeovil in the Second Round, and were leading Barnsley 1-0 in the Third Round but conceded two in the last two minutes. If only ....

Back in league action at last, goals from Adie Mann and Dale Watkins secured a 2-1 victory at Redditch on October 30th, but in the next game, the first home league fixture since September, Hinckley Town, who never threatened to make the top half of the table, inflicted the Diamonds' first League defeat of the season by taking advantage of poor defensive play to record a 3-2 victory. It was the only home League defeat of the season and it marked Kevin Shoemake's last appearance for the club.

After a late equaliser from Adie Mann had forced a League Cup replay against Premier Division Cambridge City, 637 spectators watched the side return to winning ways in splendid fashion, defeating Bilston Town 5-1. Fifteen months earlier Bilston had visited Nene Park for R&D's inaugural match but the rapid change in personnel at this level of football is highlighted by the fact that only five participants from that historic game were involved this time. For Rushden & Diamonds the survivors were Dave Johnson *(pictured below)*, Darrell Page, Adie Mann and Paul York whilst Bilston's Mark Bowater was their only man who played in both games.

The same scoreline in the next fixture, against visiting Tamworth, prompted the following observations from visiting journalist Sam Holliday.

"Tamworth were totally destroyed by a far superior side. In terms of their ground, their playing staff and their 'millionaires' feel, Rushden do look in a different league to the Lambs. They are the best team in the division by a mile...."

Dave Johnson

Stourbridge almost made mock of that assessment the following Saturday. The Diamonds were forced to fight back from 0-2 and 2-3 down, snatching a last minute equaliser through hat-trick hero Dale Watkins, for whom the game was a personal triumph. Watkins missed both the Hillier Senior Cup Second Round victory over Rothwell, a Glyn Davies own goal (which some sources credited to John Flower) separating the two sides, and the 2-1 defeat of Dudley Town which restored the Diamonds to second spot. However, the latter was not a convincing display. One fan was so disgruntled with the second half display that he demanded the return of the Salvation Army Band which had entertained the crowd during the interval with its repertoire of Christmas carols.

Cambridge City ended interest in the League Cup winning the replayed Second Round tie 3-1 and denying the Diamonds a derby meeting with local rivals Corby Town in the next round. Andy Kirkup gave Diamonds the lead but Laurie Ryan equalised on the stroke of half-time. Second half goals from Paul Wilkin and Ryan emphasised that there was still a gap between Premier and Midland Division. The fact that Rushden & Diamonds were still no great attraction was demonstrated by the sparseness of the crowd, just 167 paying at the gate. Playing the final half-hour for City was Wayne Goddard who joined Diamonds the following season but never appeared in a first team game, though he did make the bench on a couple of occasions.

Cambridge City winger, Paul Coe, the target of a £10,000 bid by Third Division Scarborough, joined Rushden and Diamonds in time to make his debut in the 2-0 victory over Leicester United, a game in which Shaun Diver wore a Diamonds shirt for the last time. The star of the show was Andy Kirkup who celebrated the birth of his son, Adam, by netting both goals as the Diamonds avenged the previous season's shock defeat that had been so costly in the side's promotion race.

Christmas brought league leaders, VS Rugby (including future Diamonds Ian King and Simon Mason), to Irthlingborough for a game which attracted a 2,000 plus crowd to Nene Park for the first time since the formation of the new club. Mickey Nuttell who, with midfielder Paul Richardson was included in an FA representative side to meet the British Universities XI in the New Year, opened the scoring after nine minutes to register his twentieth goal of the season, the first to feature on the electronic scoreboard which had been acquired from Millwall's original Den in Cold Blow Lane. Chances were squandered, however and the visitors came back strongly in the second half gaining a 71st minute equaliser through Ashley Warner. The dismissal of strong man Gary Statham for an off the ball incident with Nuttell provoked a late Diamonds onslaught on the VS goal but the depleted defence held firm for a well-deserved point.

The short excursion up the A1 on New Year's Day saw an Andy Kirkup goal defeat hosts Grantham Town, but the real hero was keeper Kevin Fox who made numerous top class saves in keeping his seventh clean sheet of the season.

Glen Beech takes on Racing Warwick's Northampton-born defender Phil Murphy.

January 3rd, a Bank Holiday Monday, brought former Diamonds Mark Jameson, Ollie Kearns and Colin Waite back to Nene Park as Racing Club Warwick salvaged an unexpected point in a game spoiled by dreadful conditions underfoot. The ground lived up to its name as passes frequently foundered in the abundant surface water rendering good football almost impossible. On the stroke of half-time the veteran Kearns' looping header from the edge of the area gave the visitors a lead that they held until the second minute of injury time. As disappointed home fans began to stream from the ground resigned to defeat, substitute Richard Bailey headed goalwards from Paul Coe's corner only to see the ball stick in the mud feet from the line. Fortunately, skipper Paul Richardson reacted more quickly than those around him, lunging forward to toe past keeper Peter Bulliman and snatch a precious point.

Surely the next game, a visit to manager-less Armitage - who had conceded 11 goals in their Christmas fixture with Tamworth in which their keeper was sent off for fighting with a spectator - would bring a return to the rich scoring form of early season? Certainly the ground was as big a contrast as one could imagine with the growing splendour of Nene Park. At least two miles from the village after which the club was named, the ground was a field next to the A513, the Handsacre to King's Bromley road. There was virtually no sign of human habitation though it was sometimes possible to discern the cooling towers of Rugeley power station. The ground had a temporary look to it, the field being enclosed by rudimentary fencing. There was no turnstile, just a five bar gate, and the gateman had neither table nor cash bag to assist him as a full coach load of Diamonds fans queued patiently and politely to tender the correct money. They needed no change - there was no programme. 117 was the official attendance, way above the season's low of 35. The bumper crowd saw Mickey Nuttell open the account after 37 minutes, but it was not until seven minutes from the end of a one-sided encounter that he scored his, and the Diamonds, second. Dale Watkins added another but, thwarted by a combination of inspired goalkeeping by Darren Clayton and the woodwork, the Diamonds had to be content with a 3-0 scoreline. The result established the Diamonds in second place, five points behind leaders Valley Sports but with two games in hand.

The following week, without the suspended Mickey Nuttell, victory over Sutton Coldfield was achieved when a Dale Watkins penalty and Richard Bailey's first league goal produced a comfortable 2-0 scoreline.

The Evening Telegraph reporter's lyrical account of the next game at Forest Green Rovers, the first of three successive journeys to the West Country, eulogised over the contribution of 'midfield maestro' Glen Beech who sealed a magnificent display by curling a free kick over the defensive wall and into the top right hand corner for the Diamonds final goal in the 5-3 victory. Deprived of Kirkup, Mann and Nuttell it was feared that a lack of firepower might jeopardise chances of returning with three points, though Richard Bailey had a promising game in what was his first League start. In the event it was defensive frailty that contributed to the eight goal thriller, raw recruit Andy Hoskins opening Rovers' account after just five minutes. Dale Watkins quickly equalised, two John Flower headers from set pieces gave Diamonds a 3-1 lead, before McGrory punished a Paul Coe handling offence, beating Fox from the penalty spot. Coe's cross shot, his first goal for the club, restored the two goal advantage but Hoskins reduced the deficit to set up a tense ending. Then came Beech's blockbuster.

The win was followed by a midweek trip to Gloucester, temporary home of third placed Newport AFC. Beech repeated his free kick success, this time curling the ball into the opposite corner, to give his side a 66th minute lead and Dale Watkins hit a late second to make the game safe. The result put daylight between the Diamonds and their nearest rivals who now trailed by nine points.

Mickey Nuttell

Fourth placed Weston super Mare proved more resilient in the next game. After taking an eighth minute lead, quickly extended four minutes later, Weston defended defiantly restricting the Diamonds to a single Mickey Nuttell penalty in return. The season's second League defeat was a timely reminder that there was still plenty to be done if the promotion dream was to become a reality. Not even the most optimistic Diamonds fan could surely have believed that this would be the last defeat of the season.

A 3-0 victory over Yate Town, notable primarily for it being Tim Wooding's debut match, was followed by an ill tempered 1-1 draw on a quagmire of a pitch at King's Lynn. In the following game, Evesham keeper, Billy Turley (later to play for Northampton and Kettering), couldn't prevent his side suffering a 1-4 defeat as a revitalised Diamonds, prompted by the return from injury of the influential Adie Mann, appeared to regain their form in their hundredth competitive first team game. A well-known name in the Evesham side was striker Keith Bertschin who was replaced in the second half by Paul Busst, son of manager John and brother of Dave, the Coventry defender. Also in the Evesham line-up was John Baker, the first man ever to score against Rushden & Diamonds, but the real significance of this match was how much better and more convincing was this performance than the previous year's scrambled victory at this ground.

Kevin Fox

The next match, however, at home to Newport only served to underline the side's tendency to play better away from home as they failed to complete the double over the exiled Welsh team they had conclusively beaten less than a month previously. The visitors secured a point in a drab encounter enlivened only by Dale Watkins' splendid solo goal, typically fashioned out of nothing. Latching on to a long clearance he outpaced the defence and finished in impeccable style, lobbing the advancing keeper from outside the penalty area.

Lowly Leicester United arrived at Nene Park confident of extending a run of form that had brought just one defeat in six matches. Their line-up contained several players who would grace other local teams in future seasons, including Ian Marsden, Darren Stevens, Jason Weafer, David Tonge, Dave Tedds and Ossie Mintus - but met a Diamonds side which at last treated the home crowd to a performance more in keeping with its away form. The 4-0 victory began a sequence of six consecutive wins culminating in the thrilling 3-2 defeat of Weston super Mare on March 19th. Some of the half dozen victories were little more than routine but it was a run that emphasised the consistency of the Diamonds, particularly to their rivals, and brought Divisional manager of the month awards to Roger Ashby for both February and March.

It required a last minute penalty to defeat Bedworth at the Miners Welfare and a single Dale Watkins strike, amidst a host of missed opportunities, accounted for Bilston at Queen Street. A routine win over Bridgnorth under the Nene Park lights was marred by the injury to Paul Richardson that kept him out of the game for nine months. The visit to Yate was trickier than anticipated. The home side led for over half an hour and for most of the second half a 2-2 draw looked the likely outcome until Watkins edged Diamonds in front.

Dale Watkins in action at an undeveloped Nene Park. Paul Richardson is in support.

That set up the crunch game against Weston super Mare. The seaside team had already beaten the Diamonds but the two goal hero of that January encounter, Steve Tapp, began this game on the bench, his replacement being the much travelled Graham Withey. A wise selection it seemed when Withey put Weston in front but shortly before half time Paul York equalised. Nuttell's goal, as the hour mark approached, put the home side in control but six minutes from time Nigel Gillard (who had represented Clevedon in the opening match of the season) made it 2-2. Two minutes away from taking a point back to Somerset, a dreadful clearance by keeper Mark Stevens gifted Dale Watkins a winner which not only gave Diamonds all the points, but perhaps more importantly, put a huge dent in Weston's confidence.

This impressive Diamonds run had coincided with the arrival of young full back, Tim Wooding *(pictured right)*, formerly of Rushden Rangers, Norwich City and Bournemouth and son of Wellingborough Town skipper of the sixties, Dave. The Weston game produced a particularly promising performance from Tim, who had a hand in all three of his side's goals. The victory kept Diamonds on top of the table and extended the difference over Weston to 13 points, though Weston had three games in hand.

The winning run came to an end the following Wednesday in a goal-less draw at Clevedon's impressive Hand Stadium. Continuous rain throughout the day made the going on the soft side of heavy and for the only League match of the season Diamonds failed to score. Elsewhere on that wild night Newport went fourth by beating Grantham 1-0 and VS Rugby kept up the pressure by winning 5-1 at Yate. With nine games to go Diamonds had 77 points and were followed by VS, four points adrift and also having played 33 games. Third placed Weston had 63 points from 29 games but Newport (60 from 32) and Clevedon (58 from 29) were surely too far behind to be serious threats.

Anxious to ease what some were seeing as a formality, Roger Ashby strengthened his squad by signing 31 year old Dougie Keast from cash strapped Corby Town for a mere £3,000. The experienced midfielder, an ideal replacement for Paul Richardson, repaid part of his fee by scoring just four minutes into his debut game at Hinckley Town as his new club recorded a comfortable 4-0 victory.

Keast was ineligible for the next match, the Hillier Senior Cup semi-final against another of his former clubs, Kettering Town. A record Nene Park crowd of 2,352 saw the new pretenders to the crown of Northamptonshire's top non-league side topple the old guard 3-2. The Diamonds took a two goal lead, both opportunist goals by Andy Kirkup, before loanee winger Mark Dempster reduced the arrears. Mickey Nuttell restored the two goal cushion before Dempster scored again just four minutes from the end to set up a tense finale. If ever a game offered portents of the future this was it, as a glance at the teamsheet will reveal.

The Kettering defence enjoyed an incredible season, conceding just 24 goals in their 42 Conference fixtures, never conceding more than two in a league fixture. All bar Darren Oxbrow of the back five later played for Rushden & Diamonds.

Tuesday March 29th 1994 NFA Hillier Senior Cup Semi-Final

Rushden & Diamonds (2) **3**		**Kettering Town** (1) **2**	
1	Kevin Fox	1	Graham Benstead
2	Andy Peaks	2	Graham Reed
3	Dave Johnson	3	Nick Ashby
4	John Flower	4	Steve Holden
5	Glen Beech	5	Darren Oxbrow
6	Darrell Page	6	Robin Taylor
7	Andy Kirkup (sub: Mann 73)	7	Warren Donald
8	Paul Coe	8	Phil Brown
9	Mickey Nuttell	9	Ian Stringfellow
10	Dale Watkins	10	Peter Costello (sub: Martin 27)
11	Paul York	11	Mark Dempsey
12	Adie Mann	12	Dean Martin
14	Richard Bailey	14	Gareth Price

Referee: GM Lee (Corby)

Goals: Kirkup (30, **1-0**); Kirkup (44, **2-0**); Dempsey (45, **2-1**); Nuttell (76, **3-1**); Dempsey (86, **3-2**)

The following Saturday it was back to real business as the Diamonds travelled to Butlin Road, Rugby, for the eagerly awaited clash with title rivals, Valley Sports. Diamonds established a two goal lead, courtesy of Mickey Nuttell's thirtieth of the season and Dougie Keast's second as early as the 11th minute, but were pegged back by determined opponents who capitalised on uncharacteristic mistakes by skipper John Flower, probably affected by concussion, to salvage a point. Ashley Warner seized upon a misdirected headed back pass to reduce the arrears after 73 minutes and, deep into injury time, Ian King coolly converted a penalty after Flower had fouled the lively Warner.

There was a strong feeling of *deja vu* about the next game, away at Racing Warwick, which wasn't confined to personnel. True there were familiar faces in the opposition ranks - Mark Jameson, former Rushden Town player Russ Ashenden and Wellingborough's Shane Geary. But for the Diamonds to surrender a two goal lead and two points for the second week running was both uncanny and careless in the extreme. Dale Watkins scored in the first minute and when Paul Coe added a second ten minutes into the second half it should have been all over. But within ten minutes Warwick were level. First Garry Harrison, on loan from the Cobblers and later to play for Raunds, narrowed the margin and then Mark Jameson scored against his old club for the second time, having previously done so for Buckingham. The draw enabled mid-table Racing Club to become only the second side - along with VS Rugby - to emerge unbeaten over two games during the season.

If bad luck goes in threes, the third match of the drawing sequence had all the necessary ingredients. The home game with Grantham ended 3-3. The game got off a frantic start with Diamonds leading 3-2 with just 17 minutes showing on the scoreboard. Mickey Nuttell struck twice after Dale Watkins had opened the scoring. This was his fourth match against his former club and the third in which he had scored.

Superstitious fans need not have worried unduly. Rock bottom Armitage went down the pan in the next match, soundly beaten 4-0. Mickey Nuttell's pair extended his season's goal tally to 36, Adie Mann added a third and Dave Johnson scored his first of the campaign. Darrell Page won the race to be the first Rushden & Diamonds player to make 100 appearances. The result meant that three wins and a draw from the final four games would guarantee the Diamonds a place in the Beazer Homes Premier Division in 1994-95.

Next on the agenda was the final away match, a visit to Coles Lane, the home of Sutton Coldfield and the venue for a 2-0 defeat the previous season. It was a nerve-ridden performance from the Diamonds but they looked to have sewn it up when two second half goals left them 2-0 up with twenty minutes to play. Defenders Dave Johnson, making his 100th appearance, and John Flower, making his 99th appearance, showed the forwards the way to score. But the nerves returned when substitute Micky Richard narrowed the gap and the last eight minutes were frantic in the extreme.

In midweek Northampton Spencer of the United Counties League were brushed aside 5-0 in the final of the Hillier Senior Cup bringing the season's first silverware. Northamptonshire's top referee, Brian Hill, presided over affairs as Dale Watkins grabbed a hat-trick.

With two wins needed from the final three matches - all at Nene Park - a fourth minute Adie Mann goal against Evesham looked to have set Diamonds well on their way. But mid-table Evesham refused to lie down and, organised by Tony Grealish, capped 45 times for Ireland, the Worcestershire side made Diamonds sweat all the way.

If that was a drab encounter, the penultimate game against Forest Green Rovers contained sufficient drama to compensate the 1,504 spectators for any amount of earlier indolence. Victory would bring the Championship to Nene Park, yet had the game begun any later than the unusual time of 7.00 pm it is doubtful if the most significant result in the Diamonds' short history would have stood. All began so well. Just 56 seconds into the game Mickey Nuttell headed home Paul Coe's inswinging corner at the near post. Four minutes later he extended the lead, tapping home his 38th goal of the season after a 25 yard drive by Paul York (becoming the fourth to make 100 appearances for the club) had rebounded from the upright. Then Adie Mann's 12th minute corner deceived Rovers' seventeen year old keeper, Neil Fulton, swinging unaided into the net to mark the Diamonds century of league goals. The Championship seemed assured until, in the 56th minute, danger came from an unexpected source. The floodlights suddenly flickered, dimmed and died. Fortunately, the early kick off ensured that there was just enough natural light to complete the game, the Diamonds adding further goals through Watkins and Coe to establish a 5-0 final scoreline. As the jubilant crowd invaded the pitch the rogue lights burst into life once more, illuminating the celebrations.

Dale Watkins, Mickey Nuttell and Adie Mann celebrate after Forest Green have been beaten and the Championship of the Midland Division secured.

Meanwhile the reserve team was coming to the end of its programme in the United Counties League Reserve Division One and the club was coming to the end of its connection with the United Counties League. Next season the reserves would look west and join the Midland Combination. It was a move that Rushden & Diamonds had tried to make twelve months previously but the UCL had objected.

The final first team game was the visit of Redditch, an occasion which might well have proved an anti-climax. In the event, victory over sixth placed opponents was a fitting end to a marvellous season. Visiting keeper, Jim Arnold, was beaten seven times as the rampant Diamonds extended their tally to 109, confirming the club as winners of the Merit Cup for scoring most goals in the Beazer Homes League that season. An attendance of 1,397 was the sixth time a league match had attracted a four figure crowd to Nene Park, the 93-94 average of 966 being over three times the 92-93 average.

It is often said that one of the essential ingredients for success is a settled line-up. That was certainly true for Rushden & Diamonds as they won the Midland Division championship. The team for the final match showed just four changes in personnel from the side that had opened the campaign against Clevedon in August: Tim Wooding had replaced Alan Kurila (with Andy Peaks on this occasion not being on the bench), Dougie Keast was there in place of Paul Richardson, Andy Kirkup had given way to Glen Beech and Paul York had missed the final curtain, enabling Paul Coe to take part. To further demonstrate the stability of the squad, all four who were missing from the Redditch match were retained for the following season.

	Team v Clevedon in first match 21 August 1993		Team v Redditch in final match 7 May 1994
1	Kevin Fox	1	Kevin Fox
2	Alan Kurila	2	Tim Wooding
3	Dave Johnson	3	Dave Johnson
4	John Flower	4	John Flower
5	Paul Richardson	5	Glen Beech
6	Darrell Page	6	Darrell Page
7	Andy Kirkup	7	Paul Coe
8	Adie Mann	8	Adie Mann
9	Mickey Nuttell	9	Mickey Nuttell
10	Dale Watkins	10	Dale Watkins
11	Paul York	11	Dougie Keast
12	Andy Peaks	12	Alan Kurila
14	Richard Bailey	14	Richard Bailey

Nobody played in every game but the settled nature of the side is further illustrated by the list of leading appearances showing seven players, Flower, Fox, Johnson, Nuttell, Watkins and York, starting at least 80% of the matches. Nuttell pipped Watkins for the accolade of leading scorer but he finished one goal behind Rugby's Ashley Warner in the Midland Division charts.

Six points clear of Valley Sports and seven in front of third placed Weston, there was no doubt that Rushden & Diamonds were worthy Midland Division champions. But would they be strong enough to challenge for Beazer Premier Division honours in 1994-95?

Beazer Homes League Midland Division 1993-1994

			Home						Away					
		P	W	D	L	F	A	W	D	L	F	A	Pts
1	Rushden & Diamonds (3)	42	15	5	1	65	18	14	6	1	44	19	**98**
2	VS Rugby (-)	42	14	6	1	47	17	14	2	5	51	24	**92**
3	Weston-super-Mare (11)	42	13	6	2	47	21	14	4	3	47	18	**91**
4	Newport AFC (5)	42	16	1	4	43	14	10	8	3	41	23	**87**
5	Clevedon Town (-)	42	11	7	3	38	22	13	3	5	37	24	**82**
6	Redditch United (9)	42	12	5	4	41	21	7	6	8	38	41	**68**
7	Tamworth (10)	42	11	4	6	48	27	8	3	10	34	41	**64**
8	Bilston Town (14)	42	9	3	9	32	36	7	7	7	33	37	**58**
9	Stourbridge (7)	42	9	4	8	37	34	8	2	11	34	41	**57**
10	Evesham United (15)	42	9	3	9	28	35	7	5	9	22	25	**56**
11	Grantham Town (13)	42	7	4	10	30	32	9	2	10	47	41	**54**
12	Bridgnorth Town (16)	42	8	3	10	26	29	7	3	11	30	39	**51**
13	Racing Warwick (22)	42	6	6	9	27	34	7	6	8	26	32	**51**
14	Dudley Town (17)	42	4	7	10	33	40	9	3	9	31	21	**49**
15	Forest Green Rovers (19)	42	7	5	9	34	46	5	7	9	27	38	**48**
16	Sutton Coldfield Town (8)	42	3	5	13	25	44	9	3	9	28	31	**44**
17	Bedworth United (6)	42	6	2	13	31	41	6	5	10	31	40	**43**
18	Hinckley Town (20)	42	5	6	10	25	32	6	4	11	19	39	**43**
19	Leicester United (12)	42	5	5	11	19	40	6	4	11	15	33	**42**
20	King's Lynn (21)	42	5	7	9	25	30	4	4	13	22	42	**38**
21	Yate Town (18)	42	4	2	15	19	43	6	4	11	29	43	**36**
22	Armitage (-)	42	5	3	13	24	51	3	8	10	21	52	**35**

Figures in brackets are 1992-93 positions.

- Rushden & Diamonds and VS Rugby were promoted to the Beazer Homes Premier Division. Moor Green and Nuneaton Borough were relegated into the Midland Division.
- For the second successive season no club was relegated from the Midland Division. Two Southern Division clubs resigned: Canterbury City and Dunstable, who then folded before playing their scheduled opening fixture in the United Counties League, a home game against Desborough.
- Only two clubs from the feeder leagues were considered suitable for promotion. Ilkeston Town, West Midlands League champions, and Rothwell Town, the top United Counties League club, both joined the Midland Division..
- One club, Buckingham Town, was transferred from the Southern Division to the Midland Division. Three south-western clubs, Clevedon Town, Weston-super-Mare and Yate Town were transferred to the Southern Division.

1993-1994 Results

Beazer Homes League Midland Division

Aug	21	Clevedon Town	H	2	0	Nuttell, Watkins	641
Aug	24	Tamworth	A	1	1	Nuttell	622
Aug	30	Bedworth United	H	3	1	Flower, Nuttell 2	884
Sep	4	Stourbridge	A	1	0	Richardson	284
Sep	14	King's Lynn	H	6	0	Mann 3, Nuttell, Kirkup, Diver	901
Sep	18	Bridgnorth Town	A	2	0	Mann, Diver	165
Oct	2	Dudley Town	A	2	2	Nuttell 2	237
Oct	30	Redditch United	A	2	1	Mann, Watkins	146
Nov	6	Hinckley Town	H	2	3	Mann, Kirkup	647
Nov	13	Bilston Town	H	5	1	Nuttell 2, Watkins, Mann, Diver	637
Nov	20	Tamworth	H	5	1	York, Nuttell, Watkins, Kirkup, own goal	701
Nov	27	Stourbridge	H	3	3	Watkins 3	603
Dec	4	Dudley Town	H	2	1	Richardson, Kirkup	738
Dec	18	Leicester United	A	2	0	Kirkup 2	191
Dec	27	VS Rugby	H	1	1	Nuttell	2054
Jan	1	Grantham Town	A	1	0	Kirkup	502
Jan	3	Racing Warwick	H	1	1	Richardson	1019
Jan	8	Armitage	A	3	0	Nuttell 2, Watkins	117
Jan	15	Sutton Coldfield Town	H	2	0	Watkins, Bailey	906
Jan	22	Forest Green Rovers	A	5	3	Watkins, Flower 2, Coe, Beech	287
Jan	26	Newport AFC	A	2	0	Beech, Watkins	422
Jan	29	Weston super Mare	A	1	2	Nuttell	495
Feb	5	Yate Town	H	3	0	Flower, Nuttell, Bailey	810
Feb	8	King's Lynn	A	1	1	Watkins	383
Feb	12	Evesham United	A	4	1	Nuttell 2, York, Flower	224
Feb	19	Newport AFC	H	1	1	Watkins	991
Feb	26	Leicester United	H	4	0	Nuttell, Mann 2, Bailey	855
Mar	1	Bedworth United	A	2	1	Watkins, Nuttell	292
Mar	5	Bilston Town	A	1	0	Watkins	189
Mar	8	Bridgnorth Town	H	2	0	Beech, Coe	844
Mar	12	Yate Town	A	4	2	Bailey 2, Beech, Watkins	238
Mar	19	Weston super Mare	H	3	2	York, Nuttell, Watkins	1310
Mar	23	Clevedon Town	A	0	0		469
Mar	26	Hinckley Town	A	4	0	Keast, Watkins 2, Nuttell	262
Apr	2	VS Rugby	A	2	2	Nuttell, Keast	1233
Apr	9	Racing Warwick	A	2	2	Watkins, Coe	249
Apr	12	Grantham Town	H	3	3	Watkins, Nuttell 2	723
Apr	16	Armitage	H	4	0	Nuttell 2, Johnson, Mann	945
Apr	23	Sutton Coldfield Town	A	2	1	Johnson, Flower	345
Apr	30	Evesham United	H	1	0	Mann	1186
May	2	Forest Green Rovers	H	5	0	Nuttell 2, Mann, Watkins, Coe	1504
May	7	Redditch United	H	7	0	Wooding, Keast, Watkins, Flower, Mann 2, Nuttell	1397

1993-1994 Results

FA Cup

Aug	28 PQ	Rocester	A	1	0	Nuttell	169
Sep	11 1Q	Sutton Coldfield Town	H	2	0	Watkins, Mann	536
Sep	25 2Q	Rothwell Town	H	1	1	Nuttell	990
Sep	28 2QR	Rothwell Town	A	2	0	Watkins 2	929
Oct	9 3Q	Burton Albion	H	4	0	Nuttell, Mann, Richardson, Watkins	1201
Oct	23 4Q	Bromsgrove Rovers	H	1	3	Kirkup	1521

FA Trophy

Oct	16 2Q	Burton Albion	H	0	1		812

Dr Martens Cup

Sep	7 P.1	Grantham Town	A	3	1	Kirkup, Flower, Watkins	188
Sep	21 P.2	Grantham Town	H	3	2	Watkins, Kurila, Nuttell	621
Oct	19 1.1	Bedworth United	H	2	0	Nuttell, Watkins	402
Oct	26 1.2	Bedworth United	A	0	0		216
Nov	9 2	Cambridge City	H	2	2	Nuttell, Mann	419
Dec	7 2R	Cambridge City	A	1	3	Kirkup	167

NFA Hillier Senior Cup

Oct	12 1	Cogenhoe United	H	4	2	Nuttell 3, Watkins	437
Nov	30 2	Rothwell Town	A	1	0	own goal	203
Mar	29 SF	Kettering Town	H	3	2	Kirkup 2, Nuttell	2352
Apr	26 F	Northampton Spencer	H	5	0	Watkins 3, Flower, Wooding	1254

- The FA Cup was won by Manchester United who beat Chelsea 4-0 in the final. Four non-League sides reached the Third Round proper. Pride of place went to Kidderminster Harriers who won 2-1 at Birmingham City and went as far as the Fifth Round. In the Fourth Round they beat Preston North End 1-0 to put them into the last sixteen where, at the Aggborough ground deemed unsuitable by the Football League, Lee Chapman scored the only goal of the game for West Ham United. Bath City drew 0-0 at Stoke City before losing the home replay 1-4. Sutton United went down by the odd goal of five at Notts County and Bromsgrove Rovers, as related in the text, lost narrowly to Barnsley. Seven non-League sides beat Football League opposition: Bath City (Hereford United), Bromsgrove Rovers (Northampton Town), Halifax Town (West Bromwich Albion), Macclesfield Town (Hartlepool United), Nuneaton Borough (Swansea City), Sutton United (Colchester United & Torquay United) and Yeovil Town (Fulham).

- In the FA Trophy final, Woking (3rd in the Conference) beat Runcorn (5th in the Conference) 2-1. Enfield and Guiseley were the beaten semi-finalists.

- In the Dr Martens sponsored Southern League Cup, Southern Division runners-up Sudbury Town beat Premier Division Gresley Rovers in both legs of the final. Sudbury's success came after they had been knocked out of the competition in the third round. However their conquerors, Gravesend & Northfleet had fielded an ineligible player so Sudbury were reinstated.

1993-1994 Teams
Beazer Homes League Midland Division

		Bailey	Beech	Coe	Diver	Flower	Fox	Hillier	Johnson	Keast	Kirkup	Kurila	Mann	Nuttell	Page	Peaks	Richardson	Shoemake	Watkins	Wooding	York
Clevedon	H					4	1		3		7	2	8	9	6		5		10		11
Tamworth	A					4	1		3		sb	7	8	9	6	2	5		10		11
Bedworth	H					4	1		3		7	2	8	9	6		5		10		11
Stourbridge	A					4	1		3		7	2	8	9	6		5		10		11
King's Lynn	H				sb	4			3		7	2	8	9	6		5	1	10		11
Bridgnorth	A				sb	4			3		7	2	8	9	6		5	1	10		11
Dudley	A				3	4					7		8	9	6	2	5	1	10		11
Redditch	A							2	3			7	8	9	6	4	5	1	10		11
Hinckley	H								3		7	2	8	9	6	4	5	1	10		11
Bilston	H				sb		1		3		7	2	8	9	6	4	5		10		11
Tamworth	H						1	sb	3		7	2	8	9	6	4	5		10		11
Stourbridge	H				sb		1		3		7	2	8	9	6	4	5		10		11
Dudley	H		sb		sb	4	1		3		7	10	8	9	6	2	5				11
Leicester United	A	sb		8	10	4	1		3		7	2		9	6	sb	5				11
VS Rugby	H			11		4	1		3		7	8		9	6	2	5		10		
Grantham	A		sb	8		4	1		3		7	2		9	6		5		10		11
Racing Warwick	H	sb	7	8		4	1		3			2		9	6		5		10		11
Armitage	A		7	8		4	1		3					9	6	2	5		10		11
Sutton Coldfield	H	sb	9	8		4	1		3		7				6	2	5		10		11
Forest Green	A	7	9	8		4	1		3						6	2	5		10		11
Newport	A		7	8		4	1		3			sb		9	6	2	5		10		11
Weston s Mare	A	sb	7	8		4	1		3			2		9		6	5		10		11
Yate	H	sb	7	8		4	1		3					9		6	5		10	2	11
King's Lynn	A	sb	7	8		4	1		3					9		6	5		10	2	11
Evesham	A		7	sb		4	1		3				8	9	6		5		10	2	11
Newport	H	sb	7	sb		4	1		3				8	9	6		5		10	2	11
Leicester United	H	sb	7	sb		4	1		3				8	9	6		5		10	2	11
Bedworth	A		7	11		4	1		3				8	9	6		5		10	2	
Bilston	A	sb	7	11			1		3				8	9	6	4	5		10	2	
Bridgnorth	H		7	11			1		3				8	9	6	4	5		10	2	sb
Yate	A	8	5	7		4	1		3					9	6				10	2	11
Weston s Mare	H	8	5	7		4	1		3			sb		9	6				10	2	11
Clevedon	A	8	5			4	1		3		7			9	6				10	2	11
Hinckley	A	sb	5			4	1		3	8	7		sb	9	6	2			10		11
VS Rugby	A		5	sb		4	1		3	8	7			9	6	2			10		11
Racing Warwick	A	sb	5	3		4	1			7			8	9	6				10	2	11
Grantham	H	sb		7		4	1		3	5			8	9	6				10	2	11
Armitage	H			7		4	1		3	5			8	9	6				10	2	11
Sutton Coldfield	A			7		4	1		3	5		8		9	6				10	2	11
Evesham	H	sb	5	7		4	1		3	sb			8	9	6				10	2	11
Forest Green	H		sb	7		4	1		3	5			8	9	6				10	2	11
Redditch	H		5	7		4	1		3	11			8	9	6				10	2	

1993-1994 Teams   Cup Competitions

		Bailey	Beech	Coe	Diver	Flower	Fox	Hillier	Johnson	Kirkup	Kurila	Mann	Nuttell	Page	Peaks	Richardson	Shoemake	Watkins	Wooding	York
FA Cup																				
Rocester	A					4	1		3	7	2	8	9	6	sb	5		10		11
Sutton Coldfield	H	sb				4			3	7	2	8	9	6		5	1	10		11
Rothwell	A				sb	4			3	7	2	8	9	6		5	1	10		11
Rothwell	H					4			3	7		8	9	6	2	5	1	10		11
Burton Albion	H					4	1	2	3	7		8	9		6	5		10		11
Bromsgrove	H	sb				4			3	7	2	8	9	6	sb	5	1	10		11
FA Trophy																				
Burton Albion	H				sb	4	1	8	3	7			9	6	2	5		10		11
Dr Martens Cup																				
Grantham	A	sb				4	1		3	7	2	8	9	6		5		10		11
Grantham	H				sb	4			3	7	2	8	9	6	5		1	10		11
Bedworth	H					4			3	7	8		9	6	2	5	1	10		11
Bedworth	A	10				4		2	3	7		8	9	6		5	1			11
Cambridge City	H				sb		1	2	3	7	10	8	9	6	4	5				11
Cambridge City	A	sb	8		10	4	1		3	7	2		9	6		5				11
Hillier Cup																				
Cogenhoe	H	sb			7	4	1	2	3	sb		8	9		6	5		10		11
Rothwell	A		sb		10	4	1		3	7	2	8	9		6	5				11
Kettering	H		5	8		4	1		3	7		sb	9	6	2			10		11
Northmptn Spencer	H	sb	5	7		4	1		3		sb	8	9	6				10	2	11

Paul Coe (left) and Alan Kurila, both of whom made their final Rushden & Diamonds appearances in the 1993-94 season.

1993-1994 Appearances

	Start						Substitute						Total					
	L	C	T	LC	CC	Tot	L	C	T	LC	CC	Tot	L	C	T	LC	CC	Tot
Richard BAILEY	4			1		**5**	13	2		2	2	**19**	17	2		3	2	**24**
Glen BEECH	22			1	2	**25**	3				1	**4**	25			1	3	**29**
Paul COE	23				2	**25**	4					**4**	27				2	**29**
Shaun DIVER	2			1	2	**5**	5	1	1	2		**9**	7	1	1	3	2	**14**
John FLOWER	35	6	1	5	4	**51**							35	6	1	5	4	**51**
Kevin FOX	37	2	1	3	4	**47**							37	2	1	3	4	**47**
Darren HILLIER	1	1	1	2	1	**6**	1					**1**	2	1	1	2	1	**7**
Dave JOHNSON	40	6	1	6	4	**57**							40	6	1	6	4	**57**
Dougie KEAST	8					**8**	1					**1**	9					**9**
Andy KIRKUP	18	6	1	6	2	**33**	1				1	**2**	19	6	1	6	3	**35**
Alan KURILA	18	4		5	1	**28**	2				1	**3**	20	4		5	2	**31**
Adie MANN	25	6		4	3	**38**	1				1	**2**	26	6		4	4	**40**
Mickey NUTTELL	40	6	1	6	4	**57**							40	6	1	6	4	**57**
Darrell PAGE	39	5	1	6	2	**53**							39	5	1	6	2	**53**
Andy PEAKS	20	2	1	3	3	**29**	1	2				**3**	21	4	1	3	3	**32**
Paul RICHARDSON	30	6	1	5	2	**44**							30	6	1	5	2	**44**
Kevin SHOEMAKE	5	4		3		**12**							5	4		3		**12**
Dale WATKINS	40	6	1	3	3	**53**							40	6	1	3	3	**53**
Tim WOODING	18				1	**19**							18				1	**19**
Paul YORK	37	6	1	6	4	**54**	1					**1**	38	6	1	6	4	**55**
MAXIMUM	42	6	1	6	4	**59**							42	6	1	6	4	**59**

Goalscorers

	L	C	T	LC	CC	Total
Mickey NUTTELL	29	3		3	4	39
Dale WATKINS	23	4		3	4	34
Adie MANN	14	2		1		17
Andy KIRKUP	7	1		2	2	12
John FLOWER	7			1	1	9
Richard BAILEY	5					5
Glen BEECH	4					4
Paul COE	4					4
Paul RICHARDSON	3	1				4
Shaun DIVER	3					3
Dougie KEAST	3					3
Paul YORK	3					3
Dave JOHNSON	2					2
Tim WOODING	1				1	2
Alan KURILA				1		1
own goal	1				1	2
TOTAL	109	11	0	11	13	144

1993-94 Playing Record

HOME	P	W	D	L	F	A	Pts
League	21	15	5	1	65	18	50
FA Cup	4	2	1	1	8	4	
FA Trophy	1	0	0	1	0	1	
League Cup	3	2	1	0	7	4	
County Cup	3	3	0	0	12	4	
TOTAL	32	22	7	3	92	31	
AWAY							
League	21	14	6	1	44	19	48
FA Cup	2	2	0	0	3	0	
FA Trophy	-	-	-	-	-	-	
League Cup	3	1	1	1	4	4	
County Cup	1	1	0	0	1	0	
TOTAL	27	18	7	2	52	23	
TOTAL							
League	42	29	11	2	109	37	98
FA Cup	6	4	1	1	11	4	
FA Trophy	1	0	0	1	0	1	
League Cup	6	3	2	1	11	8	
County Cup	4	4	0	0	13	4	
TOTAL	**59**	**40**	**14**	**5**	**144**	**54**	

Attendance Summary

HOME	Total	Ave	High		Low	
League	20296	966	2054	VS Rugby	603	Stourbridge
FA Cup	4248	1062	1521	Bromsgrove	536	Sutton Coldfield
FA Trophy	812	812	812	Burton	812	Burton
League Cup	1442	481	621	Grantham	402	Bedworth
County Cup	4043	1348	2352	Kettering	437	Cogenhoe
TOTAL	30841	995	2352	Kettering	402	Bedworth
AWAY						
League	7352	350	1233	VS Rugby	117	Armitage
FA Cup	1098	549	929	Rothwell	169	Rocester
FA Trophy	-	-	-	-	-	-
League Cup	571	190	216	Bedworth	167	Cambridge
County Cup	203	203	203	Rothwell	203	Rothwell
TOTAL	9224	318	1233	VS Rugby	117	Armitage
TOTAL						
League	27648	658	2054	VS Rugby H	117	Armitage A
FA Cup	5346	891	1521	Bromsgrove H	169	Rocester A
FA Trophy	812	812	812	Burton H	812	Burton H
League Cup	2013	336	621	Grantham H	167	Cambridge A
County Cup	4246	1062	2352	Kettering H	203	Rothwell A
TOTAL	**40065**	**679**	**2352**	Kettering H	**117**	Armitage A

SEASON THREE

1994 - 95

"'Three years she grew in sun and shower
Then nature said, 'A lovelier flower
On earth was never sown'"

Wordsworth

Back (l to r): Billy Jeffrey, Andy Kirkup, Tim Wooding, Dave Johnson, Steve Spooner, Dale Watkins, Pete Brown.

Centre (l to r): Richard Bailey, Kevin Wilkin, Mickey Nuttell, Andy Lomas, Martin Davies, John Flower, Darren Collins, Julian Capone.

Front (l to r): Adie Mann, Garry Butterworth, Paul York, Roger Ashby, Dougie Keast, Ian King, Andy Peaks.

During the summer of 1994 the Diamond Centre opened and the South Stand was fully ready for the new season. This enabled the portakabins at the west end to be removed thus clearing the site for the construction of the West Stand, later to be named after Peter DeBanke. On the footballing side there were a number of changes designed to strengthen the side for the greater challenges of the Beazer Homes League Premier Division.

Although there had only been a gap of three seasons when there had not been a club named Rushden in the Premier Division only eleven of the twenty-one that had visited Hayden Road would visit Nene Park. Bromsgrove, Dover and Farnborough had been promoted to the Conference whilst Bashley, Moor Green, Poole, Waterlooville, Wealdstone and Weymouth had been relegated to the lower divisions of the league. Dartford, the first team to be beaten by the Russians in the Premier Division, had gone out of business but by 1994 had reformed and were playing in the Kent League, albeit on the ground of Erith & Belvedere.

Rushden & Diamonds made two big signings. Both were for transfer fees that caused large intakes of breath at the time but both turned out to be bargains. From Enfield of the Diadora Isthmian League came Darren Collins for a fee of £20,000. Collins had spent three seasons at Northampton Town scoring 11 times in his 68 appearances before being signed by Trevor Gould, then manager of Aylesbury United. At the Buckinghamshire club Collins had played in the same team as future Diamonds Nick Ashby and Simon Mason as well two former Kettering Wrights, Andy and Owen. He then moved to Enfield, playing with Al James Hannigan under the managership of Graham Roberts.

From another London club came Garry Butterworth, an ever present the previous season in the Dagenham & Redbridge side that had finished sixth in the Conference. Born in Peterborough, he had made over 120 appearances for his home town club before he moved to Dagenham in the summer of 1992 after having spent a couple of months on loan at Kettering. His fee was decided by a tribunal, the verdict being £22,000, considerably less than Dagenham's manager, John Still, had hoped for.

Another new signing was the afore-mentioned Simon Mason who had spent the previous season with Diamonds' fellow promoted club VS Rugby. Leicester born, he'd played for Shepshed and Leicester United before moving to Aylesbury.

Predictable departures during the close season included Shaun Diver and John Coe (who made permanent his return to Rothwell Town), but there was surprise at the release of Glen Beech, who had played a prominent role in the promotion campaign producing a number of outstanding performances. Manager Roger Ashby attributed his decision to the need to plan for the future. *"It was a difficult decision to make. But sometimes your mind has to over-rule your heart and, at thirty-three, Glen is not getting any younger. We have to look ahead."*

Defender Alan Kurila was transfer listed with a year of his contract still to run. He did not appear again in the first team, a fate which also befell Paul Coe who eventually returned to Cambridge City. Goalkeeper Kevin Shoemake and defender Darren Hillier, who joined Nuneaton Borough, were two others who had played their last games for Rushden & Diamonds.

The opening pre-season game was a goalless draw against a Norwich City side containing such familiar names as Bryan Gunn, Mark Bowen and Mike Milligan. In the next Nene Park 'friendly', over 2,000 spectators saw Darren Collins open his account with two goals as the Diamonds overcame his old club, Northampton Town, by 3-2. Among the Cobblers players on view were goalkeeper Billy Stewart and striker Dean Trott, both destined to confront Rushden & Diamonds in future encounters.

The reserves, continuing under the stewardship of Kenny Mist, were looking forward to their first season in the Midland Combination Reserve Division. *"We are quite optimistic about the coming season, especially the thought of the challenge of a new league to compete in, visiting new grounds and playing in a better standard of football,"* Kenny wrote in a early programme. Whilst his side proved to have a extremely successful season his hopes for the quality of the new surroundings were over-optimistic. In the first game Stratford Town reserves were beaten 11-1.

John Flower with the Maunsell Cup.

As a consequence of having won the Hillier Senior Cup the previous season, the Diamonds played in the Maunsell Cup against Peterborough United. Goals from Mickey Nuttell and Dale Watkins, both former Posh players, gave the Diamonds a morale-boosting 2-1 success over their former club. Garry Butterworth was another Peterborough 'old boy' to derive considerable pleasure from the result against a Posh side that included Scott Cooksey (Bromsgrove) and Ashley Warner (VS Rugby) who had played at Nene Park the previous season whilst David Morrison was experiencing a Nene Park bench for the first time.

First team preparations were completed with a 2-0 victory over Phil Neal's Coventry City side, including several Premier Division stars, and expectations were high for the first match of the league campaign - the visit of Cheltenham Town on August 20th.

Unsurprisingly, Roger Ashby fielded the majority of the team that had played so well in the pre-season friendlies, although the absence of the injured Darrell Page gave patient Andy Peaks an early opportunity to claim a regular place in the side. A crowd of 1,610, more than double that which watched the corresponding fixture against Clevedon in 1993-94, saw the visitors score two second half goals and inflict a disappointing 2-0 defeat. The Diamonds cause was hardly helped by injury to full back Tim Wooding and the loss of central defender, John Flower, dismissed after 75 minutes for a fierce tackle on the elusive Jimmy Smith. After Jimmy Wring had given the Robins a 62nd minute lead only a string of fine saves by Kevin Fox prevented a goal rush as the beleaguered home defence struggled to contain the lively visiting attack. It was no surprise when substitute Jason Eaton added a second six minutes from time to give a more realistic final scoreline.

Rushden & Diamonds (0) **0**			**Cheltenham Town** (0) **2**		
1	Kevin Fox		1	Martin Thomas	
2	Tim Wooding	(sub: Kirkup)	2	Matthew Lovell	
3	Dave Johnson		3	Bob Bloomer	
4	John Flower		4	Chris Banks	
5	Dougie Keast		5	Vaughan Jones	
6	Andy Peaks		6	Neil Smith	
7	Darren Collins		7	Lee Howells	
8	Garry Butterworth		8	Simon Cooper	
9	Mickey Nuttell		9	Jimmy Smith	(sub: Eaton)
10	Dale Watkins	(sub: Mason)	10	Martin Boyle	
11	Paul York		11	Jimmy Wring	(sub: Cook)
12	Andy Kirkup		12	Jason Eaton	
14	Simon Mason		14	Shane Cook	

Referee: DC Madgwick (Aylesbury)

Goals: Wring (62, **0-1**), Eaton (84, **0-2**)

The visit to Gravesend and Northfleet - promoted as champions of the Southern Division - three days later assumed increased importance as the league 'new boys' attempted to make an early impact on the competition. It was a victory for the Midland champions as the side returned from Kent with all three points, Dale Watkins' third minute decider securing a 1 - 0 victory.

Darren Collins had proved provider, supplying the cross for Watkins' goal at Northfleet, but turned scorer in the next fixture at Halesowen. His double helped the Diamonds to a comfortable 4-2 success, but the game was most notable for the midfield performance of Garry Butterworth whose selection as the Dolben Insurance 'Man of the Match' was the first in a lengthy list of similar accolades.

But two away victories were followed by two moderate Nene Park performances. Goals from Darren Collins and John Flower, playing in his last game before a three match suspension, saw off bottom markers Trowbridge 2-1, the winner coming late in the second half. On the Bank Holiday Monday there was another late goal but this time it gave Burton Albion a point, Darren Grocutt punishing poor defending from a free kick to snatch an 85th minute equaliser after the Diamonds, thanks to a Dale Watkins double, had led 2-1.

Diamonds then made it three wins out three on the road despite conceding two more goals in a turbulent game at Crawley after which there were reports of crowd troubles. Diamonds came from 2-1 down to win 4-2 with Paul York sent off near the end for his second yellow card.

MAUNSELL CUP WINNERS

Back (l to r): Andy Kirkup, Garry Butterworth, Tim Wooding, Dave Johnson, John Flower, Kevin Fox. Front: Dougie Keast, Dale Watkins, Paul York, Darrell Page, Mickey Nuttell

Unbeaten in the last five games and with a perfect away record, the side travelled to Eastwood Hanley for an FA Cup First Qualifying Round tie. It is more accurate to report the destination as the picturesque Clough Hall Park, home of Kidsgrove Athletic, as Eastwood's own ground had suffered persistent vandalism and was currently awaiting urgent renovation. If ever an FA Cup fixture contained the essential ingredients for an upset this was it, the matchday programme previewing the game as 'a classic David and Goliath encounter'.

165 spectators watched the Potteries side, then seventeenth in the North West Counties League, take the lead after 37 minutes, somewhat against the run of play. A free kick from assistant boss Mick Bates curled around the five man wall, was parried by Diamonds debutant keeper, Lee Crane *(right)*, and then lashed high into the roof of the net by a jubilant Jason Robinson. Remarkably the underdogs held on tenaciously to the slender lead, surviving a constant barrage as the Diamonds sought to salvage pride. Substitute Julian Capone, also making his debut, marked his arrival twenty minutes from time with a pin-point cross which Mickey Nuttell headed high and wide of the target. It proved a costly miss. Spurning the temptation to concede an equaliser and use the much needed replay revenue to fund ground improvements, Eastwood opted for glory, a series of fine saves by John Stanway sealing a famous victory.

The Diamonds team of talents had a week to lick its wounds before embarking upon another route to Wembley - in the FA Trophy. It would prove a longer, and infinitely more rewarding journey. Not that that was apparent from the opening game, a scoreless draw of mind-numbing tediousness against Diadora strugglers, Hendon. Just about the only point of interest was that in charge of the match was top referee Graham Poll.

The replay saw the Diamonds hit four away goals for the third time in the season. The turning point in the game was the tactical switch that brought substitute Adie Mann into the action after the interval. With the sides level at 1-1, the resultant domination of midfield ensured better service to the front men. Within ten minutes of the restart, Darren Collins had scored a second goal, Dale Watkins extended the lead twenty minutes later, and with Hendon struggling to contain a rampant Rushden added his second during the eight minutes of additional time allowed by referee Graham Barber.

An 8-0 demolition of Desborough Town showed how irrelevant the Hillier Senior Cup could be, though it did provide the opportunity for Julian Capone to score his first goal for the club. It was far from ideal preparation for the trip to old Midland Division rivals, Gresley Rovers. Although the prolific strike force scored three times, recovering from a two goal deficit to lead 3-2 at half time, the defence shipped four in a dreadful display that incurred the wrath of manager Ashby.

He made wholesale changes for the next game, a Dr Martens Cup first round first leg tie against Rothwell Town, dropping Tim Wooding, Dave Johnson and Darrell Page. A reorganised line-up (including, for the last time, Simon Mason who was appearing against one of the many clubs he would subsequently represent) took time to settle and with better finishing, a little luck and a less lenient referee, the Midland Division newcomers might have taken an advantage to Cecil Street for the return. Ryan Smythe hit the bar, Ku Akeredolu shot wide from close range and Kevin Fox was forced to handle several yards outside his area to prevent a certain Rothwell goal. John Coe, impressive at the heart of the Bones defence, summed up the mood of his Rothwell team mates after the goalless draw. *"We came here determined not to lose, and left feeling we ought to have won."*

Crawley Town, who arrived the following Saturday after a string of recent victories over Cheltenham, Dorchester and Sittingbourne, could harbour no such thoughts on leaving Nene Park. In fact they could hardly get away quickly enough after suffering a 0-5 thrashing by an inspired Diamonds side that finally produced the sort of devastating home performance that had long been promised. With Wooding and Johnson restored to the defence, Ashby introduced two loanees, keeper Chris Mackenzie and sweeper, Kenny Webster. Mackenzie was well known in the county, having served Corby Town with distinction before joining Hereford United. Webster had moved to Peterborough after being a trainee at Arsenal. Both enjoyed quiet debuts as a Dale Watkins double in the first twenty-six minutes took his season's tally to twelve, Nuttell, Mann and Collins adding further goals to complete the rout.

A week later, on October 15th, the Diamonds really were on the Wembley trail, their opponents in the 2nd Qualifying Round of the FA Trophy being the Diadora side Wembley. The North London side made all the early running, going ahead on the half hour when Guiliano Grazioli (later to find national fame with Stevenage Borough) volleyed past Chris Mackenzie from the edge of the penalty area. When the same player hit the bar just two minutes later it proved to be the visitors' last serious threat and second half goals from Collins and Mann took their side through into the next round- and another meeting with Crawley Town.

Three days later Rothwell Town were despatched 2-1 in the Dr Martens Cup second leg, Mickey Nuttell being sent off for an elbowing offence, Ku Akeredolu's consolation coming too late to disturb the ten men.

The next league fixture at Dorchester provided several lessons for the Diamonds hierarchy as well as giving further lie to the old footballing adage that two goals away from home is enough to win any game, the home side hitting four in return. The Diamonds scored first and last but it was another disappointing defensive performance. The folly of a late departure for a journey of this length, particularly one via the still to be by-passed Newbury, was demonstrated by the arrival of the team less than half an hour before the start. The supporters were even later, most just managing to scramble into the superbly appointed Avenue Stadium in time to see Steve Richardson put the Magpies 2-1 up.

A comfortable 3-1 Hillier Senior Cup victory over a Northampton Spencer side which included Frankie Belfon and Adie Mann's younger brother, Ian, brought a two goal reward for Mickey Nuttell, whose golden touch of 1993-94 had temporarily deserted him. Once again, however, success against lowly opposition was quickly put into perspective on the following Saturday when Beazer Premier visitors, Gloucester City returned to the west country with all three points. Although Adie Mann's centre-come-shot deceived keeper David Coles to cancel the Dougie Keast own goal which had gifted City an 11th minute lead, poor marking from a corner shortly before half time allowed the unmarked Dave Mitchell a simple tap in after Karl Bayliss's header had struck the bar. The Diamonds' quest for an equaliser was made infinitely more difficult by the 65th minute dismissal of John Flower for an elbowing offence on Harris. Given his poor disciplinary record this second sending off of the season (both against Gloucestershire clubs) would guarantee a lengthy absence from the side. Indeed it provoked Roger Ashby to question publicly Flower's future with the club.

The Gloucester City game was Kenny Webster's last playing appearance for the Diamonds. The Peterborough United defender had made little impression during his loan spell at Nene Park but would enjoy considerable success at Stevenage Borough, winning a Vauxhall Conference championship medal in 1995-96. He ended his loan spell consigned to the substitutes bench for the entire game at Burton Albion. Missing from the Diamonds line-up were the suspended Mickey Nuttell, flu-stricken John Flower, and Adie Mann who was omitted for 'tactical reasons'. Andy Peaks and Darrell Page returned with Garry Butterworth filling the sweeper role in a five man defence. The game took place on November 5th, but fireworks were confined to the dying stages of both halves. Behind after 37 minutes, Tim Wooding levelled from 20 yards in first half injury time. Three points seemed assured when Darren Collins put his side 2 - 1 ahead with just two minutes remaining, however an equaliser at the death denied the Diamonds a deserved victory. As at Nene Park in August, the Albion saviour was Darren Grocutt. Mackenzie's loan spell also ended after this match. Like Webster, his time at Nene Park had been unimpressive but before the new year he had been restored to Hereford's first team, a position he retained for the next season and a half. It was also the final, and 114th, appearance for Darrell Page. Never criticised for lack of effort, he had been a stalwart throughout the Midland Division days. After a short stay with Wealdstone he moved to Raunds and assisted them into the Dr Martens League.

The League Cup Second Round tie against Midland Division Bedworth United saw the debut of a new goalkeeper, Martin Davies, and the re-instatement of Adie Mann. The latter celebrated his recall with a fine opening goal as the Diamonds returned to winning ways with a 4-2 victory. Davies, a Swansea born 20 year old, was on loan from Coventry City where he was third choice behind Steve Ogrizovic and Jonathan Gould.

There was another new face in the line-up for the next league game against old rivals, VS Rugby. Ian King had netted for the Warwickshire side in the corresponding fixture in 1993-94 while on loan from Stoke City. His eventual release by new manager, Lou Macari, triggered widespread interest from Football League and Conference clubs, including Northampton Town, but Roger Ashby stepped in to offer the 19 year old an attractive eighteen month contract. He marked his debut with a goal from a stunning twenty-five yard free kick as the Diamonds recorded an impressive 4-1 victory. It was an unhappy return to Nene Park for Simon Mason and the game was a graphic demonstration that whilst some fans had been disappointed that Diamonds had not stormed to the top of the Premier Division, they had adjusted much better than the side which twelve months previously had virtually matched them step for step.

Paul York in Premier Division action against Burton Albion at Nene Park.

As the ET reporter queried sardonically after the trip to Trowbridge, *"What form of intelligent life arranges fixtures that send Rushden to the west country in midweek and to Corby next Saturday?"* In the event, the side returned from Wiltshire with a point, and it might easily have been three, from a match that had no shortage of talking points. Striker Mickey Nuttell was drafted into the centre of defence (leaving new central defender Steve Shea on the bench - the nearest he got to a first team appearance), Dale Watkins took his league goals tally to eleven, and Trowbridge manager, the former Rushden Town and Irthlingborough player, Steve Rutter, played two joker cards. Making a double substitution a quarter of an hour from time, the numbers held up did not correspond to the players who left the pitch. However it proved an inspired tactical switch when one of the replacements, Matty Brown, scored an equaliser just two minutes after the change to salvage an unlikely point.

The shorter journey to the Rockingham Triangle brought maximum reward. It was the first ever local derby between Rushden and Diamonds and the Steelmen but turned out to be a very one-sided affair. Goalkeeper Kevin Fox, recalled from a month's loan to Raunds Town after Martin Davies had withdrawn with glandular fever, was called into action in the opening minutes, denying John Ashdjian, but it was one-way traffic thereafter. Ian King's neat chip over the stranded Paul Beresford after 21 minutes coincided with the departure of the injured Dale Watkins. Fears that Watkins' absence might blunt the Diamonds attack proved groundless. In his first league appearance of the season, substitute Richard Bailey seized his chance with alacrity scoring two goals in a ten minute spell to give his side a 3-0 lead. Mickey Nuttell, restored to a striking role, made it four and only the woodwork and a brave performance by Beresford kept the final score respectable. Corby's tenth successive defeat, a club record, was indicative of the changing power base in Northamptonshire football. Once the top non-league side in the county (from 1965 to 1968 Corby was in the Southern Premier, a division higher than Kettering), the Steelmen were overwhelmed by a team intent on achieving that status, and beyond.

The third, and final, qualifying round of the FA Trophy provided Crawley Town with the opportunity to gain revenge for their thrashing at Nene Park seven weeks earlier. Again the Sussex side left Irthlingborough defeated, though the margin was substantially reduced. Diamonds needed an Adie Mann winner a quarter of an hour from time to put them in the First Round Proper. There were few racing pulses in the Nene Valley when the draw was made the following Monday. Trophy fever had yet to bite and the prospect of the visit of fellow Beazer Premier side Sudbury Town did little to stir the emotions.

December began with a trip to Leek, newly transferred from the Northern Premier League, and the surprise return to first team football of midfielder Paul Richardson. Seriously injured nine months previously, 'Tigger' signalled his comeback with the Diamonds' first goal, sparking a recovery which transformed a 0-2 half-time deficit into a 3-2 lead. Unfortunately, Leek then raised their own game snatching an equaliser with twelve minutes left, and then so dominating the final stages that they might well have taken all three points.

A Mickey Nuttell goal earned a point in the 1-1 draw with Halesowen Town in Rushden & Diamonds' 100th League game. Malcolm Hazlewood netted an injury time equaliser for the visitors. Hazlewood was a survivor from Halesowen's Wembley FA Vase triumph in 1985, a season in which Irthlingborough Diamonds had lost to Hucknall Colliery Welfare in the last 32 and Rushden Town had gone out at Evesham United three rounds earlier.

The Peter DeBanke terrace

Progress in the League Cup was maintained as goals from King, York and Collins saw off Baldock Town 3-0 in a routine Third Round home win. A similar performance brought three points at the expense of Solihull Borough, though Diamonds had allowed the visitors to grab a sixth minute lead. The west terrace, dedicated to Peter DeBanke who had been connected with both clubs, was opened for the first time.

So, as the festive period approached there was much to retain the fans' interest. Promotion remained a possibility and the side was still involved in three cup competitions. Results over the holiday period increased the feeling of optimism. Three consecutive victories propelled Diamonds to third place in the table - but that was as good as it got.

The Boxing Day trip to Cambridge City saw a Dale Watkins hat-trick secure three points after former Diamonds winger Paul Coe had threatened to spoil the party with a 55th minute equaliser and the long New Year's Eve trip to the Sussex coast saw Hastings succumb 0-2, Nuttell and Watkins getting the second half goals.

The side marked its rise to third place with its fourth successive win, taking its unbeaten run to thirteen matches, with the 3-1 defeat of Chelmsford City on an afternoon when all other local games fell foul of the wintry weather. A new Nene Park record crowd of 2,523 saw Dale Watkins open the scoring after just five minutes - his fiftieth goal since joining the Diamonds from Grantham less than two years previously. Chelmsford equalised but Ian King restored the lead shortly after half-time, his dipping free-kick comprehensively beating City's former R&D keeper Kevin Shoemake from twenty yards. Those watching on the Peter DeBanke terrace, getting its first real test, had a perfect view and were also able to appreciate Watkins' second goal which made the game safe seven minutes from the end.

A perfect start to 1995 but five days later there was a tough nut to crack. Worcester City came to Nene Park with an enviable record having conceded just four goals in ten away matches. When Darren Collins opened the Diamonds account after 21 minutes it seemed that the visitors ultra-defensive strategy had back-fired. However, their only attack of note brought an undeserved equaliser eleven minutes later when veteran striker Keith Bertschin (a colleague of Brian Talbot at Ipswich) converted a cross from former Rushden & Diamonds player, Peter Green, at the far post.

The unbeaten run came to an end in the next match at VS Rugby when an inspired performance by home keeper, Paul Batchelor, denied the Diamonds at least a share of the spoils. He saved Mickey Nuttell's 38th minute penalty and within two minutes his side was in front through Simon Mason, who had begun the season at Nene Park. Valley Sports' victory was assured twenty minutes from time when old adversary, Gary Statham, added a second. Steve Spooner, a veteran of over 400 League appearances for Derby, Halifax, Chesterfield, Hereford, York, Rotherham, Mansfield and Blackpool made his debut as a 78th minute substitute, eleven days short of his 34th birthday.

DOUGIE KEAST

Edinburgh born and Leicester based, Keast has spent virtually all his football career with Northamptonshire clubs: Kettering, Corby, Rushden & Diamonds and Rothwell.

A goal-less draw in the League Cup at Worcester the following Monday allowed the Diamonds to get some of the effects of their poor performance at Rugby out of their system and enabled them to approach the FA Trophy tie with Sudbury Town with a little more confidence. Not that any was required on the Saturday, heavy rain rendering the Nene Park pitch unplayable, perhaps an unsurprising fate for a match sponsored by the County Cricket Club! By Tuesday the weather had relented and Roger Ashby's side booked its place in the second round with a convincing 3-1 victory. Steve Spooner, making his home debut, opened the scoring after 17 minutes and further goals from Collins and Watkins put the game beyond the visitors. Glen Beech, who had joined Sudbury in the summer had moved on by the time of this game but there were a number of players with local connections in the visitors' side: the experienced Trevor Quow, formerly of Northampton and Kettering (and an occasional spectator at Nene Park and hence the subject of a number of rumours linking him with the club); Richard Harradine who had joined Sudbury from Thrapston; and ex Poppy Bobby Mayes, scorer of Sudbury's late consolation penalty.

Confidence in the Diamonds ability to catch front markers, Hednesford Town, had been high at the turn of the year but by now Hednesford led Rushden by fourteen points. Hopes then took another tumble with a disappointing result at Cheltenham. The Robins, who had inflicted a 2-0 defeat in the opening league game back in August, went one better capitalising upon two unforced errors by Garry Butterworth and an undisputed penalty awarded for a blatant push in the area. Manager Ashby was sympathetic towards Butterworth, whom he described as "*easily our most consistent performer this season*", and praised the overall team effort but acknowledged that all three goals conceded were the result of "*unbelievably bad mistakes*". Jason Eaton maintained his scoring record against the Diamonds by poaching Cheltenham's second.

Facing two key cup matches in the following seven days it was imperative that the side turned in a confidence boosting performance against Sittingbourne at Nene Park on February 4th. Kevin Fox was hastily recalled from his extended loan spell with Raunds Town but he remained a spectator for much of the game. The men of Kent, without an away win all season, rarely threatened as the Diamonds dominated from the first whistle and after Collins and Watkins had established a 2-0 interval lead Rushden went nap, goals from Collins, Bailey and Spooner adding to the tally. The visitors introduced substitute Tom Planck for the second half but physicists in the 1417 crowd were reassured to see that the Sittingbourne score remained constant at nil.

The first of the cup ties brought Worcester City to Irthlingborough for the Dr Martens Cup replay. Keith Bertschin's equaliser in the league draw on January 7th had been the visitors only goal of 1995, but when David Benton's dipping 20 yarder beat Kevin Fox to record his side's first goal in 9 hours 54 minutes of action it was far too late to affect the result. The Diamonds were already leading 3-0 and a place in the semi-finals was assured. Peter Green's return to Nene Park was made even more miserable for him by being substituted just before Benton's consolation.

Importantly, supporters had witnessed a hugely competent display before the eagerly awaited FA Trophy tie with Conference side Farnborough Town. The pairing of Diamonds with a Conference club had brought the Trophy run alight and there was keen anticipation to see how the squad measured up to a member of the non-league elite. However, the vagaries of the English climate were clearly demonstrated by events on Saturday February 11th. Rothwell Town travelled north to Gateshead, the Diamonds south to Farnborough. Rothwell found the International Stadium bathed in spring sunshine and enjoyed an early lead against their Conference opponents, including Kenny Cramman, before suffering a heavy defeat.

The Diamonds, and their large contingent of travelling fans, endured frustration as a waterlogged pitch brought a belated postponement both on the Saturday and in mid-week. Any fans who relieved their frusration with a smirk at Kettering's exit from the Trophy would later pay dearly for such thoughts - the Poppies would not be the last Northamptonshire side to suffer at the feet of Boreham Wood!

The trip to Atherstone the following Saturday certainly wasn't wasted. By half-time, goals from King, Watkins (2), Collins and Keast had established a 5-0 lead. The second period brought further goals, from hat-trick hero Watkins, and Kevin Wilkin who marked his Diamonds debut with a diving header. Wilkin, once of Cambridge City, was on loan from Northampton Town where his career was blighted by serious injury. Atherstone's solitary reply came from the penalty spot after David Johnson was rather harshly adjudged to have fouled Russell.

Two days later the Trophy tie with Farnborough finally took place on a quagmire of a pitch that was probably in a worse condition than when the game was called off the previous week. The difficult conditions brought the best out of the Diamonds, particularly experienced midfielders, Dougie Keast and Steve Spooner, who inspired their side to a famous victory. The deciding goal came in the 56th minute when Farnborough keeper Maik Taylor failed to hold Spooner's speculative shot and the prolific Watkins pounced to settle the tie. The Conference side came close to snatching a last minute equaliser when Murray Jones headed into Kevin Fox's arms from just six yards but the underdogs held on, setting up a Third Round meeting with Beazer Homes rivals, Halesowen Town.

After the heroics at Cherrywood Road there was disappointment when the Diamonds returned to League action. Gresley Rovers, so often a thorn in the side during the Midland Division days, had already registered a 4-3 victory back in October. Rovers' 1-0 triumph at Nene Park owed something to the Diamonds poor finishing (the Evening Telegraph used a figure of speech that involved a banjo and the rear end of a cow), rather more to goalkeeper Bob Aston's virtuosity and most to Stuart Evans, who nodded home at the far post after Martin Devaney had won the initial header at a corner.

The League Cup semi-final first leg against Leek Town at Nene Park provided a welcome diversion, the Diamonds establishing a two goal lead by virtue of Dale Watkins' 12th minute opener and a Tim Wooding 'special' six minutes from the end.

The second goal appeared to have wrecked the visitors exercise in containment and home fans anticipated a place in the final with justifiable confidence. Leek supporters probably shared their rivals' opinion, only 210 spectators turning up for the second leg the following week. However, the danger of counting goal advantage, rather like chickens, was never better illustrated than in the return. Leek were level after half an hour, but it was two goals within a minute during extra-time that finally accounted for the Diamonds.

Before that, however, was the slight matter of the FA Trophy tie against Halesowen. With a place in the last eight at stake, Wembley fever was beginning to hit the area. There was little tension in the match, however, but no complaints from the home fans who watched their favourites hit half a dozen in front of another new Nene Park record crowd (2,547). Kicking off at 2.30 pm in an attempt to reduce traffic problems caused by holding snooker matches at the Diamond Centre on the same day, the game was effectively over before the other seven ties had started. Two goals up after ten minutes and with a third coming on the half-hour mark, this was an awesome performance from the Diamonds. Mickey Nuttell, recalled for Kevin Wilkin who was cup-tied due to an earlier loan spell at Sudbury, got the first and third, Darren Collins was also on target twice with Dale Watkins and Ian King completing the rout. Halesowen's solitary replay - just before half-time they cut the arrears to 1-4 - came from the afore-mentioned Evran Wright who had spent the previous season at Walsall. There was press conjecture that long-serving winger Andy Kirkup might make two trips down Wembley Way, his loan club Raunds Town having booked a place in the FA Vase semi-finals after beating Basildon United, though he didn't often get in the Raunds team!

The Trophy draw sent Diamonds to either North London or South Wales but bad weather in the Principality meant that the replay was abandoned with the score 1-1. It would be the following Monday before it was known whether Enfield or Merthyr Tydfil would be the quarter final destination. Before that came the disastrous League Cup second leg at Leek and the return fixture with county rivals, Corby Town. Another 2,000 plus spectators were present at Nene Park to see the rock bottom Steelmen crushed as the Diamonds achieved another 6-1 score-line, Dale Watkins hitting his second hat-trick within a month. On the losing side were Glen Beech and Paul Smith (who had played in the last ever Irthlingborough Diamonds game), son of Chris, a director of Rushden & Diamonds.

Enfield returned to Merthyr on the Monday and won 1-0. But Roger Ashby and his men had an eye on a more local trophy, the Hillier Senior Cup. Before the semi-final at Cecil Street, Rothwell opened their floodlight improvement appeal. Typically the first contribution came from the visiting chairman but there was no on-field hospitality, goals from Ian King and Kevin Wilkin just after the interval clinching a final place against Kettering.

The most optimistic supporters still clung to the belief that the League could be won. With horrendous fixture congestion looming this was never realistic and a single goal defeat at Gloucester (City's scorer was Keith Knight, later to be sent off at Nene Park when representing Cheltenham in a crucial Conference fixture) went some way to confirming the obvious. Nevertheless the squad continued to take the League seriously as shown by the 5-0 whipping they handed out to Leek Town. An opener from Dale Watkins and two goals each for Nuttell and Collins provided sweet revenge for the recent League Cup semi-final defeat. Injury to Watkins, who was taken off midway through the first half after being professionally fouled, put a dampener on proceedings. He was out for a month and would certainly play no part in the Enfield tie which followed the rout of Leek by just four days. Dave Johnson's appearance in this match enabled him to become the first Rushden & Diamonds player to make 100 League appearances.

Darren Collins' return to Enfield got off to a bad start, Gary Abbott firing the Londoners in front after just 11 minutes. But before half-time, another cracking long-range drive from Tim Wooding brought the equaliser. Kevin Fox, loaned to Raunds earlier in the season, performed heroics to deny the home side a winner and indeed, the Diamonds might have won the tie with the game's very last kick when Mickey Nuttell's shot rebounded to safety from the underside of the crossbar, but that would have been harsh on an Enfield side whose defence was superbly marshalled by Al-James Hannigan.

The replay, held three days later, remains arguably the most exciting game staged at Nene Park since Irthlingborough Diamonds' remarkable Vase triumph over Basildon back in 1981. (It was the FA Vase, quarter final replay; with five minutes to go Basildon led 4-2, after extra time Diamonds had won 6-4). Another record Nene Park crowd, 3,007, saw the Diamonds stage an astonishing fight back from 1-3 down to earn a place in the semi-final. Darren Collins proved the goalscoring hero netting twice against his former club, but it was a marvellous team performance. Dougie Keast had given his side the lead but Enfield replied with three goals in thirteen minutes either side of the interval. Collins reduced the arrears and substitute Adie Mann snatched an equaliser five minutes from the end of normal time but only courageous defending, with Andy Peaks outstanding, denied Enfield a winner. Collins had the last word, scoring early in extra time, but much of the credit for the victory should go to manager Ashby and the inspired tactical switch at 1-3 which moved the striker from a wide position to a more effective central attacking role.

There were thirteen Premier Division fixtures, a two-legged Trophy semi-final and a Hillier Cup Final still to play. There were six Saturdays left.

Having beaten Enfield on the Tuesday, it was back at Nene Park on the Thursday for a league fixture against Gravesend & Northfleet. There were five changes in the side. Amongst the incomers were keeper Lee Crane, making his first appearance since the FA Cup disaster against Eastwood Hanley, Kevin Wilkin and Andy Kirkup, recalled from Raunds. The match was a personal triumph for Wilkin who scored four times against the club that a few days earlier had made him an offer as the Diamonds ran out 6-2 winners. Dave Johnson continued to set records, becoming the first man to make 150 first team appearances for the club.

Two days later, on April 1st, the side was in action once more, but the effort of playing four games in eight days inevitably took its toll. Once again Roger Ashby shuffled his pack introducing new keeper Andy Lomas from Stevenage Borough, but a below-par performance brought a 2-2 draw against Atherstone United who had been drubbed 7-1 six weeks previously.

Kevin Wilkin netted one of the goals against the Adders and he was on target 48 hours later as the Diamonds took a surprise lead at table-topping Hednesford Town. The Pitmen fought back to go 3-1 up before Darren Collins reduced the arrears with just eight minutes remaining. Fatigue no doubt played a major part in the eventual outcome as first substitute Mickey Gynn and then Henry Wright (yes, Evran's brother!) scored to give Hednesford a 5-2 victory.

The afternoon of Saturday, April 8th 1995 will be forever etched upon the memory of Rushden and Diamonds fans as Nene Park hosted the first leg of the FA Trophy final against Woking - who had risen to become one of the current giants of non-league football and had won the FA Trophy the previous season. The day before, however, the Diamond Centre was officially opened by HRH the Prince of Wales. The Centre with its many facilities was often a source of amazement to visiting fans. It was, however, a source of year-round revenue for the club and a resource to be used by the community. It also helped significantly in attracting increasing attendances to matches, enticing those who would never be attracted by a draughty terrace and a crumbling urinal.

Umbro FA Trophy Semi-Final First Leg

Rushden & Diamonds (1) **1**		**Woking** (0) **0**	
1	Martin Davies	1	Laurence Batty
2	Tim Wooding	2	Mark Tucker
3	Dave Johnson	3	Lee Tierling (sub: Rattray)
4	Andy Peaks	4	Colin Fielder
5	Steve Spooner	5	Kevan Brown (sub: Alexander)
6	Dougie Keast	6	John Crumplin
7	Ian King	7	Lloyd Wye
8	Garry Butterworth	8	Andy Ellis
9	Mickey Nuttell	9	Scott Steele
10	Adie Mann	10	Darran Hay
11	Darren Collins	11	Clive Walker
12	Paul York	12	Kevin Rattray
14	Richard Bailey	14	Tim Alexander
G	Andy Lomas	G	Tim Read

Referee: T Holbrook (Wolverhampton)

Goal: Mann (19, **1-0**)

The ground record was shattered as 4,375 spectators crammed into the stadium to watch the Diamonds outplay their illustrious visitors. Twice Ian King seemed certain to open the scoring, shooting wide when well placed and then watching his drive rebound from the inside of the post across the face of the goal to safety. It was Adie Mann *(left)* who eventually made the deserved breakthrough in the 19th minute, beating Batty with a low shot from just outside the penalty area. It proved the only goal of the game. Woking came more into the match during the second period but rarely threatened the Diamonds goal, Andy Peaks, Tim Wooding and the immaculate Martin Davies giving outstanding performances in defence. Yet, well as the Diamonds had played, most supporters doubted that one goal would be enough to take the side to Wembley. Would Woking be a different proposition in the return the following Saturday?

But before the second leg Roger Ashby's side were required to meet Hednesford in midweek and duly suffered their second defeat in eight days against the championship favourites. Darren Collins gave the Diamonds an early lead but Brendan Hackett scored his first Nene Park goal when he equalised for Hednesford. Henry Wright put the visitors 2-1 up and although Kevin Wilkin equalised, Joe O'Connor gave the Pitmen three valuable points with an 82nd minute winner.

And so to Woking. The Diamonds side showed changes from the first encounter. Tim Wooding was missing with a chest infection, Dougie Keast dropping back to fill the full back berth, Dale Watkins returned after injury but Adie Mann was surprisingly replaced in midfield by Paul York. Woking lived up to expectations playing with greater urgency, control and purpose than in the previous game and deservedly went ahead through Kevin Rattray after 18 minutes to level the aggregate scores. Darren Collins (a losing semi-finalist against Woking the previous season) mysteriously failed to appear for the second half and was replaced by Mann. It was no surprise when veteran Clive Walker - utterly subdued at Nene Park and decidedly quiet until this fateful intervention - took Woking to Wembley with the deciding goal in the 67th minute. The Diamonds made a brave attempt to get back into the game pushing substitute John Flower forward but the Conference side's defence, superbly organised by the outstanding Mark Tucker, dealt comfortably with their best efforts. Woking went on to Wembley and retained the Trophy by defeating Kidderminster Harriers deep into extra time.

After the quarter-final success against Enfield, Evening Telegraph reporter Craig Tregurtha had referred somewhat disparagingly to "*a club which only a few years ago was playing in front of a half filled shack*", demonstrating little knowledge of previous FA Vase or FA Cup runs. However after the Woking game, there could be little objection to his description of the Diamonds as "*new county standard bearers*."

Hardly surprisingly the Easter Monday league game against Cambridge City proved to be a complete anti-climax after the excitement of the Trophy encounter. The Beazer Homes title race was now restricted to two serious contenders. Hednesford had 83 points from 37 games and were trailed by Cheltenham, six points adrift but with two games in hand. Rushden & Diamonds were seventh, already mathematically defeated, 28 points behind Hednesford and with 9 games to play. It was a deflated Diamonds side, taunted by visiting fans for their Wembley 'near-miss', but they had enough character to stutter to a 2-1 victory. For City, Diamonds old boy Paul Coe but them in front, but it was City old boy Kevin Wilkin who got both the home side's goals.

Devoted Rushden Town fans would have been able to cast their minds back just over four years to March 1991 when table-topping City visited Hayden Road and were thrashed 4-1, a result which moved the Russians six points clear of the relegation zone. The Andys, Kirkup and Peaks, were the only Rushden men to play in both games.

To increase the fixture congestion, the Hillier Cup Final was abandoned at half-time when the Nene Park floodlights failed. At the time Kettering were trailing to a Steve Spooner goal. The match was replayed on the first available date: July 29th!

Then followed the most stupid part of the season: four games in five days.

Saturday: Go to Solihull. Draw 0-0.

Sunday: Home to Hastings. Fall behind early, then win 3-1 thanks largely to a brace of goals from Andy Kirkup. Kevin Slinn makes his R&D debut at full back.

Monday: Go to Chelmsford. Come back from two down to draw 2-2, Kirkup scoring two minutes from time.

Tuesday: Day off.

Wednesday: Go to Sittingbourne. Martin Davies commits professional foul in fourth minute. Off he goes. Andy Lomas comes off the bench; Richard Bailey is sacrificed. Sittingbourne score from the penalty and eventually win 3-1. Diamonds' consolation is scored by Kirkup who was making his hundredth appearance. John Flower plays his last game for R&D.

So to the penultimate Saturday. Eight days left of the season and a leisurely schedule that involves just four games. A Tim Wooding free-kick looked to have earned three points at Worcester but City levelled with a twice-taken penalty after Garry Butterworth was adjudged to have fouled Kieran Hemstock. Martin Davies foiled Phil Mason's original attempt but was helpless with the retake, awarded after

Steve Spooner was spotted encroaching into the area. Goals from Richard Bailey and the prolific Kirkup combined to beat Dorchester 2-1. As a consequence Diamonds moved above their visitors into fifth place. Julian Capone made his first starting appearance in this game which was the last time the gate for a league match at Nene Park dropped below 1,000.

The season ended with a double-header against Sudbury Town. The Suffolk side were playing for their Premier Division survival and earned three precious points from the home encounter, a powerful header from central defender Chris Tracey consigning the visitors to a 0-1 defeat. Paul York became the second Rushden & Diamonds player to make 150 first team appearances; at Worcester a few days earlier he had become the second to make a century of League appearances.

Summer arrived with a vengeance for the return at Nene Park two days later. On a hot, energy sapping afternoon, the Diamonds fought back from a 0-2 deficit to snatch a draw with goals by Andy Kirkup and Adie Mann. Both clubs had reason to be pleased with the outcome. Sudbury gained the point that safeguarded their Premier place and the game attracted a crowd of 1,793 (some no doubt intrigued by the penalty competition involving snooker stars) who showed their appreciation for the Diamonds' many creditable performances throughout the season. The side had played 66 matches in all, reached the FA Trophy semi-final, finished fifth in the Beazer Homes Premier Division, scored ninety-nine league goals and were poised to make a determined bid for the title in 1995-96.

Andy Kirkup

Beazer Homes League Premier Division 1994-1995

			Home					Away					
		P	W	D	L	F	A	W	D	L	F	A	Pts
1	Hednesford Town (13)	42	17	3	1	60	21	11	6	4	39	28	**93**
2	Cheltenham Town (2)	42	13	6	2	46	14	12	5	4	41	25	**86**
3	Burton Albion (11)	42	10	8	3	29	19	10	7	4	26	20	**75**
4	Gloucester City (10)	42	11	5	5	42	23	11	3	7	34	25	**74**
5	Rushden & Diamonds (-)	42	12	5	4	57	26	7	6	8	42	39	**68**
6	Dorchester Town (18)	42	11	4	6	47	31	8	6	7	37	30	**67**
7	Leek Town (-)	42	11	4	6	43	25	8	6	7	29	35	**67**
8	Gresley Rovers (14)	42	10	5	6	40	33	7	7	7	30	30	**63**
9	Cambridge City (17)	42	11	3	7	34	23	7	5	9	26	32	**62**
10	Worcester City (15)	42	8	5	8	29	20	6	10	5	17	14	**57**
11	Crawley Town (5)	42	11	3	7	38	28	4	7	10	26	43	**55**
12	Hastings Town (12)	42	10	7	4	36	23	3	7	11	19	34	**53**
13	Halesowen Town (3)	42	10	3	8	49	37	4	7	10	32	43	**52**
14	Gravesend & Northfleet (-)	42	7	10	4	15	11	6	3	12	23	44	**52**
15	Chelmsford City (6)	42	10	3	8	38	32	4	3	14	18	28	**48**
16	Atherstone United (4)	42	6	6	9	28	31	6	6	9	23	36	**48**
17	VS Rugby (-)	42	8	8	5	31	24	3	6	12	18	37	**47**
18	Sudbury Town (-)	42	8	4	9	26	31	4	6	11	24	46	**46**
19	Solihull Borough (16)	42	3	11	7	17	26	7	4	10	22	39	**45**
20	Sittingbourne (8)	42	11	4	6	37	28	0	6	15	14	45	**43**
21	Trowbridge Town (7)	42	5	10	6	24	24	4	3	14	19	45	**40**
22	Corby Town (9)	42	4	6	11	23	42	0	4	17	13	71	**21**

Figures in brackets are 1993-94 positions.

- Hednesford Town were promoted to the Vauxhall Conference, not without controversy. There were claims that their new ground had not been completed on time.
- Two clubs were relegated into the Beazer Premier; Stafford Rangers (who had been promoted to the Conference from the Northern Premier) and Merthyr Tydfil (who would have retained their Conference place had Hednesford's ground not been ready).
- Leek Town were transferred back to the Unibond (Northern Premier) League.
- Solihull Borough and Corby Town were relegated to the Midland Division. Champions Newport AFC and runners-up Ilkeston Town made the opposite journey. Sittingbourne and Trowbridge Town were relegated to the Southern Division and were replaced by Salisbury City and Baldock Town.
- Armitage, Burnham and Wealdstone left the Beazer Homes League and were replaced by Cinderford Town, Fleet Town and Paget Rangers. Bottom but one in the Midland Division, Grantham Town were repreieved when the ground of Raunds Town was graded unsatisfactory.

1994-1995 Results

Beazer Homes League Premier Division

Aug	20	Cheltenham Town	H	0	2		1610
Aug	23	Gravesend & Northfleet	A	1	0	Watkins	821
Aug	27	Halesowen Town	A	4	2	Collins 2, Watkins, Johnson	781
Aug	29	Trowbridge Town	H	2	1	Collins, Flower	1489
Sep	3	Burton Albion	H	2	2	Watkins 2	1556
Sep	6	Crawley Town	A	4	2	Watkins, Nuttell 2, Collins	601
Oct	1	Gresley Rovers	A	3	4	Nuttell, Keast, Watkins	787
Oct	8	Crawley Town	H	5	0	Watkins 2, Nuttell, Mann, Collins	1543
Oct	22	Dorchester Town	A	2	4	Watkins, Wooding	637
Oct	29	Gloucester City	H	1	2	Mann	1553
Nov	5	Burton Albion	A	2	2	Wooding, Collins	762
Nov	12	VS Rugby	H	4	1	Mann, Collins, King, Watkins	1653
Nov	15	Trowbridge Town	A	1	1	Watkins	329
Nov	19	Corby Town	A	4	0	King, Bailey 2, Nuttell	786
Dec	3	Leek Town	A	3	3	Richardson, Collins, Nuttell	485
Dec	10	Halesowen Town	H	1	1	Nuttell	1346
Dec	17	Solihull Borough	H	3	1	Johnson, King, Nuttell	1139
Dec	26	Cambridge City	A	3	2	Watkins 3	562
Dec	31	Hastings Town	A	2	0	Nuttell, Watkins	624
Jan	2	Chelmsford City	H	3	1	Watkins 2, King	2523
Jan	7	Worcester City	H	1	1	Collins	1731
Jan	14	VS Rugby	A	0	2		972
Jan	28	Cheltenham Town	A	0	3		920
Feb	4	Sittingbourne	H	5	0	Collins 2, Watkins, Bailey, Spooner	1417
Feb	18	Atherstone United	A	7	1	King, Watkins 3, Collins, Keast, Wilkin	402
Feb	25	Gresley Rovers	H	0	1		1878
Mar	11	Corby Town	H	6	1	Watkins 3, Collins, Nuttell, King	2137
Mar	18	Gloucester City	A	0	1		614
Mar	21	Leek Town	H	5	0	Watkins, Collins 2, Nuttell 2	1111
Mar	30	Gravesend & Northfleet	H	6	2	Wilkin 4, Nuttell 2	858
Apr	1	Atherstone United	H	2	2	Wilkin, Nuttell	1754
Apr	3	Hednesford Town	A	2	5	Wilkin, Collins	1102
Apr	11	Hednesford Town	H	2	3	Collins, Wilkin	1657
Apr	17	Cambridge City	H	2	1	Wilkin 2	1217
Apr	22	Solihull Borough	A	0	0		206
Apr	23	Hastings Town	H	3	1	King, Kirkup 2	1078
Apr	24	Chelmsford City	A	2	2	Wilkin, Kirkup	911
Apr	26	Sittingbourne	A	1	3	Kirkup	663
Apr	29	Worcester City	A	1	1	Wooding	545
May	2	Dorchester Town	H	2	1	Bailey, Kirkup	908
May	4	Sudbury Town	A	0	1		386
May	6	Sudbury Town	H	2	2	Kirkup, Mann	1793

1994-1995 Results

FA Cup

Sep 10	1Q	Eastwood Hanley	A	0	1		165

FA Trophy

Sep 17	1Q	Hendon	H	0	0		1174
Sep 20	1QR	Hendon	A	4	1	Collins 2, Watkins 2	151
Oct 15	2Q	Wembley	H	2	1	Collins, Mann	1173
Nov 26	3Q	Crawley Town	H	2	1	King, Mann	1369
Jan 24	1	Sudbury Town	H	3	1	Spooner, Collins, Watkins	1301
Feb 20	2	Farnborough Town	A	1	0	Watkins	635
Mar 4	3	Halesowen Town	H	6	1	Nuttell 2, Watkins, Collins 2, King	2547
Mar 25	4	Enfield	A	1	1	Wooding	1792
Mar 28	4R	Enfield	H	4	3	Keast, Collins 2, Mann	3007
Apr 8	SF1	Woking	H	1	0	Mann	4375
Apr 15	SF2	Woking	A	0	2		4643

Dr Martens Cup

Oct 4	1.1	Rothwell Town	H	0	0		734
Oct 18	1.2	Rothwell Town	A	2	1	Keast, Kirkup	630
Nov 8	2	Bedworth United	H	4	2	Mann, Collins, Watkins, Bailey	524
Dec 14	3	Baldock Town	H	3	0	King, Collins, York	513
Jan 16	4	Worcester City	A	0	0		455
Feb 7	4R	Worcester City	H	3	1	Collins, Wooding, King	1007
Feb 28	SF1	Leek Town	H	2	0	Watkins, Wooding	804
Mar 7	SF2	Leek Town	A	0	4		210

NFA Hillier Senior Cup

Sep 27	1	Desborough Town	H	8	0	Watkins 2, Mann 2, Nuttell 2, Capone, Mason	398
Oct 25	2	Northampton Spencer	H	3	1	Keast, Nuttell 2	704
Mar 14	SF	Rothwell Town	A	2	0	King, Wilkin	510

NFA Maunsell Cup

Aug 2		Peterborough United	H	2	1	Watkins, Nuttell	1760

♦ The FA Cup was won by Everton who beat Manchester United 1-0 in the final. Four non-League sides reached the Third Round proper: Enfield (with Al James Hannigan) lost 0-2 at Leicester City, Aylesbury United (with Steve Heard) lost 0-4 at Queen's Park Rangers, Altrincham lost 0-3 at Tottenham Hotspur and Marlow went down 0-2 at Swindon Town. Six non-League sides beat Football League opposition: Altrincham (Wigan Athletic), Enfield (Cardiif City & Torquay United), Hitchin Town (Hereford United), Kingstonian (Brighton & Hove Albion), Marlow (Oxford United) and Woking (Barnet).

♦ In the FA Trophy final, Woking beat Kidderminster Harriers 2-1 after extra time. The losing semi-finalists were Hyde United and Rushden & Diamonds.

♦ In the Dr Martens sponsored Southern League Cup, Hastings Town beat Leek Town in both legs of the final.

1994-1995 Teams Beazer Homes League Premier Division

		Bailey	Butterworth	Capone	Collins	Crane	Davies	Flower	Fox	Johnson	Keast	King	Kirkup	Lomas	Mackenzie	Mann	Mason	Nuttell	Page	Peaks	Richardson	Slinn	Spooner	Watkins	Webster	Wilkin	Wooding	York
Cheltenham	H		8		7			4	1	3	5		sb				sb	9		6				10			2	11
Gravesend	A		8		7			4	1	3	5							9		6				10			2	11
Halesowen	A		8		7			4	1	3	5		sb					9		6				10			2	11
Trowbridge	H		8		7			4	1	3	5		sb					9		6				10			2	11
Burton	H		8		7				1	3	5						4	9		6				10			2	11
Crawley	A				7				1	3	5						4	9	8	6				10			2	11
Gresley	A		8		7			4	1	3	5					11		9	6					10			2	
Crawley	H		8	sb	7			4		3	5				1	11		9						10	6		2	
Dorchester	A		8		7			4	1	3	5		sb			11		9						10	6		2	sb
Gloucester	H		8		7			4		3	5				1	11		9						10	6		2	sb
Burton	A		8		9					3	5		7		1				6	4				10			2	11
VS Rugby	H		8		9		1			3	5	7				6				4				10			2	11
Trowbridge	A		8		9		1			3	5	7						6		4				10			2	11
Corby	A	sb	8						1	3	5	7				6		9		4				10			2	11
Leek	A	10	8		7		1	4			3					sb		9		6	5						2	11
Halesowen	H	sb	8		6		1	4			3	7				10		9		2	5							11
Solihull	H	sb	8		6		1	4		3	5	7				10		9		2								11
Cambridge	A		8		11		1	4		3	6	7						9		2	5			10				
Hastings	A		8		11		1	4		3	6	7						9		2	5			10				sb
Chelmsford	H		8		11		1	4		3	6	7						9		2	5			10				
Worcester	H		8		11		1	4		3	6	7						9		2	5			10				
VS Rugby	A		8				1	4		3	6	7				11		9		2	5		sb	10				sb
Cheltenham	A	sb	8		9		1			3	5	7								4	sb		6	10			2	11
Sittingbourne	H	9	8		11				1	3	6	7								4			5	10			2	
Atherstone	A		8		11				1	3	5	7								4			6	10		9	2	
Gresley	H	sb	8		11				1	3	6	7								4			5	10		9	2	
Corby	H		8		11				1		6	7				sb		9		4			5	10		sb	2	3
Gloucester	A		8		11				1	3	6	7				sb				4			5	10		9	2	sb
Leek	H	sb	8		11				1	3	6	7						9		4			5	10			2	sb
Gravesend	H	sb	8			1				3	sb		7			10		9		4			5			6	2	11
Atherstone	H		8		11			3			6	7		1		sb		9		4			5			10	2	sb
Hednesford	A		8		11					3	6	sb		1		7		9		4			5			10	2	sb
Hednesford	H		8		11		1			3	6	7	sb			10				4			sb			9	2	5
Cambridge	H	sb	8				1	2			6	11	sb			7				4			5	10		9		3
Solihull	A	sb	8					2	1	3			sb			7		9		4			5	10		11		6
Hastings	H	10	8				1	5		3	6	7	11							4		2		sb		9		
Chelmsford	A	10	8					4			6	sb	11	1		7				2			5			9		3
Sittingbourne	A	10	8				1	4		3	6	7	11	sb				9									2	5
Worcester	A	9	8	sb			1			3	6	7	10			sb				4			5				2	11
Dorchester	H	10	8	7	9		1				6		11							4			5				2	3
Sudbury	A	10	8	sb	9		1				6	7	sb			11				4			5				2	3
Sudbury	H	11	8	sb	9				1		6		7			10				4		2	5	sb				3

1994-1995 Teams   Cup Competitions

		Bailey	Butterworth	Capone	Collins	Crane	Davies	Flower	Fox	Johnson	Keast	King	Kirkup	Mackenzie	Mann	Mason	Nuttell	Page	Peaks	Richardson	Spooner	Watkins	Webster	Wilkin	Wodding	York
FA Cup																										
Eastwood Han	A			sb	7	1				3	5		4				9	8	6			10			2	11
FA Trophy																										
Hendon	H		8		7			4	1	3					sb	5	9	6				10			2	11
Hendon	A		8		7			4	1	3	5				sb	11	9	6				10			2	
Wembley	H		8		7			4		3	5		sb	1	11		9					10	6		2	sb
Crawley	H	sb	8		10		1			3	5	7			6		9		4						2	11
Sudbury	H	9	8		11		1			3	6	7							4		5	10			2	sb
Farnborough	A	9	8		11				1	3	5	7							4		6	10			2	sb
Halesowen	H				11			8	1	3	6	7			sb		9		4		5	10			2	
Enfield	A	10	8		11				1	3	6	7					9		4		5				2	sb
Enfield	H	10	8		11				1	3	6	7			sb		9		4		5				2	sb
Woking	H		8		11		1			3	6	7			10		9		4		5				2	
Woking	A		8		11		1	sb		3	2	7			sb		9		4		5	10				6
Dr Martens Cup																										
Rothwell	H		8		7			4	1		5		sb		6	3	9		2			10				11
Rothwell	A		8		7			4		3	5		sb	1	10		9						6		2	11
Bedworth	H	sb	8		9		1			3	5		7		6				4			10			2	11
Baldock	H		8		6		1	4			3	7	sb		10		9		2	5						11
Worcester	A	9	8				1			3	6	7	sb						4		5	10			2	11
Worcester	H	9	8		11				1	3	6	7	sb						4		5	10			2	sb
Leek	H		8		11				1	3	6				7		sb		4		5	10		9	2	
Leek	A				11			8	1	3	6	7					9		4		5	10		sb	2	
Hillier Cup																										
Desborough	H		8	sb	7			4	1	3	5				11	sb	9	6				10			2	
Nptn Spencer	H		8		7			4	1	3	5		sb		11		9					10	6		2	sb
Rothwell	A		8		sb				1		6	7			11		9		4		5			10	2	3
Maunsell Cup																										
Peterborough	H		8		7			4	1	3	5		sb				9	6				10			2	11

1994-1995 Appearances

	Start						Substitute						Total					
	L	C	T	LC	CC	Tot	L	C	T	LC	CC	Tot	L	C	T	LC	CC	Tot
Richard BAILEY	9		4	2		**15**	9		1	1		**11**	18		5	3		**26**
Garry BUTTERWORTH	41		10	7	4	**62**							41		10	7	4	**62**
Julian CAPONE	1					**1**	4	1		1	1	**7**	5	1		1	1	**8**
Darren COLLINS	33	1	11	7	3	**55**					1	**1**	33	1	11	7	4	**56**
Lee CRANE	1	1				**2**							1	1				**2**
Martin DAVIES	18		4	2		**24**							18		4	2		**24**
John FLOWER	22		4	4	3	**33**			1			**1**	22		5	4	3	**34**
Kevin FOX	17		6	4	4	**31**							17		6	4	4	**31**
Dave JOHNSON	33	1	11	6	3	**54**							33	1	11	6	3	**54**
Dougie KEAST	40	1	10	8	4	**63**	1					**1**	41	1	10	8	4	**64**
Ian KING	24		8	4	1	**37**	2					**2**	26		8	4	1	**39**
Andy KIRKUP	8	1		1		**10**	8		1	5	2	**16**	16	1	1	6	2	**26**
Andy LOMAS	3					**3**	1					**1**	4					**4**
Chris McKENZIE	3		1	2		**6**							3		1	2		**6**
Adie MANN	17		3	5	3	**28**	5		5			**10**	22		8	5	3	**38**
Simon MASON	2		2	1		**5**	1				1	**2**	3		2	1	1	**7**
Mickey NUTTELL	27	1	9	4	4	**45**				1		**1**	27	1	9	5	4	**46**
Darrell PAGE	3	1	2		2	**8**							3	1	2		2	**8**
Andy PEAKS	37	1	8	7	2	**55**							37	1	8	7	2	**55**
Paul RICHARDSON	7			1		**8**	1					**1**	8			1		**9**
Kevin SLINN	2					**2**							2					**2**
Steve SPOONER	17		7	4	1	**29**	2					**2**	19		7	4	1	**31**
Dale WATKINS	28	1	7	6	3	**45**	2					**2**	30	1	7	6	3	**47**
Kenny WEBSTER	3		1	1	1	**6**							3		1	1	1	**6**
Kevin WILKIN	11			1	1	**13**	1			1		**2**	12			2	1	**15**
Tim WOODING	30	1	10	6	3	**50**							30	1	10	6	3	**50**
Paul YORK	25		3	5	2	**36**	8		5	1	1	**15**	33	1	8	6	3	**51**
MAXIMUM	42	1	11	8	4	66							42	1	11	8	4	66

1994-95 Goalscorers

	L	C	T	LC	CC	Total
Dale WATKINS	25		5	2	3	35
Darren COLLINS	17		8	3		28
Mickey NUTTELL	15		2		5	22
Kevin WILKIN	11				1	12
Ian KING	7		2	2	1	12
Adie MANN	4		4	1	2	11
Andy KIRKUP	6			1		7
Tim WOODING	3		1	2		6
Richard BAILEY	4			1		5
Dougie KEAST	2		1	1	1	5
Dave JOHNSON	2					2
Steve SPOONER	1		1			2
John FLOWER	1					1
Paul RICHARDSON	1					1
Julian CAPONE					1	1
Simon MASON					1	1
Paul YORK				1		1
TOTAL	99	0	24	14	15	152

1994-95 Playing Record

HOME	P	W	D	L	F	A	Pts
League	21	12	5	4	57	26	41
FA Cup	-	-	-	-	-	-	
FA Trophy	7	6	1	0	18	7	
League Cup	5	4	1	0	12	3	
County Cup	3	3	0	0	13	2	
TOTAL	36	25	7	4	100	38	
AWAY							
League	21	7	6	8	42	39	27
FA Cup	1	0	0	1	0	1	
FA Trophy	4	2	1	1	6	4	
League Cup	3	1	1	1	2	5	
County Cup	1	1	0	0	2	0	
TOTAL	30	11	8	11	52	49	
TOTAL							
League	42	19	11	12	99	65	68
FA Cup	1	0	0	1	0	1	
FA Trophy	11	8	2	1	24	11	
League Cup	8	5	2	1	14	8	
County Cup	4	4	0	0	15	2	
TOTAL	**66**	**36**	**15**	**15**	**152**	**67**	

Attendance Summary

HOME	Total	Ave	High		Low	
League	31951	1521	2523	Chelmsford	858	Gravesend
FA Cup	-	-	-	-	-	
FA Trophy	14946	2135	4375	Woking	1173	Wembley
League Cup	3582	716	1007	Worcester	513	Baldock
County Cup	2862	954	1760	Peterborough	398	Desborough
TOTAL	53341	1482	4375	Woking	398	Desborough
AWAY						
League	13896	662	1102	Hednesford	206	Solihull
FA Cup	165	165	165	Eastwood	165	Eastwood
FA Trophy	7221	1805	4643	Woking	151	Hendon
League Cup	1295	432	630	Rothwell	210	Leek
County Cup	510	510	510	Rothwell	510	Rothwell
TOTAL	23087	770	4643	Woking	151	Hendon
TOTAL						
League	45847	1092	2523	Chelmsford H	206	Solihull A
FA Cup	165	165	165	Eastwood A	165	Eastwood A
FA Trophy	22167	2015	4643	Woking A	151	Hendon A
League Cup	4877	610	1007	Worcester H	210	Leek A
County Cup	3372	843	1760	Peterboro' H	398	Desborough H
TOTAL	**76428**	**1158**	**4643**	Woking A	**151**	Hendon A

GARRY BUTTERWORTH

SEASON FOUR

1995 - 96

"How long a time lies in one little word!
Four lagging winters and four wanton springs
End in a word: such is the breath of Kings."

Shakespeare - Richard II

Back (l to r): Steve Spooner, Andy Kirkup, Darren Collins, Steve Stott, Tim Wooding.
Middle (l to r): Billy Jeffrey, Steve Holden, Kevin Wilkin, Graham Benstead, Andy Lomas, Nick Ashby, Brendan Hackett, Paul Richardson.
Front (l to r): Ian King, David Holmes, Neil Smith, Andy Peaks, Roger Ashby, Carl Alford, Al James Hannigan, Garry Butterworth.

The summer of 1995 brought far reaching changes to Nene Park as the club made significant strides in its inexorable march towards full time professionalism. Chairman Max Griggs appointed manager Roger Ashby in a full time capacity with prime responsibility for taking the Diamonds into the Vauxhall Conference. The club also sought to extend its community involvement through a range of initiatives including setting up regular junior soccer courses and visits to local schools.

There was an impressive list of new signings which bolstered all departments except the attack.

To keep goal came Graham Benstead, one of several players to be signed this season from Kettering Town. A veteran of over 200 League appearances for Norwich City, Sheffield United and Brentford, he had been capped for England at youth level and, much more recently, at semi-professional level.

Also signed from Kettering was Nick Ashby *(left)*, a newcomer to Rushden & Diamonds, but a former Rushden Town player. He had left Hayden Road when the Russians were demoted to join Aylesbury United; now he made the decision to play again under the managership of his father.

Central defender Glyn Creaser was another to return for a second spell under Roger Ashby, having served with him at Wolverton. Creaser was another ex Kettering Town man, although his contribution at Rockingham Road was not extensive - just eight first team appearances at the end of the 1983-84 season. He then spent three seasons with Barnet (then in the Gola League as the Conference was known) before a successful career at Wycombe Wanderers where he was a regular in the sides that won promotion to Divisions Three and Two.

Another new central defender was Al James Hannigan who had impressed for Enfield in the FA Trophy clashes the previous season. The twenty four old had also played for Harwich & Parkeston, Harlow Town and Marlow after a youthful connection with Arsenal. Signed for a fee reported at various amounts between £5000 and £10000, he had played in the Marlow side which reached the Third Round of the FA Cup in 1992-93, losing to Tottenham Hotspur at White Hart Lane.

Midfield was strengthened by the signing of two West Midlanders. Steve Lilwall came from West Bromwich Albion (73 appearances) and had plenty of Conference experience with Kidderminster. Neil Smith was signed from Beazer Premier rivals Cheltenham Town; for three successive seasons Smith's side had finished runners-up. The former Lincoln, Redditch and Shrewsbury must have been confident he wasn't going to make it four in a row.

There were also the signings that weren't. Young central defender Jason Smith was released by Coventry City and joined the pre-season mini-tour to Poole and Weymouth before deciding to return to his home town of Tiverton. There he joined the fire service, rejoined Tiverton Town and was later rewarded with a second trip to Wembley for an FA Vase final. The experienced Kevin Brock, ex Newcastle, QPR and Oxford United, never kicked a ball competitively for Diamonds. A back injury restricted his future to managing Oxford City.

There would be a new look to the Diamonds playing kit too, local firm Whitworths providing a generous three year sponsorship as Whitworths white took over from Pittards red. The club also decided to keep up with the Premiership big boys by launching its own radio station, based initially in a studio at the east end of the ground.

There were inevitable casualties as the playing staff was pruned during the close season. FA Trophy heroes Kevin Fox and Adie Mann were released, Fox joining Raunds and Mann, a little surprisingly going to Gresley, although he later had a spell at Raunds before becoming Higham Town's player-manager.

Injury plagued Paul Richardson accepted a coaching position with the club, Ian King was transfer-listed (but remained for two more seasons) whilst John Flower and Paul York were two others who made the move to Raunds.

Going on to higher things was loan keeper Martin Davies who was signed by Cambridge United.

The new season got off to a perfect start on the evening of Thursday July 27th as a capacity crowd of 4,600 watched the opening friendly game against Premier League side, Newcastle United. Kevin Keegan, who had been a guest speaker at a Sportsmans dinner at the Diamond Centre earlier in the year, brought a full strength side to Nene Park, including new signings, Les Ferdinand and David Ginola. Dale Watkins scored an impressive consolation goal as the Diamonds went down 3-1, but the fixture was further proof of the emergent club's credibility. As Keegan remarked at the time, *"There are superb facilities here which is why I was happy to bring my squad. Rushden and Diamonds is a club on the move which is reflected in both their team and facilities. They have aspirations to be in the Football League and have a lot more going for them than most clubs in their situation."*

No-one could describe what came next as a pre-season 'friendly'. The NFA Hillier Senior Cup Final against Kettering Town, held over from the previous campaign, was intensely competitive. Within four minutes Dale Watkins had been put out of the game (which allowed Andy Kirkup, retained on a non-contract basis, to stake a claim for a first-team place) and on the quarter hour mark Tim Wooding put Diamonds in front from the penalty spot. Kettering's Junior Hunter might have been lucky to have stopped on the field after that incident but only lasted a few more minutes before he saw his first red card of the season. The ten Poppies equalised three minutes from time through Ian Scott (once of Hinckley Town) who had replaced Anton Thomas (once of Leicester United). In extra time Ian Arnold put Kettering in front but Kevin Wilkin equalised within a minute and a replay was necessary.

The replay took place two days later; it had to be that soon because it had already been arranged that the winners would play Northampton Town in the Maunsell Cup later that week. Amongst the changes for the second game was the inclusion of Graham Benstead and Nick Ashby over whose eligibility there had been some doubt since this was last season's competition and last season they were Kettering players! Benstead's inclusion meant the dropping of Andy Lomas *(left)* - who had performed excellently in the first match - whilst there was no place on the bench for Darren Watts who had returned to the club after two seasons at Cogenhoe. The replay was another 2-2 draw, Kevin Wilkin again was the man who made it 2-2 and Kettering again had a man sent off; this time it was Ian Arnold. Extra time failed to separate the sides but it was Kettering who won the silverware, taking the penalty shoot-out 3-1 and providing a disappointing final appearance for Dougie Keast who soon afterwards moved to Burton Albion.

Thoughts then turned to the real business - achieving promotion from the Beazer Premier Division. Of the newly promoted sides, Newport AFC looked the most likely to worry the championship chasers. Newport had defeated the FA of Wales in a series of lengthy court battles and had won the Midland Division title based at their well-appointed brand-new Council-backed stadium in Newport. Runners-up Ilkeston Town and the duo promoted from the Southern Division, Salisbury City and Baldock Town, did not look to have title potential. Two sides came down from the Conference: Merthyr Tydfil (so there would be two trips to Wales this season) and Stafford Rangers. Both had been big clubs: eight seasons earlier Merthyr had beaten Italian giants Atalanta in the home leg of the European Cup Winners Cup whilst Rangers' most memorable match was probably their Wembley success of 1979 when Kettering born Bob Ritchie lifted the FA trophy in front of a huge contingent of disappointed Kettering fans and one disappointed future Rushden & Diamonds manager. And undoubtedly both Gloucestershire sides, Cheltenham & Gloucester, would be building strong challenges yet again.

It was Salisbury who were Diamonds' opening League opponents, the season starting yet again with a home fixture. There was no place in the starting line for the previous season's top scorer Dale Watkins whose preparations had been hindered by that Senior Cup injury.

Rushden & Diamonds (1) **3**		**Salisbury City** (0) **0**	
1	Graham Benstead	1	Steve Weaver
2	Graham Reed	2	Matthew Parkin (sub: Paskins)
3	Nick Ashby	3	Simon Browne
4	Steve Lilwall	4	Martin Blackler
5	Glyn Creaser	5	Roger Emms
6	Al James Hannigan	6	Paul Morrell
7	Andy Kirkup	7	Robbie Carroll (sub: Hobson)
8	Garry Butterworth	8	Robbie Harbut
9	Kevin Wilkin	9	Sandy Baird
10	Neil Smith	10	Ian Chalk
11	Darren Collins	11	Gary Manson (sub: Webb)
12	Steve Spooner	12	Richie Paskins
14	Dale Watkins	14	Gordon Hobson
15	Andy Lomas	15	Lee Webb

Referee: KD Hill (Royston)

Goals: Wilkin (39, **1-0**); Kirkup (71, **2-0**); Collins (77, **3-0**)
Booked: Reed, Morrell

In the side were seven men who were making their League debuts for Rushden & Diamonds. Ashby, Benstead, Hannigan and Smith had all appeared against Kettering but for Creaser, Lilwall and Graham Reed - signed on a temporary contract to cover Tim Wooding's injury - it was their first game in an R&D shirt. Reed, who numbered Frickley, Northampton and VS Rugby amongst his former clubs, increased the ex Kettering contingent to five, joining Ashby, Benstead, Butterworth and Creaser.

The 1,532 spectators, 78 fewer than the attendance for the opening game of 1994-95, witnessed a comfortable if unspectacular victory in a game officiated by future Football League referee Keith Hill who had also been in charge for the opening game against Clevedon two seasons earlier. Kevin Wilkin scored after 39 minutes but stout resistance from the visitors prevented the Diamonds from extending the lead until Andy Kirkup converted Garry Butterworth's right wing corner late in the second half. Darren Collins then added a third thirteen minutes from time to give the final scoreline a more realistic appearance and a most encouraging start.

Monday August 21st was a stiflingly hot day and there was just a smattering of Whitworths shirts in the 4,000 crowd at Chelmsford. And after the third day's play between Essex and the West Indies had finished, they moved across the car park to City's New Writtle Street ground for Diamonds' first away match. Much of the ground, which had once accommodated crowds up to 17,000, had been demolished and City appeared to be hanging onto their existence by a thread. The County Cricket Club were reported to have made an offer for the ground - they wanted it as a car park extension - and a 5-0 defeat at Gloucester in the opening game had alarm bells ringing loudly. But a four figure crowd saw the Essex men run Diamonds mightily close. It was a wonder goal from substitute Dale Watkins fifteen seconds into stoppage time that won the game but Ashby, whilst generous in his praise of Watkins, acknowledged the debt owed to the impressive Graham Benstead who produced several miraculous saves with the scores locked at 1-1.

The side recorded a third successive victory, at home to Crawley Town, a side with several big names and fancied to do well, but the 3-1 victory was marred by the dismissal of full back Graham Reed after 65 minutes. It had all begun so well for the former Cobbler who had played a vital role in setting up Garry Butterworth's opening goal. When Watkins intercepted a misplaced clearance from former Chelsea central defender Colin Pates and curled home a delightful goal from the edge of the area victory seemed assured. Graham Benstead kept the two goal lead intact saving a penalty on the stroke of half time but the visitors, inspired by the much travelled Scottish international striker David Speedie, came back strongly after the break. However seven minutes after Reed's dismissal, Watkins extended the lead with an astute chip over the stranded Ian Chatfield to provide a three goal cushion. When Pates reduced the arrears shortly after, Benstead failing to make firm contact with a right wing corner, the importance of the goalkeeper's penalty save became increasingly apparent as Crawley stormed forward in a vain attempt to save a point.

The next fixture took the Diamonds to Burton Albion where the hosts were in far from generous mood. With only one point from the opening three games the Brewers attacked relentlessly from the first whistle. Old adversary from his Gresley days, Martin Devaney, headed his side in front after just eight minutes and although a Dale Watkins equaliser brought parity at half time Albion dominated after the interval. Devaney scored his second and the ebullient Jason Rhodes grabbed a pair either side of Darren Collins face-saver but the 2-4 defeat begged questions about the durability of Roger Ashby's new look defence. The game proved to be the final appearance by Graham Reed *(left)* who was substituted after 75 minutes.

The trek to Hastings was the scene of a stern rear-guard action by the home side, who employed a tactic unfamiliar to their Saxon forebears - the offside trap. It took the Diamonds 76 minutes to breach the well organised defence, Dale Watkins heading home a Garry Butterworth free-kick for the only goal of the game which was generally undistinguished but produced a much better organised display from Diamonds who welcomed back Tim Wooding for his first start of the season.

Two seasons ago VS Rugby had matched Rushden & Diamonds virtually every step of the way as the pair were promoted from the Midland Division. Now, the Warwickshire club was floundering badly and Diamonds romped to the top of the table. A hat trick from Dale Watkins and goals from Ashby, Wilkin and Richard Bailey, who enjoyed his best ever first team display to date, contributed to an impressive 6-1 scoreline and a disappointing return to Nene Park for Darren Hillier and Simon Mason.

Wayne Bellamy is flanked by brothers Trevor Benjamin (who went on to play for Cambridge United) and Richard Bailey (right).

Having settled into impressive league form, disruption came with the start of the FA Cup campaign with a First Qualifying Round home tie against Grantham Town on September 9th. Another variety of disruption almost came from the Midland Division opposition when manager Warren Ward fired his side into a seventh minute lead. But Darren Collins took his turn to hit a hat trick and a late fourth from Kevin Wilkin saw the side move into the next round with a comfortable 4-1 victory.

Worcester City proved more resilient in the next Beazer Homes League fixture which was drawn 0-0. In fact, had Graham Benstead failed to anticipate Steve Fergusson's 28th minute penalty kick, diving to his right to make a crucial save, manager Ashby's persuasive argument for an ultra-defensive strategy would have been severely flawed. Convinced that his side's tendency to play bright, attractive football away from home had cost promotion the previous season he remarked, *"We'll still attack at Nene Park. But on our travels it will be different. After all if you win your home games and manage to pick up a point or sometimes a win away from home that's championship form as far as I'm concerned."*

Victory at home over Chelmsford City restored the side to top spot although the three points were not secured until the 88th minute, Darren Collins converting a slide rule pass from Richard Bailey. It had been an unimpressive performance by the Diamonds who were gifted an opener when visiting defender Rob Bird diverted Garry Butterworth's cross into his own net. A draw seemed inevitable when Mark Bellingham scored a deserved equaliser eight minutes from time, but then came Collins' dramatic winner.

Collins was again on target when he netted the only goal of a dull FA Cup Second Qualifying Round game against Eastwood Hanley. There was rarely any likelihood that the North West Counties League side would repeat their shock success of the previous season. Apart from an early scare when Chris Hagan rose unchallenged to head just wide of the far post the Diamonds defence was in dominant form with sweeper Andy Peaks outstanding.

Roger Ashby was determined to add to his squad and after an approach to Woking for midfielder Andy Ellis had proved fruitless, he signed Brendan Hackett from Hednesford Town. Twenty-nine year old Hackett *(left)* had been a member of Hednesford Town's Beazer Homes League Championship winning side of 1994-95 and had also represented Bilston, Stourbridge, Redditch, Dudley, Worcester, Gloucester and Telford.

Hackett made his debut in the 2-0 victory at Cheltenham, a performance which proved to be of immense importance as well as a personal triumph for Neil Smith on his return to Whaddon Road. Goals from Andy Kirkup and Darren Collins were sufficient to overcome their nearest rivals as the Diamonds established a two point lead at the top of the league.

The Diamonds warmed up for their next FA Cup tie at Sandwell Borough with a midweek home game against King's Lynn in the Dr Martens Cup. The omens for the more prestigious KO tournament were not good as Peter Morris's side made light of their inferior status to record a well merited victory. The decisive goal came twelve minutes into the second half when Brett McNamara escaped Al-James Hannigan's attention to set up a simple chance for Andrew Stanhope. However, things became less simple later.

Fortunately the lacklustre performance was followed by a sparkling display just four days later when Sandwell Borough (a club known as Ashtree Highfield when Rushden Town first encountered them) were demolished 6-1, Kevin Wilkin *(left)* scoring four times. Preferred to Dale Watkins in the starting line-up the former Cobbler justified his selection in dramatic fashion, netting twice within a minute to put his side in a strong position just thirteen minutes into the game. Despite constant Diamonds pressure, the crowd of 250, swelled to four times its normal size by a large contingent of travelling fans, had to wait until the second half for the anticipated goal glut. Collins and Wilkin extended the lead as the midfield trio of Neil Smith, Garry Butterworth and the recalled Steve Lilwall retained their firm grip on the game. Although Marcus Powell pulled one back for Sandwell with a surprise shot from outside the penalty area, further goals from the irrepressible Wilkin and his striking partner Collins saw the Diamonds ease through into the next round.

The winning run continued with a first ever success at Gresley's Moat Ground. Al-James Hannigan opened the scoring after twenty five minutes and second half goals from Collins and Butterworth sealed an important victory which consolidated the Diamonds position at the top of the table and left Adie Mann, substituted ten minutes from the end, with disappointing memories of his first encounter against his old club.

The Fourth, and final, Qualifying Round of the FA Cup sent Diamonds to another new club, Purfleet. Situated in the giant shadow cast by the Queen Elizabeth Bridge which crosses the Thames to Dartford, the club was founded in 1985 when Tommy and Harry South bought a piece of ground on which to build a hotel. On their spare land they marked out a football pitch so that they could have their own Sunday League side. In ten years the club progressed so rapidly that it had reached the Premier Division of the Isthmian League (at that time sponsored by ICIS) and was now just 90 minutes away from a first ever clash with a Football

DARREN COLLINS

Leading goalscorer for R&D 1995-96; leading scorer in Beazer Premier;
Joint leading goalscorer for R&D 1996-97;
Leading goalscorer for R&D 1997-98; second highest scorer in Vauxhall Conference.

League club. So too were Diamonds and they looked favourites from the seventh minute when they scored from their first corner, Al-James Hannigan heading home Tim Wooding's cross. Diamonds won eleven more corners during the first half - a measure of their superiority - without adding to the goals tally. Veteran striker David Crown became an increasingly important figure after the interval and when Darren Collins was sent off following a touchline flare-up in the 75th minute the game swung decidedly in the ICIS League side's favour. The threatened equaliser came just a minute from time, Crown forcing the ball past Graham Benstead after a goalmouth scramble.

With the enticing prospect of a home tie against one time winners Cardiff City in the First Round Proper, the Nene Park replay assumed even greater significance, attracting a crowd of 2,850. Fielding three strikers, Darren Collins, Kevin Wilkin and the recalled Dale Watkins, and with Andy Kirkup pushing forward from midfield, the Diamonds were committed to attack. The tactic worked as non-stop pressure eventually brought an opening goal two minutes from half time. A long ball from Nick Ashby set Collins free on the left, keeper Stuart Horne could only parry his cross and Watkins sidefooted home from six yards. A second goal within sixty seconds of the restart virtually decided the outcome, Collins heading home from Tim Wooding's free-kick. Purfleet hit back quickly through Paul Donovan but when the pacy Kirkup outstripped the visiting defence and crossed for Wilkin to beat Horne with a close range header, home fans knew that they could look forward to a visit from the Welsh Bluebirds on November 11th.

Al James Hannigan

Coincidentally the next league fixture took the Diamonds to the Principality and a visit to Penydarren Park, Merthyr, but whilst fans were focused on the visit of Cardiff there were some bizarre happenings off the field. It had been discovered that King's Lynn's Andrew Stanhope who had scored the winner in the Dr Martens Cup First Leg was actually under suspension at the time of the game. He had also played in Lynn's FA Cup victory over Canvey Island. The FA threw King's Lynn out of their competition and reinstated Canvey who then beat Hednesford and drew with Brighton & Hove Albion. The Beazer Homes League, though, did nothing so forthright, merely declaring the match void and ordering it to be replayed.

An overnight stay en route to Merthyr was followed by another excellent performance. Manager Ashby reverted to a more conservative 4-4-2 formation, the cup-tied Brendan Hackett replacing Watkins in the starting line-up. Goals from Collins, the rejuvenated Kirkup and substitute Watkins sealed the impressive 3-0 victory. The three consecutive away victories at Cheltenham, Gresley and Merthyr were probably the team's best three performances of the season; they were also the three games which probably contributed most to the eventual promotion. At the time, though, the significance seemed to be lost in all the FA Cup hype. Even the fact that Diamonds went top of the table following the Merthyr victory was greeted in low key but a study of the table after that match now shows how important it was.

			Home					Away					
	P	W	D	L	F	A	W	D	L	F	A	Pts
1 Rushden & Diamonds	11	4	0	0	14	3	5	1	1	13	5	**28**
2 Worcester City	14	4	2	1	13	6	4	2	1	11	6	**28**
3 Newport AFC	13	4	1	0	12	6	4	2	2	13	9	**27**
4 Cheltenham Town	13	4	1	1	15	4	4	1	2	11	14	**26**
5 Gloucester City	14	5	1	1	15	6	2	3	2	11	7	**25**
6 Halesowen Town	12	3	3	1	16	13	2	2	1	7	5	**20**
7 Merthyr Tydfil	13	5	0	2	19	9	1	1	4	7	17	**19**

Next, with a little reluctance, came the legal version of the first leg of the opening round of the Dr Martens Cup against King's Lynn which was treated as an opportunity to give some of the fringe players some match practice. Glyn Creaser returned for his first start since the original tie, Steve Lilwall *(left)* replaced Butterworth, Mickey Nuttell came in for Wilkin and Dale Watkins for Kirkup. Darren Collins gave the Diamonds an early lead, and with Andy Peaks marking the prolific Brett McNamara out of the game there was little danger of the Linnets repeating their earlier success. However, the inability to add to that single goal advantage, despite the introduction of substitute strikers Richard Bailey and Julian Capone, rendered the outcome of the return leg a far from foregone conclusion.

Guy Fawkes' Eve, the Saturday before Cardiff, brought bottom of the table, the once mighty Stafford Rangers, to Nene Park. Without a league win all season the visitors shocked the large crowd, and no doubt delighted watching Cardiff City scouts, by capitalising on woeful Diamonds defending to take an early lead through Warren Houghton. They held the advantage until four minutes from half time when Tim Wooding equalised with a stunning volley from eighteen yards. Stafford might have regained the lead through Ian Banks within minutes of the restart but the chance was missed and it was the home side which scored a vital second. Dale Watkins, who had suffered ill deserved abuse from sections of the crowd, converted Wooding's cross and the Diamonds at last began to play like potential champions. Two goals from Wilkin and a spectacular first for the club by Brendan Hackett brought a final 5-1 scoreline.

Preparations for the biggest game in the club's short history were disrupted by the parochial necessity of an NFA Hillier Senior Cup tie against Long Buckby. The UCL club was dispatched 4-0, Mickey Nuttell scoring twice despite carrying a knock that made him doubtful for the FA Cup tie, the other goals coming from Kirkup and Collins. Frankie Belfon turned out for the Bucks, as did Steve Gee, soon to become part of the Nene Park youth set up.

The Cardiff game was an all-ticket sell-out. By 11.15 am on the preceding Sunday 2,000 tickets for the cup tie had been snapped up by eager fans, prompting this comment from club secretary, Dave Joyce. *"The tickets were sold extremely quickly but nothing surprises me at this club any more. When I turned up at the ground there were queues all round the car park."*

There was considerable media interest too, and most of the quality broadsheets carried articles recording the club's rise from comparative obscurity to the top of the Beazer Homes League. Inevitably much was made of the Dr Martens connection but the chairman modestly underplayed his own significant contribution preferring to point up the achievements of Roger Ashby and his team.

"We pay well, but they're great lads not mercenaries. There's a real team spirit. Our targets have always been moderate. A place in the Vauxhall Conference by 1997 and the Football League by 2000."

Visiting reporters were also hugely impressed by the facilities at Nene Park and there was unstinted praise for the aesthetic appearance of the stadium. As the man from the 'Independent' wrote, *"This football ground certainly doesn't resemble an architecturally challenged hypermarket."*

After all the pre-match publicity the game itself was something of an anti-climax. Despite the presence in the press box of several journalistic heavyweights - apologies to the 'Sunday Telegraph's Julie Welch - the desired shock result never seemed likely. There wasn't even any crowd trouble to make the headlines. Cardiff's notoriously fervent fans, corralled into the uncovered east end of the ground, had their initial boisterousness doused by a sharp shower. More significantly, the boost of an early goal raised Welsh spirits and they were able to delight, good naturedly, in what was a comfortable victory.

In front of a crowd of 4,214 the Diamonds failed to do themselves justice and allowed the visitors - just four places from the bottom of the Third Division - to dominate the opening exchanges and quickly establish a two goal lead through the lively Carl Dale and impressive 17 year old centre back Lee Jarman. When Al-James Hannigan reduced the arrears a minute after the interval home hopes fluttered briefly but were dashed when City produced a thoroughly professional performance, settling the game when the elegant Gardner provided a perfect cross from the left wing and Dale flung himself forward to head powerfully past the helpless Benstead.

Rushden & Diamonds (0) **1**			**Cardiff City** (2) **3**		
1	Graham Benstead		1	David Williams	
2	Tim Wooding		2	Derek Brazil	(sub: Oatway)
3	Nick Ashby		3	Damon Searle	
4	Andy Peaks	(sub: Spooner)	4	Ian Rodgerson	
5	Neil Smith		5	Lee Jarman	
6	Al James Hannigan		6	Scott Young	
7	Andy Kirkup		7	Haydn Fleming	
8	Garry Butterworth		8	Darren Adams	(sub: Evans)
9	Mickey Nuttell	(sub: Watkins)	9	Carl Dale	
10	Kevin Wilkin		10	Nathan Wigg	
11	Darren Collins		11	Jimmy Gardner	
12	Dale Watkins		12	Andy Evans	
14	Steve Spooner		14	Charlie Oatway	
15	Steve Lilwall		15	Chris Ingram	

Referee: SW Dunn (Bristol)

Goals: Dale (28, **0-1**), Jarman (32, **0-2**), Hannigan (46, **1-2**), Dale (71, **1-3**)
Booked: Smith, Jarman

Cardiff boss, Kenny Hibbitt was generous in victory, predicting a bright future for the Nene Park club. *"It really is a magnificent set up. We'll probably play at no better venue all season. I wouldn't be surprised if in a few years we see the Diamonds in the Football League."*

There was no time for lengthy inquests. Four days later the Diamonds travelled to Butlin Road to meet VS Rugby in the Beazer Homes League. Gerald Murphy gave VS an early lead but Kevin Wilkin's hat trick secured a 3-1 victory.

Wilkin was again on target at Gravesend - fresh from knocking Colchester out of the FA Cup - when additional goals from Darren Collins and Neil Smith *(left)* earned a similar scoreline. It was the fifth successive away win but again demonstrated the Diamonds' habit of letting the opposition take the lead, the Kent side having gone in front in the seventh minute.

The midweek visit of Burton Albion, the first of three home matches in eight days, provided an opportunity to avenge the only league defeat of the season to date, a deed that was duly done. Albion, with Dougie Keast operating in midfield, were disappointingly unambitious. Diamonds needed strength and patience and deservedly triumphed through a brace of second half goals.

Atherstone United were the next side to suffer defeat at Nene Park. After taking an almost obligatory lead after six minutes through Keith Russell everything went wrong for the visitors. The Adders were demoralised as the rampant Diamonds struck seven times. Collins hit four and Hannigan, Hackett and Ashby one apiece. Three substitutions in the 67th minute, bringing Watkins, Lilwall and Nuttell into the fray, understandably affected the side's rhythm and concentration and Atherstone gained two late consolation goals. These took a little of the gloss off Andy Peaks *(right)* becoming the third man to make one hundred league appearances for Rushden & Diamonds. The result moved the Diamonds seven points clear at the top of the table and the momentum was beginning to seem unstoppable.

Baldock Town never looked like being the side to halt what now appeared to be Diamonds' irresistible surge to the title. First half goals by Collins, Kirkup and Wilkin took the season's tally to fifty, extended the winning run to ten league games and kept the 100% home league record, now eight wins in eight games.

It wasn't long before there was a salutary reminder that the path to the championship would be far from smooth.

At Crawley, the day before Mike Atherton began his mammoth innings which saved England from apparently certain defeat in the Johannesburg test match, Rushden & Diamonds showed no such resilience after having established a winning platform with goals from Tim Wooding and Darren Collins who had capitalised on a mistake by former Diamonds trialist, Howard Clark. David Speedie, derided by many for merely being a name who was collecting money, produced a superbly inspiring spell of football which reduced Diamonds to total panic. Twelve minutes from time he produced the opportunity for Bill Hudson, nephew of Chelsea's Alan, to pull a goal back and five minutes later Speedie himself sent the home crowd delirious with the equaliser to set up a frantic finish. How the disorganised defence, lacking the injured Andy Peaks, managed to hold on was a mystery, though it certainly needed a superb save from Graham Benstead to deny the former Arsenal striker, Raphael Meade in the last minute.

In midweek the return leg of the Dr Martens Cup First Round tie took place at

King's Lynn. Diamonds probably did themselves a favour by managing to lose 2-0 and hence go out on aggregate but it needed a injury time goal for Lynn to progress in the competition many thought they should have been expelled from. Deputy goalkeeper Andy Lomas might have enjoyed the game - he saved a penalty - but Al James Hannigan certainly didn't: he was sent off after two yellow cards.

The lengthy journey to Dorchester was undertaken on the Friday to avoid the traffic problems experienced the previous season. It was a generally lacklustre performance where another outstanding display by Graham Benstead and tireless efforts from midfield pair Garry Butterworth and Neil Smith preserved a precious point. Dorchester's pacy front pair, Tommy Killick and Owen Pickard, provided incessant problems for the visitors whilst keeper Ken Veysey who had conceded nine goals the previous month when he returned to his previous club, Oxford United, for an FA Cup tie was rarely troubled. The Diamonds lost Darren Collins with an ankle injury at the interval and went a goal down two minutes into the second half when Pickard lifted the ball over the stranded Benstead. The equaliser though, was an exquisitely constructed strike, Wilkin netting from Dale Watkins' pinpoint pass after the substitute had outstripped the home defence. Perhaps the most important contribution, however, came from referee Osman who turned down a strong penalty appeal late in the game after Tommy Killick's goal bound shot struck Andy Peaks on the arm.

In midweek the side returned to winning ways and it did so in style with a thrilling 3-2 victory over third placed Gloucester City. The game was a magnificent advertisement for non-league football with both sides committed to all out attack. Andy Kirkup's left foot volley opened the scoring after 20 minutes, Paul Milsom levelled five minutes before half time, Darren Collins provided a comfortable cushion with two goals in five minutes before Andy Adebowale reduced the arrears to set up a pulsating finale.

On the following Saturday, however, it was a different story as Hastings Town made the first dent in the home record. Diamonds made two changes: Ian King, made his first senior appearance of the season, replacing the injured Brendan Hackett while Garry Butterworth dropped back into the defence to accommodate newcomer Steve Stott *(right)* at the expense of Al-James Hannigan.

Non-league international Stott, a £30,000 signing from Kettering Town (who had signed him from Bromsgrove Rovers), made a disastrous start when his misplaced pass set up the opening goal for Stuart Playford after just ten minutes. A further reshuffle was necessary shortly after when Tim Wooding limped out of the action, Andy Peaks moving across to cover and allowing a reprieve off the bench for Hannigan. In the second half, willed on by a particularly fervent Peter DeBanke crowd, Stott made amends for his earlier aberration by providing the cross for substitute Watkins to volley his side level.

The 100% home record had gone but defeat for second placed Cheltenham Town stretched the Diamonds advantage at the top of the league to ten points with half the games played.

			Home					Away					
		P	W	D	L	F	A	W	D	L	F	A	Pts
1	Rushden & Diamonds	21	9	1	0	35	10	7	3	1	22	10	**52**
2	Cheltenham Town	21	6	2	3	24	12	7	1	2	21	18	**42**
3	Gloucester City	21	7	1	2	21	10	5	3	3	22	15	**40**
4	Worcester City	19	6	2	2	18	9	5	2	2	14	9	**37**
5	Halesowen Town	18	5	3	2	20	16	5	2	1	14	8	**35**
6	Merthyr Tydfil	21	7	0	4	26	15	4	2	4	15	21	**35**

Glyn Creaser was restored to the centre of defence and winger Brendan Hackett returned for the first game of the Christmas period, a Nene Park clash with Ilkeston Town. A bumper crowd of 2,312 on a Saturday traditionally associated with low crowds saw the Diamonds extend that lead to thirteen points following a convincing 3-0 success over their struggling opponents. Dale Watkins came off the bench once more to seal victory with the final goal after Wilkin and Hackett had earlier breached a five man Ilkeston back line, further boosted by the presence of the experienced Bryn Gunn in a holding midfield role. Gunn, a native of Corby, had won a European Cup medal when Nottingham Forest had beaten Kevin Keegan's Hamburg side 1-0 in Madrid.

Many supporters suffered a frustrating Boxing Day afternoon when the fixture at Baldock was aborted by referee McGirl after twenty-five goalless minutes. The frost-bound, uneven pitch was clearly unplayable from the outset and it remains a mystery why the game began at all - unless of course one subscribes to the conspiracy theory: 900 paying customers at £4 a time, and no refunds!

The Saturday trip to Halesowen and the New Year's Day home game with Sudbury also fell victims to the weather. By the time the side was next in action, three weeks after the Ilkeston game, conditions could hardly have been more different. The thaw which followed the freeze turned Atherstone's Sheepy Road pitch into a quagmire but a combination of skill, determination and excellent finishing from twin strikers Wilkin and Collins, who scored twice, earned three points.

With one of those quirks that so often happens in Cup draws, Rushden & Diamonds were once again paired with Purfleet. This time it was the FA Trophy

First Round proper, a stage to which the Diamonds had been exempted due to their record the previous season. Thoughts of Wembley soon evaporated: Fleet's Nigel Jeyes notched the only goal of the game on the hour and earnt his club a trip to Macclesfield in the next round.

In the time-honoured phrase, Diamonds could now concentrate on the league, providing, of course, they were not distracted by the heady excitement of the Hillier Cup. Heady excitement was notably absent from a bitterly cold Nene Park on the penultimate day in January when Raunds visited for the semi-final. Old boys Kevin Fox, Darrell Page, John Flower and Peter Green were part of a battling Shopmates performance which took the match to extra time and almost to a replay. It was that man again - not Tommy Hanley but Darren Collins - who removed Rushden blushes with the 117th minute winner.

It was another 1-0 victory the following Saturday but the Premier Division win over Worcester City was of much higher quality. The first half of this battle between the Division's two tightest defences saw the Diamonds at their very best. Newcomer Steve Holden, released by Kettering the previous week, made a sound start at the heart of defence, Steve Stott enjoyed his most effective game to date in midfield and Darren Collins scored the all important goal after 36 minutes. How different it was after the break. It had taken Worcester 50 minutes to win their first corner but they dominated proceedings thereafter to such a degree that Diamonds fans, management and above all the beleaguered home defence were hugely relieved to hear Jimmy Ogilvie's final whistle.

The undefeated home record came to an end on the following Saturday, February 10th, when Gravesend & Northfleet showed the form that had brought them an FA Cup visit to Villa Park. Mark Munday put the Kentishmen ahead after five minutes and although Diamonds twice equalised, Peter Mortley headed Gravesend's winning third goal five minutes from the end. It was only the Diamonds second defeat of the season but a timely reminder that the apparently unassailable lead at the top of the table was far from secure.

Halesowen Town now posed the greatest threat but the West Midlanders defeat at bottom of the table Stafford on the following Tuesday enabled the Diamonds to extend their lead to 13 points after a 3-0 success in the rearranged fixture at Baldock in front of a crowd paying half-price, some of whom remembered to bring their programmes from Boxing Day. Diamonds stood up well to the physical challenge; Steve Stott netted his first goal for the club and Darren Collins added two more to his already impressive tally. Roger Ashby expressed his relief at the result. *"This was a vital match for us and I thought the players responded magnificently. It's a big week for us now with Cheltenham on Saturday and Halesowen next Tuesday. That's why a win here was so important. It has set us up perfectly."*

In the event only the first of those games occurred in the next seven days, the Halesowen visit being postponed. 2,472 watched the Diamonds crush Cheltenham 4-1 at Nene Park, Andy Kirkup netting a double with Kevin Wilkin and

Dale Watkins *(left)* scoring the other two. It was nowhere the emphatic victory the scoreline suggests. David Elsey had fired the Robins in front after ten minutes and Watkins' equaliser came on the stroke of half-time after Cheltenham had missed a penalty. The second half, whilst containing plenty of good football, was a nerve-tingling affair. It was only in the final five minutes that Diamonds could relax after two late goals ruined the Robins' hope of an equaliser. Watkins' goal, against his future employers, was his 97th, and last, for the club.

Next on the agenda was the potentially tricky visit to Newport AFC who had dropped to mid-table after leading the Division in the early weeks of the season. Previously the Diamonds had played them at Gloucester but now the court battle was over and they were ensconced at the brand new Ysptty Stadium in their home town, the original home of Newport County, Somerton Park, being now the location of a housing estate. It needed a gutsy performance to come away with a point in front of a vociferous and partisan crowd of 1,170, nearly twice the number that had turned up for the previous game, which roared their side forward and rewarded the players with a standing ovation at the end. Behind from the 51st minute when Steve Lowndes, capped ten times for Wales, played a perfect ball to Dave Webley who scored from close range, the Diamonds fought back to level through Nick Ashby. Debutant loanee Steve Taylor, who had cost Crystal Palace £90,000 in the summer, impressed with his work rate before departing with an injury to be replaced by substitute Watkins. There was no inimitable super-sub goal this time but a draw was just reward for the side's efforts which, to paraphrase the Evening Telegraph report, *"so effectively repelled the Newport pressure that by the end of the game it had faded as completely as the rainbow over the nearby steelworks."* Garry Butterworth made his 100th appearance in this match, having missed just six games since signing for Rushden.

So the Diamonds began the final third of the season still 12 points ahead of their nearest rivals.

			Home					Away					
		P	W	D	L	F	A	W	D	L	F	A	Pts
1	Rushden & Diamonds	28	12	1	1	45	14	9	4	1	29	12	**68**
2	Halesowen Town	28	8	5	2	29	20	8	3	2	20	10	**56**
3	Gloucester City	28	8	3	3	27	15	6	4	4	24	17	**49**
4	Cheltenham Town	29	7	5	3	27	14	7	2	5	24	28	**49**
5	Merthyr Tydfil	27	9	0	5	30	19	6	2	5	19	24	**47**
6	Worcester City	27	8	4	2	26	15	5	3	5	17	15	**46**

The first of the final fourteen matches attracted only 1409, the lowest home league crowd of the season, to Nene Park for the visit of Sudbury Town. Yet again the opposition took the lead, scoring through the former Kettering and Corby striker, John Ashdjian after 11 minutes. For a time it seemed that, despite almost total Diamonds domination, especially in midfield where Steve Spooner relished his first Beazer Homes start since early September, the Suffolk side would hold out for at least a point. Everything changed from the 56th minute when Darren Collins equalised after hesitation in the Sudbury defence. Within three minutes the Diamonds were ahead through a Brendan Hackett header and only the brilliance of visiting keeper Steve Mokler prevented a defeat of epic proportions, although he was finally beaten by Andy Kirkup just two minutes from full time. Tim Wooding became the eleventh player to make a century of appearances for the club.

So commanding were Steve Holden and Al-James Hannigan at the centre of defence that the next opponents, Cambridge City, barely mustered a half-decent shot in ninety minutes. Hannigan had just returned from a loan spell at Yeovil and marked his recall with a splendid performance. Darren Collins gave the Diamonds an early lead but despite creating a hatful of chances it was not until the 72nd minute that Hannigan scored with an inswinging cross that somehow deceived Barry Piggott in the City goal.

Twelve matches to go and the next was the vital game at Halesowen which took place on Tuesday March 19th after two earlier postponements. It was third time lucky for neither side as the match ended in a goalless draw. There was excitement but few chances for either side and in particular their leading scorers, Darren Collins leading the Premier Division list with 24, and third placed Halesowen favourite, Evran Wright. The draw left Rushden nine points in front with a game in hand; they had 75 points from 31 games, Halesowen had 66 points from 32 matches.

That crucial away point ought to have made Diamonds even stronger favourites for the title but the reverse seemed to be the case. Perhaps the fact that the lead was down to single figures made stomachs flutter; perhaps the appearance in the Halesowen programme of one of football's less frequently quoted truisms did not help, *"Rushden & Diamonds have headed the League for most of the year. You only have to be top of the table for one game, that is the 42nd."*

And so began a remarkable period of inconsistency which was to put the Diamonds' promotion place in serious jeopardy. Two more points were dropped at Ilkeston in the next game. The Derbyshire side were desperately attempting to drag themselves out of the relegation zone and introduced two new strikers, Simon Grayson from Boston United and Mark Hallam from Gloucester. After on-loan keeper, former Poppy Paul Reece, had denied the visitors with a string of outstanding saves, the Diamonds took the lead through Brendan Hackett after 71 minutes. They might have gone two up ten minutes later. Referee Solomon, faced with a much simpler conundrum than his biblical counterpart, decided in his wisdom that when former Olympic decathlon gold medal winner Daley Thompson stumbled in the penalty area he had been fouled by Dale Watkins. Thompson had then appeared to handle the ball before kicking it past his own keeper with substitute Watkins following up in the belief that victory had been sealed. Ilkeston salvaged an equaliser at the death. David Taylor hared down the left and crossed for Grayson to crash home a debut goal. Rushden's loan signing, Steve Taylor, made his fourth and final appearance. This, just as the previous three, ended in his being substituted. Darren Collins failed to score on his hundredth appearance for the club; that century of games had produced a stunning sixty-two goals.

Probably the most forgettable match of the season came next, the Hillier Cup Final at Rothwell. The Bones, consolidating in their second season in the Beazer Midland Division, had beaten Kettering 5-0 in the semi-final and went on to lift the cup with an 80th minute goal from Stewart Beards, a name familiar to Irthlingborough Diamonds and Rushden Town fans. Better news, perhaps, was that Halesowen had dropped two points at Dorchester.

Whilst Rothwell fans remembered the match for a long while, Diamonds were soon able to forget it because of the news that Carl Alford *(left)* (himself a frequent spectator at Rothwell) had been signed from Kettering Town. An attempt had been made to sign him simultaneously with Steve Stott but it was only now that Kettering succumbed to the £85,000 fee. The stage was perfect for his debut as the next game was the crunch of the season: Rushden & Diamonds v Halesowen at Nene Park.

It had been three and a half weeks since the previous home game. Then victory over Sudbury had put Diamonds 15 points in front having played a game more than Halesowen. Now the difference was down to just six points, though Halesowen had played two more games. A crowd of 3481 flocked to Nene Park and saw Alford oblige with a debut goal. There wasn't much else for the home fans to get excited about. Halesowen were the better side throughout. Kevin Harrison opened the scoring after 22 minutes but Alford's equaliser came within a minute. Andy Bradley notched the winner with nearly half an hour left. The introduction of substitute David Holmes, signed on loan from Gloucester City, did not turn the tide Diamonds' way. Supporters trooped home to confirm the dreaded details on teletext. The top of the table now read:

			Home					Away					
		P	W	D	L	F	A	W	D	L	F	A	Pts
1	Rushden & Diamonds	33	13	1	2	49	17	10	6	1	32	13	**76**
2	Halesowen Town	35	10	6	2	34	21	11	4	2	25	11	**73**
3	Cheltenham Town	35	8	5	4	29	16	10	3	5	32	33	**62**

There was a further diversion on the following Tuesday, Nene Park's third international of the season. Back in November the club had been privileged to stage two matches, Sweden v Latvia and England v Latvia, in the UEFA under 18 championship. Now Irthlingborough was to host the semi-professional international against the Netherlands. As a contest it was a non-event, England going two up in thirteen minutes and eventually coasting to a 3-0 win. Three Diamonds men were selected: Steve Stott scored the first goal and Carl Alford got the second from a Nick Ashby cross.

All three were back at Nene Park forty-eight hours later for the more important fixture with Dorchester Town. The Dorset side had been due to visit Irthlingborough on a Saturday early in March. However the Dorset FA insisted that instead, Dorchester had to play a Dorset Cup tie against a Dorset Combination side on that date and hence Dorchester were forced to wend their way north on a Thursday afternoon. The effects of the long journey appeared to have taken its toll of the visitors who only arrived at Nene Park a quarter of an hour before kick off. Understandably slow to start they survived sustained pressure, aided by a profligate Diamonds strike force, but snatched the winner eleven minutes from the end when Nick Ashby's chested back pass fell woefully short of keeper Andy Lomas and was gratefully converted by the inrushing Tommy Killick. The final whistle brought discordant noises from aggrieved elements in the crowd prompting a philosophical response from manager Ashby. *"This club's come a long way in a very short space of time and the expectations are naturally high. People are not used to seeing us lose. But no-one has a divine right to win every week. I think everybody thought we'd have the title wrapped up a couple of months ago. Neither I nor the players, though, ever believed that would be the case."*

Now Halesowen really were breathing down the Diamonds necks: three points behind and Rushden had only one game in hand. For the first time for months supporters started looking at goal differences. There was some comfort for those of a nervous disposition: Rushden & Diamonds' was much better than Halesowen's.

Less than forty-eight hours later we were back at Nene Park where anxiety on the terraces found expression on the field as the players struggled to overcome a tenacious Cambridge City side, battling to avoid relegation. The Diamonds' generosity apparently knew no bounds. They gave their opponents a goal start, spurned a glorious opportunity to equalise when Carl Alford's tame penalty kick was saved by Kevin Murray and squandered countless other excellent chances.

The game turned on an inspired joint substitution, Steve Spooner *(left)* and Kevin Wilkin replacing Stott and Kirkup thirteen minutes from time. Within five minutes Darren Collins had run on to Nick Ashby's fine through pass to register his 34th goal of the season. Then, with only two minutes remaining, the impressive Spooner linked with Garry Butterworth down the right before crossing into a crowded penalty area where the predatory Alford atoned for his penalty miss in the best possible way by forcing home the winner. And there was good news from Halesowen: Burton Albion had gone home with a draw.

In the next game, at Sudbury on Easter Monday afternoon, Alford made it three goals in four appearances but finished on the losing side for the third time. Mid-table Sudbury, inspired by veteran David Crown (who had moved from Purfleet) recorded a 4-1 success, former Northampton striker Ian Brown netting all four. The evening news from Worcester was no help: Worcester 0 Halesowen 1.

There were now six matches left.

			Home					Away					
		P	W	D	L	F	A	W	D	L	F	A	Pts
1	Rushden & Diamonds	36	14	1	3	51	19	10	6	2	33	17	**79**
2	Halesowen Town	37	10	7	2	35	22	12	4	2	26	11	**77**
3	Cheltenham Town	37	9	5	4	30	16	11	3	5	35	33	**68**

A straightforward 3-0 victory over Newport AFC in front of a near 3000 crowd steadied nerves. A Darren Collins goal after just four minutes was a tremendous help and when Alford struck a minute before the break it was virtually all over. It certainly was when Nick Ashby fired in the third. Halesowen just squeezed a 2-1 victory at home to Cambridge City.

On the following Tuesday came Diamonds' match in hand. Victory was crucial, nay essential. The opposition, as fate would have it, was the old bogey team, Gresley Rovers. It was another tense evening as player-manager Paul Futcher's brave Gresley side fought every inch of the way. Collins provided the home side with the lead on the half hour but Graeme Fowkes equalised nine minutes after the break. Alford's dramatic winner came with under four minutes left. Four games left for both sides, Diamonds five points in front. Two wins and a draw would give Diamonds the title on goal difference.

So it was off to Gloucester City's Meadow Park to take on opponents suffering a financial crisis which had forced them to unload several players in the previous month. Those that were left, though, proved to be a spirited bunch. They took a 12th minute lead when former Diamonds favourite, Dave Johnson, provided the free-kick which Steve Mardenborough, a member of Darlington's Conference winning side, converted. Darren Collins equalised within four minutes and it seemed that a draw had to be the outcome. It wasn't. Unbelievably Diamonds managed to concede a injury time goal. Long throw specialist Grant Thorne hurled the ball into the Diamonds penalty area, Gary Kemp flicked on and Paul Milsom arrived unmarked at the far post to head past Benstead. A bad result but made even worse by Halesowen's victory at Gravesend which cut the Diamonds lead to a fragile two points.

Three games to go and Wednesday found Diamonds on the road to Salisbury, knowing defeat could well hand Conference football to Halesowen. It was perhaps to Diamonds advantage that Salisbury had dragged themselves clear of the relegation zone and were no longer desperate for points. Diamonds certainly were but they kept their composure well and emerged with all three thanks to two goals late in the first half from Collins and Kirkup.

The penultimate Saturday required Diamonds to travel to Stafford who were already relegated. Victory in this game and the final match the following Saturday would guarantee promotion. Diamonds were without Nick Ashby, injured at Salisbury, so Steve Lilwall stepped in for his first league start since August 21st. Steve Spooner was considered fit enough to start, though he did not last until half-time, being replaced by Steve Holden who had not fully recovered from his injury at Gloucester. As a contest the game lasted six minutes. Alford scored after two minutes and four minutes later Kirkup made it 2-0. Keeper Steve Perks was injured and had to be substituted, defender Mal Esfandiarania, an Iranian two days short of his 29th birthday, taking over. Esfandiarania, formerly with Knighton Town of the Cymru Alliance, made a series of remarkable stops, applauded with great fervour by a significantly large still-loyal Stafford following, but was beaten by Brendan Hackett before the interval and by Kirkup just before the end.

Halesowen had struggled to beat Baldock 1-0 but the ball was undoubtedly in Diamonds' court. The top of the table was now:

			Home					Away					
		P	W	D	L	F	A	W	D	L	F	A	Pts
1	Rushden & Diamonds	41	16	1	3	56	20	12	6	3	40	19	**91**
2	Halesowen Town	40	12	7	2	38	23	13	4	2	27	11	**86**
3	Cheltenham Town	41	10	6	4	35	17	11	4	6	38	37	**73**

A point on Saturday would win it for Diamonds but it was now possible that the title could come to Nene Park on the Tuesday evening. If Halesowen failed to win at Crawley, Rushden would be champions. Consequently Trumps Bar was full that evening to listen to commentary of the Crawley v Halesowen game. It was good news early on when Crawley took the lead, it became a little tedious when there was a ten minute delay to mend a broken crossbar and turned into a somewhat depressing evening when a superb second half performance enabled Halesowen to complete a 3-1 victory with goals from Gary Hackett, Richard Crisp and, yes, Evran Wright. Those who were at Crawley reported that you could bet your house that Halesowen would win at Newport on the final Saturday.

And by half time on Saturday May 4th you would have bet your house on Diamonds winning - unless you'd seen some of their other home performances! It looked as easy as ABC at the interval - Alford, Butterworth and Collins having opened up a 3-0 lead. Collins's goal was more than a little controversial - he appeared to knock it out of the hands of Gary Wager before tapping it into the net, but it provided Collins with his 30th league goal of the season and ensured that he finished top of the Premier Division scoring charts.

Rushden & Diamonds (3) 3			**Merthyr Tydfil (0) 2**		
1	Graham Benstead		1	Gary Wager	
2	Andy Peaks		2	Mark Williams	
3	Steve Lilwall		3	Steve Williams	
4	Steve Holden		4	Andy York	
5	Steve Stott		5	Neil O'Brien	
6	Al James Hannigan		6	Colin Loss	
7	Andy Kirkup	(sub: King)	7	Lee Jones	
8	Garry Butterworth		8	Andy Beattie	(sub: Knight)
9	Darren Collins		9	Chris Summers	(sub: Jenkins)
10	Carl Alford		10	Paul Evans	(sub: Mitchell)
11	Brendan Hackett	(sub: Watkins)	11	Gareth Astley	
12	Dale Watkins		12	Ross Knight	
14	Ian King		14	Tony Jenkins	
15	David Holmes		15	Ian Mitchell	

Referee: RJ Harris (Oxford)

Goals: Alford (9, **1-0**), Butterworth (39, **2-0**), Collins (45, **3-0**), Evans (56, **3-1**), Knight (82, **3-2**)

Booked: Alford, Astley, O'Brien

But Diamonds lacked a surname beginning with D and the second half, especially after Evans had replied early for the Welsh side, produced an orgy of nail-biting amongst the 4664 crowd (another record). Few of them can remember exactly what happened after Ross Knight got Merthyr's second eight minutes from time. There are few who can recall precisely those frantic final minutes, played in the knowledge that Halesowen had taken the lead at Newport. Eventually, though, came the time to celebrate as the massive shield was presented in front of a pitch covered with ecstatic fans who had temporarily forgotten the trauma of the preceding six weeks and were beginning to relish the prospect of covering the entire country in the Conference.

Beazer Homes League Premier Division 1995-1996

			Home					Away					
	P	W	D	L	F	A	W	D	L	F	A	Pts
1 Rushden & Diamonds (5)	42	17	1	3	59	22	12	6	3	40	19	**94**
2 Halesowen Town (13)	42	12	7	2	38	23	15	4	2	32	13	**92**
3 Cheltenham Town (2)	42	10	7	4	38	20	11	4	6	38	37	**74**
4 Gloucester City (4)	42	13	3	5	38	24	8	5	8	27	23	**71**
5 Gresley Rovers (8)	42	10	5	6	34	27	10	5	6	36	31	**70**
6 Worcester City (10)	42	11	6	4	36	19	8	6	7	25	24	**69**
7 Merthyr Tydfil (-)	42	11	3	7	39	25	8	3	10	28	34	**63**
8 Hastings Town (12)	42	8	5	8	37	33	8	8	5	31	23	**61**
9 Crawley Town (11)	42	10	7	4	34	25	5	6	10	23	31	**58**
10 Gravesend & Northfleet (14)	42	10	5	6	34	21	5	5	11	26	41	**55**
11 Sudbury Town (18)	42	11	4	6	41	28	4	6	11	28	43	**55**
12 Chelmsford City (15)	42	7	9	5	25	22	6	7	8	21	31	**55**
13 Dorchester Town (6)	42	9	4	8	39	27	6	4	11	23	30	**53**
14 Newport AFC (-)	42	5	7	9	30	29	8	6	7	23	30	**52**
15 Salisbury City (-)	42	10	4	7	33	29	4	6	11	24	40	**52**
16 Burton Albion (3)	42	8	7	6	30	24	5	5	11	25	32	**51**
17 Atherstone United (16)	42	6	7	8	31	33	6	5	10	27	42	**48**
18 Baldock Town (-)	42	5	8	8	25	27	6	6	9	26	29	**47**
19 Cambridge City (9)	42	7	2	12	28	35	5	8	8	28	33	**46**
20 Ilkeston Town (-)	42	6	8	7	27	33	5	2	14	26	54	**43**
21 Stafford Rangers (-)	42	7	1	13	31	39	4	3	14	27	51	**37**
22 VS Rugby (17)	42	3	5	13	20	36	2	5	14	17	56	**25**

Figures in brackets are 1994-95 positions.

- Rushden & Diamonds were promoted to the Vauxhall Conference.
- No club was relegated from the Conference into the Beazer Homes League. Dover Athletic, 20th in the Conference, survived because neither of the top two in the Unibond were eligible: Bamber Bridge (ground) and Boston United ("administrative error").
- Ilkeston Town, Stafford Rangers and VS Rugby were relegated to the Midland Division. Cambridge City retained Premier Division because there was no club relegated from the Conference.
- Nuneaton Borough and King's Lynn were promoted from the Midland Division. Sittingbourne and Ashford Town came up from the Southern Division.
- Four clubs left the Beazer Homes League: Braintree Town, Bridgnorth Town, Bury Town and Poole Town. The five vacancies were filled by Cirencester Town, Dartford, Raunds Town, Shepshed Dynamo and St. Leonards Stamcroft.

Saturday May 4th 1996 and after weeks of increasing tension players and fans can finally celebrate the Southern League Championship and the club's consequent promotion to the Conference.

Gathered round the shield are (standing, left to right): Andy Lomas, Steve Spooner, Al James Hannigan, Garry Butterworth, Steve Stott, Steve Holden, Neil Smith, Andy Peaks, Nick Ashby and Brendan Hackett. The pair in front are Carl Alford (left) and Darren Collins. Ian King is behind Hannigan, Graham Benstead can be identified behind Butterworth, Steve Lilwall is almost completely obscured by Smith, David Holmes is behind Peaks (who is behind Hackett's right hand) and Kevin Wilkin is partially visible between Ashby and Hackett. Missing is Andy Kirkup, being presented with an individual award, and Dale Watkins who may own the apparently disembodied right arm behind Holden's head.

The Southern League dates back to 1894 when it was formed to provide a professional league in the south of England. At the time the Football League was exclusively northern and midlands, apart from Royal Arsenal who had joined in 1893. The first champions were Millwall, soon followed by Southampton, Tottenham Hotspur and Portsmouth. Northampton Town were champions in 1909: by this time the other county representatives, Kettering and Wellingborough had left the league. In 1920 the Southern League's First Division became the Football League's Third Division. The league continued through the depression of the thirties and picked up strongly after World War Two, though it was weakened in 1979 when it lost thirteen clubs to the newly formed Alliance Premier League (now known as the Conference).

1995-1996 Results

Beazer Homes League Premier Division

Aug	19	Salisbury City	H	3	0	Wilkin, Kirkup, Collins	1532
Aug	21	Chelmsford City	A	2	1	Spooner, Watkins	1003
Aug	26	Crawley Town	H	3	1	Butterworth, Watkins 2	1611
Aug	28	Burton Albion	A	2	4	Watkins, Collins	901
Sep	2	Hastings Town	A	1	0	Watkins	552
Sep	5	VS Rugby	H	6	1	Ashby, Wilkin, Watkins 3, Bailey	1624
Sep	16	Worcester City	A	0	0		960
Sep	19	Chelmsford City	H	2	1	own goal, Collins	1747
Sep	30	Cheltenham Town	A	2	0	Kirkup, Collins	1122
Oct	14	Gresley Rovers	A	3	0	Hannigan, Collins, Butterworth	808
Oct	28	Merthyr Tydfil	A	3	0	Collins, Kirkup, Watkins	464
Nov	4	Stafford Rangers	H	5	1	Wooding, Watkins, Wilkin 2, Hackett	2078
Nov	15	VS Rugby	A	3	1	Wilkin 3	741
Nov	18	Gravesend & Northfleet	A	3	1	Wilkin, Collins, Smith	658
Nov	21	Burton Albion	H	2	0	Wilkin, Collins	1651
Nov	25	Atherstone United	H	7	3	Hackett, Hannigan, Collins 4, Ashby	2231
Nov	28	Baldock Town	H	3	0	Collins, Kirkup, Wilkin	1922
Dec	2	Crawley Town	A	2	2	Wooding, Collins	1118
Dec	9	Dorchester Town	A	1	1	Wilkin	684
Dec	12	Gloucester City	H	3	2	Kirkup, Collins 2	1666
Dec	16	Hastings Town	H	1	1	Watkins	1924
Dec	23	Ilkeston Town	H	3	0	Wilkin, Hackett, Watkins	2313
Jan	13	Atherstone United	A	3	1	Wilkin, Collins 2	605
Feb	3	Worcester City	H	1	0	Collins	2197
Feb	10	Gravesend & Northfleet	H	2	3	Watkins (pen), Collins	1841
Feb	13	Baldock Town	A	3	0	Stott, Collins 2	858
Feb	17	Cheltenham Town	H	4	1	Watkins, Kirkup 2, Wilkin	2472
Feb	24	Newport AFC	A	1	1	Ashby	1170
Mar	5	Sudbury Town	H	3	1	Collins, Hackett, Kirkup	1409
Mar	16	Cambridge City	A	2	0	Collins, Hannigan	750
Mar	19	Halesowen Town	A	0	0		1725
Mar	23	Ilkeston Town	A	1	1	Hackett	1009
Mar	30	Halesowen Town	H	1	2	Alford	3481
Apr	4	Dorchester Town	H	0	1		1823
Apr	6	Cambridge City	H	2	1	Collins, Alford	2135
Apr	8	Sudbury Town	A	1	4	Alford	918
Apr	13	Newport AFC	H	3	0	Collins, Alford, Ashby	2914
Apr	16	Gresley Rovers	H	2	1	Collins, Alford	2250
Apr	20	Gloucester City	A	1	2	Collins	1226
Apr	24	Salisbury City	A	2	0	Collins, Kirkup	596
Apr	27	Stafford Rangers	A	4	0	Alford, Kirkup 2, Hackett	1160
May	4	Merthyr Tydfil	H	3	2	Alford, Butterworth, Collins	4664

1995-1996 Results

FA Cup

Sep	9	1Q	Grantham Town	H	4	1	Collins 3, Wilkin	1681
Sep	23	2Q	Eastwood Hanley	H	1	0	Collins	1652
Oct	7	3Q	Sandwell Borough	A	6	1	Wilkin 4, Collins 2	250
Oct	21	4Q	Purfleet	A	1	1	Hannigan	794
Oct	24	4QR	Purfleet	H	3	1	Watkins, Collins, Wilkin	2850
Nov	11	1	Cardiff City	H	1	3	Hannigan	4214

FA Trophy

Jan	20	1	Purfleet	H	0	1		1906

Dr Martens Cup

Oct	3	1.1	King's Lynn	H	0	1	*(match declared void)*	1262
Nov	1	1.1	King's Lynn	H	1	0	Collins	1098
Dec	5	1.2	King's Lynn	A	0	2		432

NFA Hillier Senior Cup 1994-1995

Jul	29	F	Kettering Town	H	2	2	Wooding (pen), Wilkin	1927
Jul	31	FR	Kettering Town	A	2	2	Collins, Wilkin *(lost on penalties)*	1509

NFA Hillier Senior Cup 1995-1996

Nov	7	QF	Long Buckby	H	4	0	Nuttell 2, Kirkup, Watkins	578
Jan	30	SF	Raunds Town	H	1	0	Collins	904
Mar	26	F	Rothwell Town	A	0	1		511

- The FA Cup was won by Manchester United who beat Liverpool 1-0 in the final. Two non-League sides reached the Third Round proper. Woking lost 0-2 at Swindon Town and Gravesend & Northfleet lost 0-3 to Aston Villa after conceding ground advantage and playing at Villa Park. Four non-League sides beat Football League opposition: Blyth Spartans (Bury), Gravesend & Northfleet (Colchester United), Hitchin Town (Bristol Rovers) and Woking (Barnet).

- In the FA Trophy final, Macclesfield Town (4th in the Conference) beat Northwich Victoria (8th in the Conference) 3-1. Two Unibond League sides, Chorley and Hyde United were the beaten semi-finalists.

- In the Dr Martens sponsored Southern League Cup, Midland Division champions Nuneaton Borough beat Premier Division Baldock Town. Moor Green and Salisbury City were the beaten semi-finalists.

1995-1996 Teams
Beazer Homes League Premier Division

		Alford	Ashby	Bailey	Benstead	Butterworth	Collins	Creaser	Hackett	Hannigan	Holden	Holmes	King	Kirkup	Lilwall	Lomas	Nuttell	Peaks	Reed	Smith	Spooner	Stott	Taylor	Watkins	Wilkin	Wooding
Salisbury	H		3		1	8	11	5		6				7	4				2	10					9	
Chelmsford	A		3		1	8	11	5		6				sb	4				2	10	7			sb	9	
Crawley	H		3		1	8	11	5		6				7					2	4	sb			10	9	
Burton	A		3		1	8	11	5		6				sb					2	4	7			10	9	sb
Hastings	A		3		1	8	11	5						7			sb	4		9	6			10	sb	2
VS Rugby	H		3	9	1	8	11	5										4		6	sb			10	7	2
Worcester	A		3		1	8	11	5		6				sb				4		9				10	7	2
Chelmsford	H		3	sb	1	8	11			5							9	4		6				10	7	2
Cheltenham	A		3		1	8	9		11	6				7			sb	4		5				10	sb	2
Gresley	A		3		1	8	9		11	6				7				4		5					10	2
Merthyr	A		3		1	8	9		11	6				7				4		5				sb	10	2
Stafford	H		3		1	8			11	6				7			sb	4		5				10	9	2
VS Rugby	A		3		1	8	9		11	6				7	sb			4		5				sb	10	2
Gravesend	A		3		1	8	9		11	6				7				4		5					10	2
Burton	H		3		1	8	9		11	6				7				4		5					10	2
Atherstone	H		3		1	8	9		11	6				7	sb		sb	4		5				sb	10	2
Baldock	H		3		1	8	9		11	6				7	sb		sb	4		5				sb	10	2
Crawley	A		3		1	8	9	4	11	6				7						5					10	2
Dorchester	A		3		1	8	9		11	6				7				4		5				sb	10	2
Gloucester	H		3		1	8	9		11	6				7				4		5	sb			sb	10	2
Hastings	H		3		1	8	9			sb			11	7				4		5		6		sb	10	2
Ilkeston	H		3		1	8	9	4	11				sb	7				2		5		6		sb	10	
Atherstone	A		3		1	8	9		11	4				7				2		5	sb	6			10	
Worcester	H		3		1	8	9				4		11	7				2		5	sb	6		10		
Gravesend	H		3		1	8	9				4		11	7				2		5		6		10	sb	
Baldock	A		3		1	8	9		11		4			7				2		5	sb	6		10		
Cheltenham	H		3		1	8	9		11		4			7				2		5	sb	6		10	sb	
Newport	A		3		1	8	9		11		4			7				2		5		6	10	sb	sb	sb
Sudbury	H		3		1	8	9		11		4			7						5	6			10	sb	2
Cambridge	A		3		1	8	9		11	6	4			7						5			10	sb	sb	2
Halesowen	A		3		1	8	9		11	6	4			7						5			10		sb	2
Ilkeston	A		3		1	8	9		11	6	4			7						5		sb	10	sb	sb	2
Halesowen	H	10	3		1	8	9		11	6	4	sb		7								5		sb	sb	2
Dorchester	H	10	3			8	9			6		11		sb		1		4				5		sb	7	2
Cambridge	H	10	3			8	9		11	6				7		1		4			sb	5			sb	2
Sudbury	A	10	3			8	9		11	6				7		1		4			5	sb			sb	2
Newport	H	10	3	sb	1	8	9		11		4			7				2			5	6				
Gresley	H	10	3		1	8	9		11		4			7				2			5	6				
Gloucester	A	10	3		1	8	9		11	sb	4			7				2			5	6				
Salisbury	A	10	3		1	8	9		11	4				7				2			5	6		sb	sb	
Stafford	A	10			1	8	9		11	4	sb			7	3			2			5	6			sb	
Merthyr	H	10			1	8	9		11	6	4		sb	7	3			2				5		sb		

1995-1996 Teams   Cup Competitions

		Ashby	Bailey	Benstead	Butterworth	Capone	Collins	Creaser	Hackett	Hannigan	Keast	King	Kirkup	Lilwall	Lomas	Nuttell	Peaks	Smith	Spooner	Stott	Watkins	Wilkin	Wooding
FA Cup																							
Grantham	H	3		1	8		11	5					9				4	6	sb		10	7	2
Eastwood Hanley	H	3	sb	1	8		11			5			sb			9	4	6			10	7	2
Sandwell	A	3		1	8		9			6			7	11			4	5				10	2
Purfleet	A	3		1	8		10			6			7	11		sb	4	5				9	2
Purfleet	H	3		1	8		10			6			7				4	5			11	9	2
Cardiff	H	3		1	8		11			6			7			9	4	5	sb		sb	10	2
FA Trophy																							
Purfleet	H	3		1	8		9		11	4			7			sb	2	5		6	sb	10	
Dr Martens Cup																							
King's Lynn	H	3	sb	1		sb	7	6	11					8		9	4	5	sb		10		2
King's Lynn	A	3	9				sb	4	11	6				7	1			5	8		10	sb	2
Hillier Cup 94-5																							
Kettering	H				8	sb	11			6	3		sb		1		4	7	5		10	9	2
Kettering	A	3		1	8	sb	11			6	10		sb				4	7	5			9	2
Hillier Cup 95-6																							
Long Buckby	H			1	8		11	4		2			7	3		9		5	6		10	sb	
Raunds	H	3	sb	1	8		9		11			sb	7				4	5	6		sb	10	2
Rothwell	A	3		1			9		11	6			7				4	5	8		sb	10	2

1995-1996 Appearances

	Start						Substitute						Total					
	L	C	T	LC	CC	Tot	L	C	T	LC	CC	Tot	L	C	T	LC	CC	Tot
Carl ALFORD	10					**10**						**0**	10					**10**
Nick ASHBY	40	6	1	2	3	**52**						**0**	40	6	1	2	3	**52**
Richard BAILEY	1			1		**2**	2	1		1	1	**5**	3			2		**7**
Graham BENSTEAD	39	6	1	1	4	**51**						**0**	39	6	1	1	4	**51**
Garry BUTTERWORTH	42	6	1		4	**53**						**0**	42	6	1		4	**53**
Julian CAPONE						**0**				1	2	**3**				1	2	**3**
Darren COLLINS	41	6	1	1	5	**54**				1		**1**	41	6	1	2	5	**55**
Glyn CREASER	9	1		2	1	**13**						**0**	9	1		2	1	**13**
Brendan HACKETT	30		1	2	2	**35**						**0**	30		1	2	2	**35**
Al James HANNIGAN	29	5	1	1	4	**40**	2					**2**	31	5	1	1	4	**42**
Steven HOLDEN	14					**14**	1					**1**	15					**15**
David HOLMES	1					**1**	1					**1**	2					**2**
Dougie KEAST					2	**2**						**0**					2	**2**
Ian KING	3					**3**	2				1	**3**	5				1	**6**
Andy KIRKUP	36	5	1		3	**45**	4	1			2	**7**	40	6	1		5	**52**
Steve LILWALL	4	2		2	1	**9**	3					**3**	7	2		2	1	**12**
Andy LOMAS	3			1	1	**5**						**0**	3			1	1	**5**
Mickey NUTTELL	1	2		1	1	**5**	5	1	1			**7**	6	3	1	1	1	**12**
Andy PEAKS	32	6	1	1	4	**44**						**0**	32	6	1	1	4	**44**
Graham REED	4					**4**						**0**	4					**4**
Neil SMITH	32	6	1	2	5	**46**						**0**	32	6	1	2	5	**46**
Steve SPOONER	10			1	5	**16**	8	2		1		**11**	18			2	5	**27**
Steve STOTT	17		1			**18**	2					**2**	19		1			**20**
Steve TAYLOR	4					**4**						**0**	4					**4**
Dale WATKINS	13	3		2	2	**20**	16	1	1		2	**20**	29	4	1	2	4	**40**
Kevin WILKIN	22	6	1		4	**33**	14			1	1	**16**	36	6	1	1	5	**49**
Tim WOODING	25	6		2	4	**37**	2					**2**	27	6		2	4	**39**
MAXIMUM	42	6	1	2	5	56							42	6	1	2	5	56

Goalscorers

	L	C	T	LC	CC	Total
Darren COLLINS	30	7		1	2	40
Kevin WILKIN	14	6			2	22
Dale WATKINS	14	1			1	16
Andy KIRKUP	11				1	12
Carl ALFORD	7					7
Brendan HACKETT	6					6
Al James HANNIGAN	3	2				5
Nick ASHBY	4					4
Garry BUTTERWORTH	3					3
Tim WOODING	2				1	3
Mickey NUTTELL					2	2
Richard BAILEY	1					1
Neil SMITH	1					1
Steve SPOONER	1					1
Steve STOTT	1					1
own goal	1					1
TOTAL	99	16	0	1	9	125

1995-96 Playing Record

HOME	P	W	D	L	F	A	Pts
League	21	17	1	3	59	22	52
FA Cup	4	3	0	1	9	5	
FA Trophy	1	0	0	1	0	1	
League Cup	1	1	0	0	1	0	
County Cup	3	2	1	0	7	2	
TOTAL	30	23	2	5	76	30	
AWAY							
League	21	12	6	3	40	18	42
FA Cup	2	1	1	0	7	2	
FA Trophy	-	-	-	-	-	-	
League Cup	1	0	0	1	0	2	
County Cup	2	0	1	1	2	3	
TOTAL	26	13	8	5	49	25	
TOTAL							
League	42	29	7	6	99	40	94
FA Cup	6	4	1	1	16	7	
FA Trophy	1	0	0	1	0	1	
League Cup	2	1	0	1	1	2	
County Cup	5	2	2	1	9	5	
TOTAL	**56**	**36**	**10**	**10**	**125**	**55**	

Attendance Summary

HOME	Total	Ave	High		Low	
League	45485	2166	4664	Merthyr	1409	Sudbury
FA Cup	10397	2599	4214	Cardiff	1652	Eastwood
FA Trophy	1906	1906	1906	Purfleet	1906	Purfleet
League Cup	1098	1098	1098	King's Lynn	1098	King's Lynn
County Cup	3409	1136	1927	Kettering	578	Long Buckby
TOTAL	62295	2077	4664	Merthyr	578	Long Buckby
AWAY						
League	19028	906	1725	Halesowen	464	Merthyr
FA Cup	1044	522	794	Purfleet	250	Sandwell
FA Trophy	-	-	-	-	-	-
League Cup	432	432	432	King's Lynn	432	King's Lynn
County Cup	2020	1010	1509	Kettering	511	Rothwell
TOTAL	22524	866	1725	Halesowen	250	Sandwell
TOTAL						
League	64513	1536	4664	Merthyr H	464	Merthyr A
FA Cup	11441	1907	4214	Cardiff H	250	Sandwell A
FA Trophy	1906	1906	1906	Purfleet H	1906	Purfleet H
League Cup	1530	765	1098	King's Lynn H	432	King's Lynn A
County Cup	5429	1086	1927	Kettering H	511	Rothwell A
TOTAL	**84819**	**1515**	**4664**	Merthyr H	**250**	Sandwell A

Crucial to the development of the club has been the increasing involvement of an increasing number of supporters. Support did not begin to grow until the second season, 1993-94, during which the Supporters Club played a major role in establishing an identity for the club and a focal point for the supporters from east Northamptonshire.

The Supporters Club is synonymous with the Wiltons, the husband and wife team that got the idea off the ground and who continue to administer the burgeoning organisation from their office in Diamond Way. Phil started the club to enable the twenty or so Rushden Town supporters who regularly travelled away with the Russians to do likewise with Rushden & Diamonds. For the first away match of 1993-94, at Tamworth, the minibus provided by Roy of Finedon was sufficient. By April the travelling contingent of 300 needed six full-size coaches to take them to Rugby.

In the summer of 1994, at one of the first functions to be held at the new Diamond Centre, KCBC, a local radio station, staged an awards evening. As well as the more usual awards, each club in the area was asked to nominate a clubperson of the year. The Rushden & Diamonds choice was Pam and Phil Wilton for the immense amount of very effective work that they had done in developing the Supporters Club. Making the presentations was the former England football captain, Billy Wright, the first man to make one hundred international appearances for England.

SEASON FIVE

1996 - 97

"The length of five long winters"

Wordsworth

Back (l to r): Andy Kirkup, Al James Hannigan, Brendan Hackett, Steve Stott, Terry Wilson, Glen Fuff, Tim Wooding, Steve Lilwall.

Middle (l to r): Pete Brown, Paul Richardson, Darren Collins, Steve Holden, Nick Ashby, Martin Davies, Graham Benstead, Kevin Wilkin, Andy Furnell, Mark Tucker, Billy Jeffrey, Kenny Mist.

Front (l to r): Kenny Cramman, Carl Alford, Neil Smith, Roger Ashby, Garry Butterworth, Ian King, Andy Peaks.

The major construction project for the summer of 1996 was the stand at the eastern end of the ground. Extra capacity was necessary to enable the club to attain the minimum 6,500 capacity to be eligible for promotion to the Nationwide League. Whilst nobody connected with the club expected progress to be that rapid (though many might have hoped) it would have been foolish not to have been ready should the opportunity have arisen. The East Stand, once planned as a double-decker, fulfilled that objective and filled the only remaining undeveloped part of Nene Park.

At that time it was necessary to have the ground suitable by December 31st, though Stevenage's legal pursuit of the Nationwide League was soon to force the date to be much later. Hence it was planned that the East Stand would be ready before Christmas, though it would be roofless. Buildings in the south eastern corner, including the Supporters Club office and the Radio Diamonds studio were demolished when construction started before the beginning of the season.

A look at the other sides in the Conference soon showed what exalted company Rushden & Diamonds had reached after four seasons of existence. The three previous champions were all there: Kidderminster Harriers, Macclesfield Town and Stevenage Borough, all of whom had been denied promotion to the Football League because their ground improvements had not been completed in time. Tradition was represented by the four clubs that had been founder members of the league in 1979 (then known as the Alliance Premier League) and had remained continuously in membership: Altrincham, Kettering Town, Northwich Victoria and Telford United. Hednesford Town was the only club that had previously played a league fixture at Nene Park (against Rushden & Diamonds that is, for in the early eighties Stevenage Borough were in the United Counties Premier Division and played against both Irthlingborough Diamonds and Rushden Town) whilst there were four other clubs against whom Rushden & Diamonds had played cup matches: Bromsgrove Rovers, Farnborough Town, Kettering Town and Woking. With no club being relegated from Division Three of the Football League and no club being promoted from the Unibond League there were only two new clubs in the Conference, the other being the ICIS League champions, Hayes.

The club made two major close season signings, both players who had impressive Conference pedigrees. Kenny Cramman was a midfielder who had played in most of Gateshead's games the previous season, scoring half a dozen Conference goals. He had spent two seasons with his home town club after signing from Bishop Auckland whom he had joined from Hartlepool United. Mark Tucker had been a virtual ever-present in Woking's defence since joining his home town club on a free transfer from Fulham. Still only twenty-four years old, he had gained an FA Trophy winners medal in both 1995 and 1996.

The major departure was the club's leading scorer, Dale Watkins, who followed Dave Johnson to Gloucester City which was also the destination of David Holmes. Steve Spooner and Mickey Nuttell both moved to Burton Albion and Andy Lomas signed for Boreham Wood.

It was not only the first team that would be competing in a new league in the forthcoming season. The club's application for the reserve team to play in the Capital League was accepted. The Capital League comprised the reserve sides of twelve Football League clubs, three Conference clubs' second strings and the reserve teams of Crawley Town and Sutton United. The Capital League by this time restricted itself to Football League and Conference clubs only: hence Rushden & Diamonds had been unable to join previously. A league of this standard was regarded as essential to keep squad members not in the first team match fit as well as providing better conditions for players recovering from injury and for assessing trialists. The Midland Combination Reserve Division had not proved sufficiently strong for these purposes but membership was nevertheless maintained. The Capital League team played all its fixtures midweek with all home games in the main stadium; the Midland Combination reserve team played mainly on Saturdays, the home matches taking place on the training pitch. Gradually the Midland Combination side became virtually a youth side.

Mark Tucker, with Max Griggs and Roger Ashby, after signing for Rushden & Diamonds.

The first team squad warmed up for their first Vauxhall Conference season with a series of fixtures against Football League clubs including West Ham United, Derby County and Arsenal. The visit of West Ham proved controversial as fans who had paid to see what they thought would be a full strength Premiership side were understandably disgruntled at finding the Hammers side was shorn of its top names and packed with reserves. With hindsight it might now be possible to reflect more philosophically upon the emergent talent on view that evening - Rio Ferdinand, Frank Lampard junior, Stan Lazaridis et al.

The first competitive game brought Dr Martens Cup winners and Beazer Midland Division Champions, Nuneaton Borough to Nene Park in the Southern League Championship Challenge match on the Saturday before the Conference season started. This is an annual match between the League winners and the League Cup winners. It provided a gentle debut for two new signings. Kenny Cramman and Terry Wilson, the former Nottingham Forest and Scotland under-21 international who was attempting to resurrect a promising career cruelly cut short by injury and who had been signed by Diamonds on a temporary basis. Against moderate opposition, Diamonds recorded a comfortable 3-0 victory over a side whose best known name was former Cobbler Warren Donald. Darren Collins demonstrated that he had lost none of his sharpness by scoring twice, and his expected striking partner Carl Alford hit the third after he had come on as a half-time substitute to prove his recovery from a pre-season injury.

The victorious team (most of them) and others after beating Nuneaton.

Back (l to r): Darren Collins, Billy Jeffrey, Tim Wooding, Kevin Wilkin, Brendan Hackett, Steve Stott, Andy Peaks, Roger Ashby, Steve Lilwall.

Front (l to r): Paul Richardson, Al James Hannigan, Andy Kirkup, Carl Alford, Kenny Cramman, Terry Wilson.

And so the Diamonds travelled to Cheshire on August 17th for their inaugural Conference fixture against Altrincham - one of the greats of post-war non-league football. The line-up included just two new faces from the side that had won the Beazer Premier Division back in May, namely Cramman and central defender Jim Rodwell, who had represented both Bedworth and Halesowen in previous games against the Diamonds. Rodwell had been drafted into the squad at late notice, and at a considerable price, when key signing Mark Tucker proved unfit, a fate which also befell Tucker's expected partner at the heart of the defence, Steve Holden. Terry Wilson was ineligible, still awaiting international clearance after playing in Scandinavia during the summer.

Altrincham (2) **4**			**Rushden & Diamonds** (1) **3**		
1	Matt Dickins		1	Graham Benstead	
2	Mark Maddox		2	Andy Peaks	
3	Darren Heesom		3	Nick Ashby	
4	Paul France		4	Steve Stott	
5	Barry Butler	(sub: Carroll)	5	Jim Rodwell	
6	Neil Doherty		6	Al James Hannigan	
7	Stuart Terry		7	Kevin Wilkin	
8	Paul Cain	(sub: Pybus)	8	Garry Butterworth	
9	Neil Hardy		9	Carl Alford	(sub: Hackett)
10	Ian Horrigan		10	Darren Collins	
11	Chris Sharratt		11	Kenny Cramman	
12	Steve Carroll		12	Brendan Hackett	
14	Darren Pybus		14	Tim Wooding	
15	Jerome John		15	Ian King	

Referee: A Kaye (Bradford)

Goals: Cramman (17, **0-1**), Sharratt (38, **1-1**), Terry (43, **2-1**), Collins (47, **2-2**), Cramman (54, **2-3**), Ashby (o.g.) (82, **3-3**), Hardy (89, **4-3**)

Booked: Maddox

The game was a seven goal thriller with enough twists in the script to last all season as Rushden fans suffered most conceivable emotions. Those who battled their way up the overcrowded M6 must have wondered if they would ever get there: the Cobblers certainly struggled as they made a similar journey, ending in a late kick off at Wigan. Before the Cobblers had even kicked off the Diamonds were in trouble, Carl Alford pulling up lame after just a few minutes. He continued until the twenty-ninth minute before being replaced by Brendan Hackett but by that time his side were in front, Kenny Cramman striking a hammer-blow from the edge of the penalty area to open the scoring. Altrincham, belatedly stung into action, subjected the visiting defence to a lengthy period of sustained pressure and then two dreadful errors at the back gifted the Robins a half-time lead. Graham Benstead failed to cut out a right wing cross allowing Sharratt a simple far post header and then compounded the mistake by hitting his clearance from Nick Ashby's back pass against the onrushing Terry, rebounding into the net. Fears of a second half rout were quickly allayed when Darren Collins levelled three minutes after the restart and Kenny Cramman converted Kevin Wilkin's beautifully weighted through pass to restore the advantage. Leading 3-2, the Diamonds were just eight minutes from the perfect start to their Conference campaign when defensive frailty consigned the side to a defeat it arguably did not deserve. As the game entered its closing stages Nick Ashby deflected a Neil Hardy cross past the hapless Benstead and inside the near post. Sensing an unlikely victory, the Altrincham manager, the pugnacious John King, urged his players forward as they won a corner in the final minute. The Diamonds failed to clear, Hardy pounced and the points were lost. Most supporters felt that the side would play much worse and win but they were perhaps glossing over the defensive problems, which, many felt, would disappear when first choice defenders Holden and Tucker were available.

Kenny Cramman

Optimistic illusions lasted only until the following Tuesday evening. *Slough Town 5 Rushden & Diamonds 0* was a crushing scoreline as glaring defensive deficiencies were exposed against one of the Conference's more moderate lights - and this despite Jim Rodwell's towering performance which helped prevent a even more calamitous score-line. Trailing 0-1 at half-time to a Cliff Hercules header, the Diamonds folded after the break conceding four goals in twenty-four minutes. Former Enfield striker, Gary Abbott, prompted from midfield by Simon Stapleton and aided by another less than convincing goalkeeping display from Graham Benstead, scored a hat-trick. Manager Ashby was far from pessimistic after the game, *"Obviously having five players out hasn't helped. So far we haven't been good enough - but we will be. There are 40 games to go and I'm very positive."*

The first Conference game at Nene Park attracted 2112 spectators, many of whom thought, or hoped, that the two opening defeats were isolated events. One or two even remembered that when Lincoln City won the Conference they had lost their first two games heavily. Delusions lasted twelve minutes: Darren Vicary capitalised upon poor defending to put Northwich ahead. From that point, though, the reshaped defence which included Tim Wooding and Garry Butterworth, dropping back to replace Al James Hannigan (who moved back to Enfield), played with more purpose. Early in the second half, Ian King *(right)*, making his first Conference start, set up the equaliser for Darren Collins. It proved to be enough to secure the first ever Conference point.

Two days later, August Bank Holiday Monday, the side travelled to fellow newcomers Hayes with both sides in search of that elusive first win. Neither found it. The now familiar unforced defensive error gifted Hayes an early lead before Carl Alford opened his season's account with an equaliser on the half hour. When the other results had been collated it emerged that Hayes were one off the bottom and that Rushden & Diamonds were one place lower.

Terry Wilson made a belated league debut in the home game against Stalybridge Celtic and goalkeeper Martin Davies, re-signed after a year at Cambridge United, made his first appearance of the season. The changes made little difference against a mediocre Celtic side who had five men booked by referee Keith Hill who had twice refereed Diamonds' opening Beazer Homes matches and who had now been promoted to the Conference. Diamonds could not take advantage of the brief absence through injury of Celtic keeper Harvey Willetts but some face was saved by Kenny Cramman's equaliser four minutes from time.

The Tuesday home game with Macclesfield resulted in a fourth consecutive 1-1 draw but this was by far the best performance of the season to date with Rushden raising their game against better opposition. After conceding yet another early goal from a set piece, the Diamonds rallied to match their high riding opponents in every department once Terry Wilson had dealt 'authoritatively' with dangerman Tony Hemmings. Roger Ashby's bold decision to play three strikers eventually paid dividends. The deserved equaliser was late in coming, however, Kevin Wilkin glancing home Wilson's inswinging corner in the 87th minute.

The long awaited victory eventually arrived on September 7th at the seventh time of asking. Halifax's dilapidated Shay Ground was the venue and inevitably Halifax were gifted the opening goal, Garry Butterworth colliding with Martin Davies and Micky Norbury tapping in. Eight minutes later Jim Rodwell equalised with his first goal for the club and, in the second half, impressive strikes from Darren Collins and Kenny Cramman wrapped up a 3-1 success in which Andy Furnell made his debut twenty minutes from time.

Two days later the side recorded a second away victory, this time at the Drill Field, Northwich. Perhaps at last the Diamonds were getting the hang of the Conference. Nevertheless it was no great surprise when they went a goal down after nineteen minutes, Lee Steele outjumping taller defenders to head home a corner. However Rushden recovered to take three points on the back of a sound defensive display with Jim Rodwell, Garry Butterworth and Terry Wilson particularly impressive. It was Wilson who scrambled home the equaliser - his only goal for the club - a minute before half-time and with only six minutes remaining Rodwell powered a header past Dean Greygoose for his second goal in two matches.

There followed an interruption to the Conference programme with the start of the FA Cup campaign. The club must have come close to having been exempted to the Fourth Qualifying Round by virtue of having reached the First Round Proper the previous season, but it was not close enough and again they had to start at the First Qualifying Round. Drawn in section 13, Diamonds knew they would be at home in the next two rounds if they won their first game in which they were drawn away to West Midlands Police or Westfields. Westfields, from the West Midlands League, caused a minor upset by winning against opponents from the Midland Alliance, a higher league, and thus Rushden travelled to deepest Herefordshire rather than sampling the delights of the mobile stand at the Police's Tally Ho headquarters next to Edgbaston cricket ground.

The Westfields ground is situated a couple of miles south east of Hereford city centre, close to the river Wye with Dinedor Hill to the south and Backbury Hill to the east. Not that the players had much time to admire the surroundings as, despite leaving Nene Park at 10.30, they somehow did not arrive at the ground until ten minutes before the scheduled start, delaying the kick-off by a quarter of an hour. After Kevin Wilkin had opened the scoring, former Peterborough United striker Andy Furnell *(right)* hit a hat-trick as the Diamonds cantered to a 4-0 victory in what was often little more than a training ground romp. The Conference side hit the woodwork five times and frittered countless chances to extend their goals tally.

The good form continued into the next league game. The confidence gained from three successive away wins was evident in the first twenty minutes against midweek visitors Farnborough Town as the Diamonds dominated the early stages without conceding a sloppy goal. As the half progressed, however, the visitors began to settle, Diamonds lost their rhythm, play became ragged and an uncharacteristic error by Garry Butterworth let in Chris Boothe for a simple goal three minutes before the break. The second half saw Farnborough provide an object lesson in how to 'kill' the game, defending deep, retaining possession and making their opponents chase the ball. Somewhat inevitably they scored a second when Martin Davies's poor clearance reached Phil Wingfield whose speculative shot was deflected past the stranded keeper. The defeat ended a seven game unbeaten run and the first home Conference victory was still awaited.

The visit to Woking on September 21st served to provide a true measure of the Diamonds deficiencies. Veteran Clive Walker, who had proved the catalyst for the Cards' FA Trophy Semi-Final second leg triumph back in 1995, again inspired his side to victory. Roger Ashby gave a Conference debut to Richard Bailey and when the young striker's drive rebounded from the upright after a quarter of an hour Kevin Wilkin was on hand to force the ball home. Within eight minutes Woking were level, Walker calmly netting from the penalty spot after Tim Wooding had brought down David Timothy. The scores remained level at half-time but Walker was being allowed a deal too much space and it seemed only a matter of time before he made the Diamonds pay. With only nine minutes of the second period gone he collected the ball wide, teased two defenders and put over a tantalising cross. Tim Wooding inexplicably headed it back into play and Tommy Jones scored with a twenty yard drive. Five minutes later, Walker, the former Chelsea star, scored his second, coolly sidestepping Martin Davies before rolling the ball into the net. And within sixty seconds he had completed his hat-trick, stroking home another penalty after the beleaguered Davies had brought down former Kettering man Junior Hunter. The three goals originated from quite awful defensive errors and although Richard Bailey gave the final score some respectability with his first Conference goal there was no doubting the difference in class between the two sides.

Yet there was no such gulf in evidence when the Diamonds met defending Champions and current league leaders, Stevenage Borough at Nene Park three days later. Encouraged by the season's best gate so far of 3,288 the side responded to manager Ashby's demand for self examination by turning in a courageous performance, rendered all the more creditable as the Diamonds played for over an hour with only ten men. Once again the opposition scored an early goal from a set piece. After twenty minutes of even play former Diamond Kenny Webster's corner was knocked on by Efetobor Sodje for John Ugbah to get the vital touch just ahead of the prolific Barry Hayles. Six minutes later Carl Alford was dismissed, Stamford based referee Mr Bryan attributing malicious intent to his challenge on goalkeeper Des Gallagher. Most neutral observers regarded his attempt to win the loose ball as at worst over-zealous. There was no capitulation, in fact the ten men played as ten men so often do - they played like twelve, and only heroics from the overworked Gallagher prevented a deserved equaliser.

"Surely", wrote Evening Telegraph reporter, Steve Harrison, *"'the Diamonds have now turned the corner."*

September 28th brought runaway leaders of the Dr Martens Premier Division, Gresley Rovers, to Nene Park in the Second Qualifying Round of the FA Cup. In addition to Steve Lilwall, recalled to the side after a lengthy absence, the home line-up included the enigmatic Ian King. The prodigal winger opened the scoring after twenty-three minutes, Carl Alford converted Kevin Wilkin's pin-point cross ten minutes later and the first home win of the season was virtually assured. Further goals from Collins and Alford sealed a 4-0 victory which demonstrated the gulf between the Conference and the Dr Martens League and set up a Third Round meeting with the winners of the Desborough Town v Bilston Town tie at Nene Park. Gresley had been Rushden & Diamonds bogey side in earlier seasons and it was perhaps fitting that such a result against such opposition should have occurred in Andy Kirkup's 166th and final appearance for the club.

Buoyed by cup success the side travelled to Hednesford to renew acquaintance with another of their former Beazer Homes League adversaries. It was a frustrating affair, the Diamonds playing well enough to earn a point and getting nothing, Hednesford deserving little and getting all three. Missed chances were at the heart of the visitors failings, Kevin Wilkin spurning a golden opportunity to put his side ahead on the half hour. It proved a costly miss as, within seconds, Bernard McNally's scorching volley flew past Martin Davies from fully twenty-five yards. Hednesford keeper, Scott Cooksey denied Wilkin, Alford and Cramman as the Diamonds pushed forward relentlessly in search of an equaliser but, as struggling sides frequently complain, down at the bottom invariably means down on your luck. George Lawrence, later to feature briefly as a potential Diamonds player, was an unused substitute for Hednesford.

Would it be lucky thirteen when Welling United visited Nene Park for the thirteenth Conference fixture of the season? It would certainly be a crucial fixture with Diamonds still looking for their first home win. Rushden were one place away from a relegation spot and Welling were just two places higher.

			Home					Away					
		P	W	D	L	F	A	W	D	L	F	A	Pts
17	Welling United	10	2	0	3	7	11	1	2	2	8	9	**11**
18	Halifax Town	12	3	1	2	12	9	0	1	5	3	15	**11**
19	Rushden & Diamonds	12	0	3	2	3	6	2	1	4	11	17	**10**
20	Hayes	10	1	4	1	4	4	0	2	2	4	7	**9**
21	Bath City	11	2	0	2	5	6	0	3	4	8	15	**9**
22	Stalybridge Celtic	11	1	1	3	4	6	0	2	4	4	14	**6**

Diamonds did enjoy a crucial piece of luck, Lewis Watts heading Ian King's chip into his own goal as early as the fifth minute but after that they dominated and completed a comprehensive 3-0 victory to break the Nene Park duck. Winger David Morrison, on loan from Peterborough United, made his first appearance, club skipper Neil Smith returned as a second half substitute after a long-term injury, the gate was another impressive 2,000 plus and things looked set fair for the anticipated climb up the table.

A thrilling 3-2 victory at Dover in the Spalding Cup - if the Conference's League Cup can ever be described as thrilling - with Kevin Wilkin's winner coming in the last minute after Dover had been two up, supported grounds for optimism. Sadly, however, the club was about to enter the darkest period in its brief history.

The dark age would have begun earlier if Bilston Town, the Dr Martens Midland Division side had not scorned two simple chances to equalise Darren Collins' sixtieth minute goal in the Third Qualifying Round of the FA Cup. Bilston, who had struggled to beat Desborough Town in the previous round, made a rethink necessary for those who had discerned a huge gap between the Conference and the Dr Martens League after Gresley had been despatched a fortnight earlier. Bilston, of course, had been the first ever opponents of Rushden & Diamonds back in August 1992. Those spectators who attended both games would have found something in common: a disappointing, or even dire, performance by the home side though on this occasion they survived to become a numbered ball in the velvet bag the following Monday. Just one player had survived from 1992: Bilston's Danny Williams came on as a seventy-first minute substitute in 1996: four years earlier he had come on ten minutes sooner.

There were two items of interest on the following Monday. The good news was a home draw against Bognor Regis Town in the FA Cup, the bad news was the defeat at Kidderminster. It was perhaps not too surprising that the visit to title chasing Harriers proved fruitless but the side played significantly better. Martin Davies *(left)* gave an outstanding display in goal but Kim Casey's goal early in the second half was enough to send Diamonds home pointless. One third of the Conference fixtures had now passed; only thirteen points had been harvested.

Roger Ashby's programme notes for the following Saturday's fixture against Gateshead, the first test for the newly-opened Nene Park roundabout, included a personal tribute to Andy Kirkup, transferred earlier in the week to Gloucester City. Andy, written off so often during his time at Nene Park, had frequently confounded his critics by forcing his way back into the first team reckoning. However, despite the side's poor start to its Conference campaign he had failed to start a single match, his ten league and cup appearances all confined to the replacements bench. He could count himself fortunate to miss the Gateshead game. It was certainly the Diamonds worst performance in the Conference to date. Had the 0-4 defeat been inflicted by one of the league's top sides there might have been some excuse. But this was a very mediocre, bottom half team so effectively orchestrated by the outstanding veteran Kenny Lowe that the Diamonds scarcely had a kick. Kenny Cramman, desperately trying to impress against his former team mates, was stretchered off in the dying minutes of the game - it summed up his and the Diamonds day.

At least there was progress in the FA Cup, victory over Bognor Regis Town of the ICIS League Division One sending the Diamonds into the First Round Proper for the second successive season. Bognor might not have been in the top division of their League but their FA Cup record suggested they were not to be taken lightly; in the previous season they had reached the Second Round, going out at Peterborough. Manager Ashby elected to play with three central defenders, Jim Rodwell *(below)*, Steve Holden (his first appearance of the season) and Andy Peaks

with the onus placed on full backs Tim Wooding and Steve Lilwall to get forward as often as possible. The new formation struggled to make an impact until Brendan Hackett was introduced at the expense of Lilwall for the last twenty-five minutes. He made an immediate impact running at the Bognor defence and when one of his forays down the left flank was ended illegally, Wooding's free-kick was glanced inside the far post by Darren Collins. Eleven minutes later Hackett produced another penetrating run followed by a powerful shot which the Bognor keeper could only parry and a grateful Collins pounced to make the game safe. Referee Coxhead took exception to Alford's exuberant celebration and decided it merited a booking - by his name ye shall know him!

Monday's cup draw brought little joy - Boreham Wood of the ICIS Premier away. If fans were unfamiliar with the name it would, ere long, become indelibly imprinted on their memories. However, before the prospect of FA Cup glory could be savoured there were vital Conference points to be gleaned. The long trip to Southport brought cold comfort as the side slipped to second from bottom following a 1-2 defeat. The team performed well for much of the game but the eventual outcome hinged on a crucial lapse in concentration. After Ian King had blasted his team in front with the sort of twenty yard shot that was once his trademark (it was only the ninth goal conceded by Southport - the meanest defence in the league) the Diamonds seemed to be heading for at least a point. While Martin Davies and

Andy Peaks were in commanding form at the back, Carl Alford and Darren Collins posed a real threat in attack. Only the brilliance of former Cobbler Billy Stewart in the Southport goal prevented the visitors from extending the lead. There was no denying the quality of the equaliser, Brian Butler timing his run from midfield perfectly to score from the edge of the area, but the 78th minute winner was a gift. Scorer Andy Whittaker was one of four unmarked Southport players who might have knocked home the corner kick. Steve Lilwall, withdrawn midway through the second half, did not appear again for the first team.

The home fixture with Dover provided the intriguing prospect of seeing the two most expensive men to move between two non-Football League clubs in opposition. Both got on the scoresheet - within a minute of each other! It was Dover's David Leworthy, a £50,000 buy from Farnborough, who opened the scoring but Carl Alford struck to salvage a precious point as Diamonds just kept their heads above the bottom three.

Alford's return to Rockingham Road the following Tuesday was a low-key affair. The Hillier Cup pairing of Kettering v Rushden & Diamonds certainly showed that there was no seeding in the draw. The attendance of fewer than 2,000 also showed how low down on fans' priorities the County Cup is. Nevertheless there was some action on the pitch and the result went Kettering's way after Rushden had taken a sixth minute lead, Steve Holden scoring his only goal for the club. Craig Norman equalised early in the second half from a penalty awarded for Holden's challenge on Tony Lynch. Then, two minutes from the end, Leroy May, previously yellow-carded for holding an animated pitchside discussion with visiting supporters, punished Martin Davies for an horrendous fly-kick by intercepting and rolling the ball into the empty net from twenty yards.

It hardly represented ideal preparation for the First Round Proper FA Cup tie at Boreham Wood where Mark Tucker made his first appearance of the season replacing the injured Andy Peaks in the sweeper role. The opening Boreham Wood goal, after a mere nine minutes, was simplicity itself. Giant centre-half Gary Nisbet helped on a long throw and Terry Robbins, once of Tottenham Hotspur, forced the ball past Martin Davies. Minutes later Davies dived bravely at the feet of the dangerous Tony Samuels to prevent a second. Sustained Diamonds pressure brought a twenty-eighth minute equaliser through Brendan Hackett but thereafter defences dominated with Steve Holden and Tucker outstanding in the visiting back line and a Nene Park replay was necessary. As this was the competition proper, rather than the qualifying rounds, the replay could not be staged for another ten days.

Instead it was possible to play the Spalding Cup tie against Stevenage Borough who fielded at least half a team of reserves. Watched by the smallest Nene Park crowd of the season, Borough were punished when Darren Collins struck midway through the second half with the only goal of the game. Terrace talk was less of the game and more of the prospect of an FA Cup Second Round visit to Luton Town.

The difficult trip to Morecambe produced a 0-2 defeat but the performance was much worse than the scoreline indicated. The game followed what had become a familiar pattern. The Diamonds dictated the first half-hour without seriously threatening the home goal and then conceded a goal from a set piece in the opposition's first serious attack. Having conceded a second, again after failing to clear from a set piece Rushden gradually lost all semblance of shape adopting what seemed to be a curious 5-1-4 formation as they attempted to chase the game. Three second half substitutes were used: one of them, David Morrison, did not play for Diamonds again. He returned to Peterborough and was soon sold to Leyton Orient. It was also the last appearance for Terry Wilson, one of the three withdrawn: he had often shown touches of great class but the injuries had taken their toll on his pace. Few could draw comfort from this match, the tenth league defeat of the season and a display that had the word "relegation" stamped right through it. Indeed as the hardy band of Diamonds supporters returned to their coach after the game, braving yet another icy squall from across Morecambe Bay, they probably wondered just what they were doing there. The hugely impressive Mark Tucker probably felt the same.

As the sides lined up for their FA Cup replay, Rushden & Diamonds and Boreham Wood knew they were fighting for a visit to Kenilworth Road, Luton, in the Second Round. For Boreham Wood it would be a local derby which could only have been surpassed by, perhaps, a trip to Watford and it was the Hertfordshire side that seemed to want it more. A Nene Park crowd of 2,619 watched the ICIS Premier side match their Conference opponents in every department as the Diamonds threw away the advantage of an early Kevin Wilkin goal, losing their discipline, shape, and the game itself. Poor defending from a corner enabled Steve Heffer to level the score a minute before half-time. Richard Bailey replaced the ineffective Ian King after the break but it was Boreham Wood who took the lead, Terry Robbins flooring Martin Davies as he attempted to punch clear and Tony Samuels heading into the unguarded net. Steve Holden and Brendan Hackett were booked by Nationwide League referee d'Urso for dissent, the former then compounding his offence by unceremoniously depositing Dean Samuels into touch and receiving a red card. It was Dean Samuels, the younger of the brothers, who put the game beyond the Diamonds in the final minute capitalising upon an unintentional pass from the referee. The indefatigable Darren Collins reduced the arrears in injury time but it was too little too late and a disappointed and angry home support eventually disappeared into the night..

The St. Andrew's Day visit of Bath City was crisis time:

			Home					Away					
		P	W	D	L	F	A	W	D	L	F	A	Pts
17	Dover Athletic	18	2	5	2	13	16	1	4	4	9	13	**18**
18	Bromsgrove Rovers	19	4	2	3	17	12	1	0	9	4	21	**17**
19	Bath City	18	3	2	4	9	12	0	5	4	11	18	**16**
20	Halifax Town	17	3	2	4	15	17	0	3	5	5	17	**14**
21	Rushden & Diamonds	18	1	4	3	7	11	2	1	7	12	22	**14**
22	Hayes	17	2	4	3	7	8	0	2	6	6	16	**12**

Cometh the hour, cometh the man. The Diamonds' saviour turned out to be Julian Capone *(left)* who was in his third season with the club but was making only his second starting appearance. His inclusion in place of the injured Ian King against the fellow-strugglers from the west country provided a rare opportunity for the former Raunds Town and Bedford Town midfielder to display the range of skills that can make him one of local football's most entertaining players. He capped an outstanding game by scoring the Diamonds third goal in the 4-1 victory - only the second home league win of the season - and played before 1,853, the lowest home Conference gate of the season. In truth Bath were a poor side, struggling financially now that tenants Bristol Rovers had left Twerton Park. Their side included some names who had visited Nene Park much earlier in the history of Rushden & Diamonds. Nicky Brooks and Shaun Penny had both featured for Clevedon Town in the opening match of the Midland Division campaign in August 1993, and veteran Graham Withey had appeared for Weston-super-Mare in a crucial promotion battle in March 1994.

Capone's impact was brief; injured late in the victory over Bath it was another seven weeks before he was fit enough to resume. Thus another reshuffle was necessary for the trip to Telford United. Kenny Cramman replaced Capone and the transfer-listed Carl Alford found a place on the bench. Any supporter trying to keep up to date by watching Ceefax must have thought that Alford had been transferred overnight when his name came up as having scored for Halifax! That was an error and there must have been suspicions from any fans consulting this service that the whole thing was an error. Diamonds scorers kept appearing on the screen! First it was *Collins 41*, then *Rodwell 60*. And eventually the Alford error was corrected and *Alford 67*, *Alford 86* and *Collins 90* all appeared as Rushden ran out 5-0 winners. And it was true! What a debut it was for full back Simeon Hodson, signed the previous week from Kidderminster Harriers. Formerly with half a dozen Football League clubs including West Bromwich Albion and his native Lincoln City, he had been a Conference winner with Kidderminster, and had found himself at Telford - the club he later joined - with the responsibility of marking his former Harriers team mate, Corby born Jon Purdie.

The result lifted the side to seventeenth place, its highest position since mid October, but the inconsistency that had blighted the first Conference campaign returned with a vengeance in the home encounter with Bromsgrove Rovers on December 14th. Rovers were two points and three places below Diamonds and when Carl Alford opened the scoring after just four minutes beating Chris Taylor at his near post a third successive league victory looked on the cards. But enforced changes at the heart of defence where Andy Peaks and Nick Ashby replaced the suspended Rodwell and Holden, contributed to aerial vulnerability. Both Bromsgrove goals resulted from poorly defended corners, former Diamonds loanee Steve Taylor powering home the first after 25 minutes with Chris Smith following up Darren Grocutt's initial header to nod the winner on the hour. Taylor, who had failed to score in an unimpressive loan spell at Nene Park in which he never finished a game, may have surprised the cynics in the crowd when he scored but he then produced his Diamonds form, being substituted at the interval. Those among the 2,144 spectators who had chosen a trip to Nene Park in preference to a more seasonal shopping expedition no doubt felt they had made the wrong decision even though they were present to see the Airwair Stand at the eastern end of the ground in use for the first time.

The prospect of forthcoming successive games against league leaders Kidderminster Harriers hardly filled supporters hearts with joy. The first encounter saw the Diamonds bow out of the Spalding Cup, losing 0-1 at Aggborough. It may sell Spalding a few balls but this competition does little to excite supporters, a gathering of fewer than 1000 being present at Kidderminster.

The league game at Nene Park was a different matter. Full of entertainment, it nevertheless provided a painful reminder of how fickle is footballing fortune. It also demonstrated that there was an element of consistency within the Diamonds' inconsistency. The three best visiting sides, Macclesfield, Stevenage and Kidderminster were met with the three best performances. And it needed to be good against Kidderminster who came to Nene Park as the title favourites, eleven points in front of Macclesfield. Roger Ashby gave a debut to his latest loan signing, Sammy Ayorinde *(left)* a Nigerian striker who had joined his current club, Leyton Orient, from Sturm Graz, one of the top Austrian sides. Diamonds were good value for their 1-0 lead, though the penalty (the only one awarded to Diamonds in the entire season), converted by Carl Alford, was a little dubious. Only seconds away from a morale boosting victory the Diamonds suffered a cruel blow in injury time. Nick Ashby, protecting the inside of the post at a corner, was adjudged to have handled a fierce shot. That it was goal bound was indisputable but whether the hapless defender could have taken evasive action was in considerable doubt. Watford referee Harvey was in no doubt that it was a penalty. He dismissed the forensic evidence, a ball-sized circular muddy mark on Ashby's chest, and then dismissed Ashby. Neil Doherty dispatched the penalty. Two wrongs may have made a right but Rushden's fans were in a far from philosophical mood.

The Boxing Day visit to Kettering, and Kettering's New Year's Day visit to Nene Park, fell foul of the cold weather. The logic of arranging such games at holiday time seemed dubious. Rushden v Kettering games will attract big gates whenever they are played so it seemed sensible to leave the holiday dates, when there are always bumper crowds, for more mundane fixtures - and ones which will incur lower policing costs.

But while Northamptonshire namby-pambies were stopping inside because it was a bit cold, further north, where men are men, football was still being played. Thus on Saturday December 28th off we went to Stalybridge. The snow on Snake Pass was impressive - so impressive that the return journey was made via Woodhead. The snow on the pitch at Celtic's Bower Fold ground was much less deep though it was crisp and even. It was not relished by Rushden & Diamonds but Stalybridge had no such qualms. *"We played on much worse than this at Gateshead on Boxing Day"*, they said and the view was shared by the Merseyside referee. The snowbound pitch hardly favoured Sammy Ayorinde who was making his second, and final, appearance in a Rushden shirt: obviously he hadn't been at Graz in the winter. Former Cobbler Dean Trott and ex-Poppy Ian Arnold ran the Diamonds back four ragged, and although Steve Charles opening goal was somewhat fortuitous there was nothing lucky about Trott's powerful drive which secured Celtic a comfortable 2-0 win. It was a low-key finish to Neil Smith's appearances for the club; captain in the title winning side, a series of injuries blunted his talents. Steve Holden was another for whom this was his last appearance: he too had been troubled by a number of injuries.

It was fully three weeks before the wintry weather relented, deepening the gloom amongst the inactive Nene Park ranks. The resumption of action on January 18th saw visitors Farnborough Town gain a 2-1 victory in the FA Trophy, two players with tenuous county links contributing to their success. Former Rushden Town player Dick Underwood would have been proud of the fearsome left foot volley with which his nephew Jon opened the scoring and Pat Gavin, whose two goals had ensured Northampton's Third Division survival back in 1993, set up Phil Wingfield for the decisive second.

The return fixture at Cherrywood Road the following Saturday offered an immediate opportunity for revenge. The chances of revenge were boosted considerably by the inclusion of two new signings, both of whom had played against Diamonds earlier in the season. Twenty-eight year old Oxford born midfielder Simon Stapleton was signed from Slough Town whom he had joined after Football League experience at Bristol Rovers and Wycombe Wanderers.

David Leworthy *(right)* was six years older and had packed a huge variety of experiences into his career. After an apprenticeship with his home town club Portsmouth, where he made one first team appearance (as a substitute in a goalless draw with Newport County), he moved across Portsmouth Harbour to Fareham Town, then in the Southern Premier. Whilst there he was spotted by Tottenham Hotspur. His Spurs debut was at Highbury where Arsenal won 2-0 with goals from Charlie Nicholas and Brian Talbot. During his brief time as a Spurs first team player Leworthy scored three goals in the top division, the most important probably being the winner in a 3-2 success at Newcastle in which Glen Hoddle scored Spurs' second. The following season he was sold to Oxford United for £150,000 where he spent four years before joining Reading. Three years later he was snapped up by Farnborough. His move to Dover in 1994 for £50,000 made him the most expensive player to move between two non-League sides. That was a distinction he held until Carl Alford moved to Nene Park. Now he found himself alongside Alford on the ground of one of his former clubs. It was almost inevitable that it would be a dramatic return. Two down after twenty-five minutes thanks to goals from Jon Underwood and Dean Coney (another much travelled striker of a similar age to Leworthy), it was a twenty-five yard volley of breath-taking quality that blasted Diamonds back into the game. Not to be outdone, Stapleton also scored on his debut, netting a quarter of an hour from the end to earn a valuable point in a manner which boosted morale considerably.

Leworthy, who had already treated the Nene Park crowd to a marvellous display of front running when appearing in a Dover shirt back in November, was to prove a vital acquisition in the struggle for Conference survival. Diamonds fans awaited the visit of Morecambe with relish, excited at the prospect of seeing Leworthy in a Rushden shirt. For a while it seemed that the match would end in disappointment as Jamie Udall headed Morecambe in front early in the second half, beating Graham Benstead *(left)* who, in the absence of Martin Davies, was playing his first game since August. The last twenty minutes had just begun when the Diamonds levelled with a brilliant goal. Simeon Hodson played the ball into Leworthy on the edge of the area, the striker exchanged passes with Carl Alford and then drove the ball past the helpless Steve McIlhargey from an impossibly acute angle. Six minutes later Kenny Cramman's beautifully struck twenty-five yard free-kick rocketed into the net for the winner.

Seven days later the Nene Park crowd was up by more than 20% for the visit of Hednesford Town. The upturn in form and fortune produced an optimistic air amongst the home supporters: victory could take Diamonds out of the bottom three, albeit on goal difference:

			Home					Away					
		P	W	D	L	F	A	W	D	L	F	A	Pts
17	Hayes	26	5	5	5	15	16	2	2	7	12	20	**28**
18	Bromsgrove Rovers	29	5	3	5	23	17	3	1	12	9	28	**28**
19	Halifax Town	25	5	3	5	19	22	2	4	6	11	24	**28**
20	Rushden & Diamonds	25	3	5	4	15	16	3	2	8	19	26	**25**
21	Dover Athletic	27	3	6	3	17	20	2	4	9	16	30	**25**
22	Bath City	28	4	3	5	11	15	0	5	11	14	43	**20**

It was too optimistic as it turned out, for a well-organised visiting team took advantage of the home team's frequent loss of possession and marked Benstead's last game with two second half goals.

For both Hednesford and Rushden the next game was at Macclesfield. The size of the Diamonds' task can be gauged by the fact that on the Tuesday Hednesford crashed 0-4. It meant that second-placed Macclesfield were now only four points behind leaders Kidderminster and had a game in hand. Saturday February 15th was going to be a tough day.

The day seemed anything but tough for those supporters who lunched at the renowned Cat & Fiddle pub, just below the peak of Shining Tor on Axe Edge moor. The sun shone brilliantly in a cloudless sky: a few miles to the west and a thousand feet lower could be discerned the town of Macclesfield. It surely wouldn't be this idyllic at the Moss Rose.

It certainly wasn't. Within a couple of minutes midfield anchorman Steve Stott had suffered an injury. That would have been bad enough in normal circumstances but with Garry Butterworth missing it seemed to be disastrous. Stott soldiered on for a while, helping repel non-stop pressure as the Silkmen laid siege to the visitors' goal. Macclesfield also suffered an early injury and replaced defender Mark Bradshaw (who moved to Halifax in the summer and won a second Conference medal) with forward John Askey on the half-hour mark. Five minutes later Stott had to retire from the fray and, amazingly, Diamonds immediately took the lead. Julian Capone, in only his second appearance since his sensational Conference debut back in November, crossed for David Leworthy to glance a header into the far corner of Ryan Price's goal. Within two minutes, though, Macclesfield were level, Steve Wood equalising after Martin Davies had parried Phil Power's fierce cross shot. Diamonds survived an early second half scare, Davies saving a penalty from loanee Richard Landon (who had had a full-time career at Plymouth Argyle and Stockport County since appearing at Nene Park for Bedworth United in 1993) after Jim Rodwell was adjudged to have handled Peter Davenport's cross. It proved a brief reprieve. The hugely impressive Chris Byrne, signed from Unibond League Droylsden after his release from Crewe Alexandra, burst through from midfield to net the Macclesfield winner. Rushden's performance could justifiably be termed "brave" but it just was not good enough. Bath's victory at Halifax meant that the bottom team in the Conference now was Rushden & Diamonds.

A week later came the trip to Gateshead and whilst most travelling supporters ploughed up the A1 a few opted for the arguably more civilised mode of rail and sampled the privatised Great North Eastern Railway service. Saturday rail travel brings together supporters of a wide variety of clubs. On the two and a quarter hour journey from Peterborough to Newcastle representatives of a number of clubs, including Berwick Rangers (home to Stenhousemuir) and Cowdenbeath (home to Montrose), were encountered though there was no rational explanation for the two Northampton fans who boarded at Peterborough and alighted at Doncaster: Rovers were playing the Cobblers at Sixfields.

Football fans certainly suffer for their devotion and none of those observed en route to the International Stadium could have suffered more than did Diamonds fans at Gateshead. Overhead there were sunny periods but a howling easterly gale was blowing in from the North Sea to ensure that there was no fog on the Tyne. Initial good news was that Garry Butterworth was back in the side. Stott was still injured and was replaced by Simon Stapleton whilst central defender Matt Crossley *(right)*, on loan from Wycombe Wanderers, made his debut for Diamonds, replacing Mark Tucker whose injury-plagued time with the club meant that his last appearance had been at Macclesfield. Carl Alford, having another disappointing spell, and having been pointedly asked by Roger Ashby why the England non-League manager had called up the veteran Leworthy rather than Alford, was relegated to the bench. Facing the raw, driving wind (in which lesser mortals found it difficult to even stand up), the Diamonds line-up made determined attempts to keep a clean sheet to half-time. They were within six minutes of achieving their aim when Paul Proudlock punished a poor Martin Davies clearance from a corner by driving home from the edge of the penalty area. Try as local hero Kenny Cramman, the inspirational Leworthy, and the ever-involved Capone might, there was no way back. It was the Diamonds eighth odd goal defeat and certainly not the first occasion that they had paid the supreme price for poor defending at set pieces. It was a depressing end to the Rushden career of Nick Ashby who limped off eighteen minutes from the final whistle. With their team six points adrift of fourth from bottom Halifax Town, despondent fans facing the long trek home began to contemplate less arduous trips to Baldock, Boston or even Boreham Wood in the coming season. The league table they contemplated for the whole of the following week was:

			Home					Away					
		P	W	D	L	F	A	W	D	L	F	A	Pts
17	Gateshead	29	**4**	4	7	21	21	4	**4**	6	17	24	**32**
18	Hayes	30	6	5	5	20	16	2	3	9	13	25	**32**
19	Halifax Town	27	6	3	6	26	27	2	4	6	11	24	**31**
20	Bromsgrove Rovers	31	5	3	6	23	20	3	1	13	9	30	**28**
21	Bath City	32	5	3	7	16	22	1	5	11	19	47	**26**
22	Rushden & Diamonds	28	3	5	5	15	18	3	2	10	20	29	**25**

Three of the players were able to temporarily forget the problems as they joined the England semi-professional squad for the trip to Dublin. Garry Butterworth, Kenny Cramman and David Leworthy all played the full ninety minutes but finished on the losing side as the Irish won 2-0.

Meanwhile the board was considering the replies to the national advertisements for a player-coach to assist Roger Ashby, a post which had been held in abeyance since the approach to Woking's Clive Walker earlier in the season. One of the responses came from Brian Talbot *(left)*, the forty-three year old former Ipswich, Arsenal and England star. Talbot was not unknown at Nene Park, indeed he had on one occasion presented Irthlingborough Diamonds players with their United Counties League trophies at the end of season dinner. Talbot was present for the fixture against Slough Town at Nene Park on March 1st and moved to the dug-out in the second half as Diamonds strove to hold on to a 2-1 lead, both goals scored by Julian Capone. An injury to Matt Crossley made matters more difficult and an injury time equaliser from Mark Fiore deprived Diamonds of two vital points. To emphasise how disappointing this was, Slough's equaliser ended their run of five consecutive defeats but it still meant that they had not won a Conference game since November 23rd.

Before the following week's visit to Kettering there was plenty of off-field interest. It was soon agreed by all that Brian Talbot should assume the title and responsibility of Head Coach and that Roger Ashby should spend more time preparing for the expansion of the club's youth programme. Ashby cited immense pressure and excessive criticism as reasons for the change in role, *"The last few weeks have been very difficult for me. There has been a lot of criticism, especially from outside sources and no-one likes that. I don't need it. It hasn't been a very pleasant time for me. It's not something I have experienced in management before and it's not something I would like to go through again."* Chairman Max Griggs expressed his appreciation for the former manager's immense contribution to Rushden & Diamonds by appointing him Sports Development Director, *'an ambassador for the club, who will continue to develop the highly successful soccer clinics, school visits and behind the scenes activities on the football side.'* Roger Ashby's impressive record stands scrutiny. Out of 282 games under his charge, the Diamonds won 161 (57%), drew 61 (22%) and lost only 60 (21%). They won the Southern League Premier and Midland Divisions, the NFA Senior Cup, the Maunsell Cup and reached the semi-finals of the FA Trophy. Over the same period attendances at Nene Park rose from 300 to average around 2,500.

Brian Talbot had thirteen games left. His task was simple to state: safeguard the club's Vauxhall Conference place. The practicalities of the task would be far less simple. Ironically the first of Talbot's thirteen took the new coach to Rockingham Road where he had spent a troubled four month spell back in 1992. The teams for the match at Kettering are included because it shows the first Rushden & Diamonds side under Talbot's control although there was not a great deal the new man could do about team selection as he had only seen the one game. Thus there was only one change from the team that played against Slough. Matt Crossley was injured and returned to Wycombe whilst Kenny Cramman took over the problematical left back position. Darren Collins continued on the bench.

Kettering were unbeaten in eight matches and had won the last five home games. In stark contrast, the visitors had won only one of their previous eleven matches. Yet the Diamonds overturned the form book, as so often happens in local derbies, with a scintillating five goal display which stunned the huge home contingent in the 4,628 crowd. Kevin Shoemake, restored to the Poppies goal after a seven weeks absence because Northampton Town required loan keeper Billy Turley to play for their first team at Hereford, suffered from a mixture of bad luck and poor judgement as goals from Alford and Hackett put his former club 2-0 up. Just before the break the lively and often under-rated Chris Pearson (who had played for Hinckley Town against Rushden & Diamonds in Diamonds' sixth competitive fixture back in 1992) got a goal back to raise the hopes of the home supporters. But a speculative forty yarder from David Leworthy restored Rushden's two goal advantage on the hour and effectively killed the game. In the closing ten minutes Leworthy accepted a misplaced pass from Kettering player-manager Steve Berry to extend the lead and Garry Butterworth rifled home his first goal of the season to complete a remarkable 5-1 scoreline.

Saturday March 8th 1997

Kettering Town (1) 1 | **Rushden & Diamonds (2) 5**

	Kettering Town			Rushden & Diamonds	
1	Kevin Shoemake		1	Martin Davies	
2	Rob Marshall		2	Simeon Hodson	
3	Jamie March		3	Kenny Cramman	
4	Craig Gaunt		4	Andy Peaks	
5	Richard Nugent		5	Jim Rodwell	
6	Steve Berry	(sub: Dowling)	6	Steve Stott	(sub: Stapleton)
7	Tarkan Mustafa	(sub: Dudfield)	7	Julian Capone	
8	Craig Norman		8	Garry Butterworth	
9	Neil Lyne		9	Carl Alford	(sub: Collins)
10	Tony Lynch		10	David Leworthy	
11	Chris Pearson		11	Brendan Hackett	
12	Luke Dowling		12	Darren Collins	
14	Lawrie Dudfield		14	Simon Stapleton	
15	Paul Miles		15	Richard Bailey	

Referee: AD Hall (Birmingham)

Goals: Alford (7, **0-1**); Hackett (36, **0-2**); Pearson (43, **1-2**); Leworthy (62, **1-3**); Leworthy (81, **1-4**); Butterworth (83, **1-5**).

Booked: Berry, Norman

Brian Talbot retained the 4-4-2 formation, employed so effectively at Rockingham Road, in the next game at fellow relegation strugglers Bromsgrove Rovers. It wasn't a pretty game, indeed it resembled a good many that the Diamonds had lost earlier in the campaign. This time, however, they grafted away getting their reward in the 75th minute when David Leworthy intercepted a poor back pass to keeper Chris Taylor and set up Carl Alford for the only goal of the game. Alford went off for the last few minutes. His replacement was Richard Bailey, for whom this was his last appearance; two-thirds of the total of seventy that he made were as substitute.

A new record Nene Park crowd of 5,170 turned up on the evening of March 18th for the return game with Kettering Town. They saw Diamonds clinch a hard fought game with a Steve Stott header just before half time. In the second period, Kettering, playing towards their supporters in the packed Airwair Stand, did everything but equalise, Martin Davies, in his last appearance, helping to keep them at bay.

A fourth consecutive victory was achieved at the expense of Telford United, the 2-0 success gained on the back of a several fine performances, notably Garry Butterworth and Steve Stott in midfield, Jim Rodwell at the back and debutant Steve Cherry *(right)*, the former Derby County, Notts County and Watford goalkeeper. It was Cherry's second Nene Park appearance in a week, having appeared in the opposition ranks for Kettering Town. Cherry demonstrated his impeccable handling, positional play and distribution, inspiring confidence throughout the back line. Telford, though, played a part in their own downfall with Mark Kearney getting himself dismissed for a second yellow card shortly after Rodwell had given Diamonds a twenty-third minute lead.

The winning run was maintained at Welling where the side enjoyed several slices of the luck that had eluded them earlier in the season to achieve an unlikely victory courtesy of David Leworthy's cleverly executed eighty-second minute goal. Twice the ball had struck the woodwork with keeper Cherry beaten only to rebound to safety in a first half dominated by the home team but Rushden's new found resilience saw them weather the storm and sneak that all important goal.

A 1-1 draw at Dover brought the five match winning streak to an end, the first points dropped since Brian Talbot had taken over. Brendan Hackett beat an inspired Ron Fearon in the Dover goal to put the Diamonds ahead, but with a total shot count of 13 to 5 in their favour they really should have done better. Gary Stebbing's long range equaliser represented the home side's only real shot in anger as the Rushden defence, superbly marshalled once more by Andy Peaks, dealt efficiently with the spasmodic Dover attacks.

During the following week Brian Talbot strengthened his squad before the transfer deadline by signing four players as emergency cover on non-contract terms. George Lawrence, a former Southampton and Oxford United striker, had played a major role in the consecutive Maltese championships won by Hibernians when Talbot was their coach. Amongst Lawrence's finest moments must have been the goal he scored in each leg of the UEFA Cup tie against Dinamo Minsk when the Maltese side lost 5-6 on aggregate. Hakan Hayrettin, ex Leyton, Barnet, Torquay, Wycombe, Cambridge and Doncaster, former Watford apprentice Mark Jones and Craig Allardyce from Blackpool, son of Bolton Wanderers stalwart and Notts County manager Sam, completed the quartet.

The Easter Monday game with Hayes attracted a crowd of 3,134 who witnessed a thrilling game with the Diamonds twice coming from behind to earn a deserved point. The game was a tale of two substitutes, the visitors highly rated 18 year old Jason Roberts (who subsequently went to Wolverhampton Wanderers for big money) coming off the bench after twenty-three minutes to add his precocious skills to a Hayes side already 1-0 up through Joe Francis. Darren Collins equalised but shortly after half time Andy Cox rose unchallenged to head home Jon Brady's corner. Enter Carl Alford after seventy-six minutes. Within a further seven the club's record signing had put his side on level terms with a fine header from Kenny Cramman's cross. Kevin Wilkin came on for the last half hour, his last appearance for the club. It was his 95th appearance and he scored 43 goals, a scoring record which is even more impressive when it is realised that he only made the starting line-up on 66 occasions. The draw increased the unbeaten run to seven, a sequence which had seen Rushden & Diamonds rise to the heady heights of sixteenth place, eight points in front of the relegation zone now occupied by Bromsgrove, Bath and, plummeting swiftly, Altrincham.

Alford celebrated his inclusion in the starting line-up against Southport with the two goals which paved the way to a comfortable win, even though two of the goals came in the final ten minutes. A third from David Leworthy sealed a victory largely achieved through the patient passing game so favoured by coach Talbot. So, on the second occasion that the Grand National had been abandoned, Rushden & Diamonds, just as in 1993, won 3-0.

Leworthy, Garry Butterworth and Kenny Cramman were again selected for the England semi-professional side and had a mid week excursion to the Netherlands. All three played in the goalless draw against the Dutch, Leworthy being regarded by at least one reporter as *"the pick of the visitors"*. The match was played in the unlikely venue of Appingedam in Groningen province, in the extreme north-east of the country where korfball is the major sport.

Having gone nine games without defeat, another season of Conference football seemed assured. Defeat at Bath, however, in a five goal thriller, was a salutary reminder that survival couldn't be taken for granted. Few could deny that City deserved the three points for their battling performance in their own desperate bid to remain in the Conference, yet for much of the match Diamonds had shown that they too could battle. They came from behind to lead 2-1 with scores from Carl Alford and Simon Stapleton *(left)* but lost it in the last quarter of an hour, David Mehew's winner coming fully seven minutes into injury time.

There was then a nine day break in which Diamonds aficionados found the FA Trophy semi-final replay to be the major interest. Dagenham & Redbridge's line-up included Glyn Creaser but there were three times as many ex Diamonds in the Gloucester team. It was one of them, David Holmes, who gave Gloucester an early lead but Dave Johnson, Dale Watkins and the rest of their City colleagues missed a Wembley trip as Creaser's side came back to win 2-1.

After their rest the side travelled to Broadhall Way and watched Stevenage Borough demonstrate the standards at which the Diamonds must aim if they are to claim front-runners credentials. Still nursing slender title aspirations, Borough gave Brian Talbot's side a footballing lesson in the second half. The 4-1 score-line was a fair reflection of the ninety minutes play, but the game hinged on two incidents involving referee Coxhead. With Stevenage leading 1-0 through the prolific Barry Hayles, reserve keeper Richard Wilmot upended the goalbound David Leworthy and was shown the appropriate red card. Within minutes the stand-in, midfielder Jason Soloman, flapped at a Brendan Hackett cross, Garry Butterworth headed goalwards, Efetobor Sodje allowed the ball to slip between his legs and Carl Alford got the final touch to equalise. Diamonds' domination lasted just three minutes. Hackett's innocuous challenge on Paul Barrowcliff was adjudged worthy of a red card and, somewhat bemused, the 'culprit' left to join Wilmot, presumably not literally, in an early bath. The second half was all Stevenage, and particularly Dean Hooper who enjoyed the freedom of the right flank. Goals from Sodje, Fulham loanee Michael Mison and Ryan Kirby ensured a resounding victory for the home side.

With only three games left the home fixture against Halifax Town on April 26th assumed vital significance. Conference survival was not yet mathematically certain. The last three games were all at Nene Park but two of them were against relegation candidates and the other was against Woking.

			Home					Away					
		P	W	D	L	F	A	W	D	L	F	A	Pts
17	Rushden & Diamonds	39	6	7	5	25	22	6	3	12	31	38	**46**
18	Halifax Town	39	8	4	7	32	32	3	7	10	16	36	**44**
19	Welling United	39	7	2	10	20	26	4	7	9	26	33	**42**
20	Bath City	39	8	4	7	23	25	2	6	12	25	52	**40**
21	Bromsgrove Rovers	40	7	4	9	28	30	4	1	15	12	33	**38**
22	Altrincham	39	5	3	11	20	29	3	9	8	22	36	**38**

It was a dour struggle in the rain and Halifax had the best of the few chances created but Micky Norbury squandered them and the Diamonds eventually clinched the game eleven minutes from time when Brendan Hackett produced a moment of pure class to score the goal which ensured that Nene Park would host Conference football in 1997-98. Receiving the ball wide on the left he controlled instantly, turned and fired a fifteen yard angled shot into the top corner of the Halifax net. Whilst Rushden fans went off to celebrate, the soaked and bedraggled Halifax supporters went off to face the strong possibility of starting the new campaign in the Unibond League. Elsewhere Bath and Welling had both won and Halifax's last two games were against Macclesfield and Stevenage.

Woking were the visitors in the penultimate game of the season. The return visit of the FA Trophy Semi-Final opponents of two seasons earlier had long been anticipated as one of the games of the season. But following the drama and the outcome of the previous match the sense of anti-climax was palpable. For much of the time the game resembled a pre-season friendly with both sides seemingly content to go through the motions. It warmed up a little in the second half after Justin Jackson's shot had received a wicked deflection off Jim Rodwell to put the visitors 1-0 up. This reversal spurred the Diamonds into action and, after Laurence Batty had produced the save of the season to deny Kenny Cramman, Darren Collins ran on to Steve Stott's through pass to score with characteristic coolness. Clive Walker, earmarked unsuccessfully as the new player-coach prior to Brian Talbot's appointment, was decidedly out of sorts suggesting he might indeed be seeking a change of clubs in the close season. But that would not be until after another trip to Wembley where this time Woking would face Dagenham & Redbridge in the FA Trophy final.

The fact that Diamonds had made themselves safe with the win against Halifax undoubtedly reduced Irthlingborough's collective consumption of valium but it also meant that the real drama was elsewhere. Whilst Rushden and Woking were drawing 1-1 at Nene Park, it was the same score at Farnborough where an equaliser five minutes from time deprived Bath of two of the three points they had looked like getting. Halifax were back in with a chance but the following day they looked as if they were on their way down when they trailed Macclesfield by two goals as they went into the last ten minutes. Amazingly they fought back to gain a point and with both Bath and Halifax winning on the final Saturday the Yorkshire side survived by just one point. Undoubtedly they will point to their spirited comeback against Macclesfield as the reason for their having one more season in the Conference, but if Chris Boothe had not got that late equaliser for Farnborough then Bath would have survived and Halifax would have been travelling to Alfreton, Bamber Bridge and Colwyn Bay.

And so the season finished as it had begun - with a game against Altrincham. If it had been a long, hard struggle for the Diamonds the visitors had suffered even more cruelly. Their unbroken period amongst non-league football's elite had come to an end. The Unibond was now a certainty. Yes, Alfreton, Bamber Bridge and Colwyn Bay would be on their fixture list for next season. How distant that dramatic seven goal opening day match now seemed. Where was the Altrincham supporter who had said, *"See you on the last day of the season. If both sides play like they have today, it'll be the title decider"*? A third of the way through the season his assessment of Altrincham was not too wide of the mark. The Cheshire side were sixth in the Conference; two thirds of the way through the season they had dropped to fourteenth and by the time they arrived at Nene Park they were twenty-first, having won their first game of 1997 the previous week after fifteen consecutive matches without a win.

The season's final game, which the Diamonds won 3-2, was a mixture of good, bad and very indifferent football, and mostly memorable for the wrong reasons. Garry Butterworth's season ended prematurely when he and Ian Horrigan were dismissed three minutes from time for an altercation which sparked a free-for-all amongst the players. And this after he had received two 'Player of the Year' trophies and headed his side into the lead from Darren Collins' cross. An own goal and an Ian King strike put Diamonds three up but in a sloppy finish they conceded two goals in the final seven minutes. Craig Allardyce became the only one of the four emergency signings to appear for the first team when he replaced the injured Jim Rodwell early in the game. Making their final Diamonds bow were Ian King, who scored the third goal, Andy Furnell and somewhat surprisingly, David Leworthy.

Head coach Brian Talbot had been at the helm for thirteen games. There was nothing unlucky about the revival which saved the club's Conference status, but considerable improvements were still required if the Diamonds were to compete with the league's top sides in 1997-98.

With just over ninety minutes to go before kick-off Wally Valentine of Radio Diamonds interviews Brian Talbot (or vice-versa!).

GM Vauxhall Conference 1996-1997

			Home					Away					
	P	W	D	L	F	A	W	D	L	F	A	Pts
1 Macclesfield Town (4)	42	15	4	2	41	11	12	5	4	39	19	**90**
2 Kidderminster Harriers (7)	42	14	4	3	48	18	12	3	6	36	24	**85**
3 Stevenage Borough (1)	42	15	4	2	53	23	9	6	6	34	30	**82**
4 Morecambe (9)	42	10	5	6	34	23	9	4	8	35	33	**66**
5 Woking (2)	42	10	5	6	41	29	8	5	8	30	34	**64**
6 Northwich Victoria (8)	42	11	5	5	31	20	6	7	8	30	34	**63**
7 Farnborough Town (10)	42	9	6	6	35	29	7	7	7	23	24	**61**
8 Hednesford Town (3)	42	10	7	4	28	17	6	5	10	24	33	**60**
9 Telford United (13)	42	6	7	8	21	30	10	3	8	25	26	**58**
10 Gateshead (5)	42	8	6	7	32	27	7	5	9	27	36	**56**
11 Southport (6)	42	8	5	8	27	28	7	5	9	24	33	**55**
12 Rushden & Diamonds (-)	42	8	8	5	30	25	6	3	12	31	38	**53**
13 Stalybridge Celtic (14)	42	9	5	7	35	29	5	5	11	18	29	**52**
14 Kettering Town (16)	42	9	4	8	30	28	5	5	11	23	34	**51**
15 Hayes (-)	42	7	7	7	27	21	5	7	9	27	34	**50**
16 Slough Town (17)	42	7	7	7	42	32	5	7	9	20	33	**50**
17 Dover Athletic (20)	42	7	9	5	32	30	5	5	11	25	38	**50**
18 Welling United (19)	42	9	2	10	24	26	4	7	10	26	34	**48**
19 Halifax Town (15)	42	9	5	7	39	37	3	7	11	16	37	**48**
20 Bath City (18)	42	9	5	7	27	28	3	6	12	26	52	**47**
21 Bromsgrove Rovers (11)	42	8	4	9	29	30	4	1	16	12	37	**41**
22 Altrincham (12)	42	6	3	12	25	34	3	9	9	24	39	**39**

Figures in brackets are 1995-96 positions.

♦ Macclesfield Town were promoted to Nationwide Division Three and won promotion at the first attempt.

♦ Relegated from Division Three were Hereford United who, had they won their final game against Brighton & Hove Albion, would have survived and Brighton would have been relegated.

♦ Promoted from the Unibond League were champions Leek Town, from the ICIS League champions Yeovil Town and from the Dr Martens League second placed Cheltenham Town. The ground of Dr Martens champions Gresley Rovers was not considered to be satisfactory.

♦ Bath City and Bromsgrove Rovers were relegated to the Dr Martens League, Altrincham were relegated to the Unibond League. To maintain the correct numbers, Gravesend & Northfleet transferred from the Dr Martens to the ICIS.

♦ The Dr Martens League lost Gravesend & Northfleet (transferred to the ICIS), Sudbury Town (resigned) and Buckingham Town (relegated). The new trio was Blakenall, Brackley Town and Wisbech Town.

1996-1997 Results

GM Vauxhall Conference

Aug	17	Altrincham	A	3	4	Cramman 2, Collins	1037
Aug	20	Slough Town	A	0	5		1325
Aug	24	Northwich Victoria	H	1	1	Collins	2112
Aug	28	Hayes	A	1	1	Alford	1043
Aug	31	Stalybridge Celtic	H	1	1	Cramman	2156
Sep	3	Macclesfield Town	H	1	1	Wilkin	2242
Sep	7	Halifax Town	A	3	1	Rodwell, Collins, Cramman	948
Sep	9	Northwich Victoria	A	2	1	Wilson, Rodwell	769
Sep	17	Farnborough Town	H	0	2		2298
Sep	21	Woking	A	2	4	Wilkin, Bailey	2768
Sep	24	Stevenage Borough	H	0	1		3288
Sep	30	Hednesford Town	A	0	1		1252
Oct	5	Welling United	H	3	0	own goal, Stott, Cramman	2296
Oct	14	Kidderminster Harriers	A	0	1		2603
Oct	19	Gateshead	H	0	4		2214
Nov	2	Southport	A	1	2	King	1225
Nov	9	Dover Athletic	H	1	1	Alford	2110
Nov	23	Morecambe	A	0	2		1040
Nov	30	Bath City	H	4	1	Collins, Wilkin 2, Capone	1853
Dec	7	Telford United	A	5	0	Collins 2, Alford 2, Rodwell	900
Dec	14	Bromsgrove Rovers	H	1	2	Alford	2144
Dec	21	Kidderminster Harriers	H	1	1	Alford	2529
Dec	28	Stalybridge Celtic	A	0	2		788
Jan	25	Farnborough Town	A	2	2	Leworthy, Stapleton	961
Feb	1	Morecambe	H	2	1	Leworthy, Cramman	2145
Feb	8	Hednesford Town	H	0	2		2618
Feb	15	Macclesfield Town	A	1	2	Leworthy	1304
Feb	22	Gateshead	A	0	1		632
Mar	1	Slough Town	H	2	2	Capone 2	1980
Mar	8	Kettering Town	A	5	1	Alford, Hackett, Leworthy 2, Butterworth	4628
Mar	15	Bromsgrove Rovers	A	1	0	Alford	1109
Mar	18	Kettering Town	H	1	0	Stott	5170
Mar	22	Telford United	H	2	0	Rodwell, Leworthy	2554
Mar	25	Welling United	A	1	0	Leworthy	747
Mar	29	Dover Athletic	A	1	1	Hackett	1671
Mar	31	Hayes	H	2	2	Collins, Alford	3134
Apr	5	Southport	H	3	0	Alford 2, Leworthy	2218
Apr	12	Bath City	A	2	3	Alford, Stapleton	960
Apr	21	Stevenage Borough	A	1	4	Alford	2836
Apr	26	Halifax Town	H	1	0	Hackett	2629
Apr	29	Woking	H	1	1	Collins	2589
May	3	Altrincham	H	3	2	Butterworth, own goal, King	2521

1996-1997 Results

FA Cup

Sep	14 1Q	Westfields	A	4	0	Wilkin, Furnell 3	518
Sep	28 2Q	Gresley Rovers	H	4	0	King, Alford 2, Collins	1875
Oct	12 3Q	Bilston Town	H	1	0	Collins	1605
Oct	26 4Q	Bognor Regis Town	H	2	0	Collins 2	1844
Nov	16 1	Boreham Wood	A	1	1	Hackett	1567
Nov	26 1R	Boreham Wood	H	2	3	Wilkin, Collins	2619

FA Trophy

Jan	18 1	Farnborough Town	H	1	2	Wilkin	1759

Spalding Cup

Oct	8 1	Dover Athletic	A	3	2	Cramman, Wilkin 2	723
Nov	19 2	Stevenage Borough	H	1	0	Collins	1073
Dec	16 3	Kidderminster Harriers	A	0	1		811

NFA Hillier Senior Cup

Nov	12 2	Kettering Town	A	1	2	Holden	1862

Southern League Championship Match

Aug	10	Nuneaton Borough	H	3	0	Collins 2, Alford	1210

♦ The FA Cup was won by Chelsea who beat Middlesbrough 2-0 in the Final. Three non-League sides reached the Third Round proper, all going out with glory: Stevenage Borough went down 0-2 to Birmingham City to whom they conceded ground advantage, Hednesford Town beat York City 1-0 and Woking drew 1-1 at Premiership Coventry City losing the Kingfield replay 1-2. In the Fourth Round Hednesford went to Middlesbrough's Cellnet Stadium and took the lead. Five minutes from the end it was 1-1 but goals from Jan-Aage Fjortoft and Fabrizio Ravanelli enabled Middlesbrough to scrape through 3-2. Non-league sides defeating Football League opposition were: Hednesford Town (Blackpool and York City), Stevenage Borough (Leyton Orient), Sudbury Town (Brighton & Hove Albion) and Woking (Millwall and Cambridge United).

♦ In the FA Trophy Final, Woking beat Dagenham & Redbridge 1-0 with a goal from Darren Hay late in injury time. Stevenage Borough and Gloucester City were the beaten Semi-finalists.

♦ In the Spalding Cup, the Conference's top two sides met in the two-legged Final. A 1-1 draw at Macclesfield and a 0-0 draw at Kidderminster meant that Kidderminster Harriers took the cup because of their away goal.

♦ In the NFA Hillier Senior Cup, Kettering Town took the silverware for the twenty-eighth time when they beat Ford Sports 3-1 in the Final at Rockingham Road. The Daventry side was competing in the Senior Cup for the first time, beating Desborough Town, Raunds Town and, in the Semi-Final, Corby Town. The other beaten Semi-Finalist was Cogenhoe United.

1996-1997 Teams Vauxhall Conference

		Alford	Ashby	Bailey	Benstead	Butterworth	Capone	Cherry	Collins	Cramman	Davies	Furnell	Hackett	Hanigan	Hodson	Holden	King	Kirkup	Leworthy	Lilwall	Morrison	Peaks	Rodwell	Smith	Stapleton	Stott	Tucker	Wilson	Wilkin	Wooding
Altrinchm	A	9	3		1	8			10	11			sb	6								2	5			4			7	
Slough	A		3		1	8			10	11			7	6			sb	sb				2	5			4			9	sb
Northwch	H	9	3		1	8			10	6			11				7	sb					5			4			sb	2
Hayes	A	9	3		1	8			10	6			11				7						5			4				2
Stalybrge	H	9	3			8			10	11	1		7				sb	sb					5			4		6	sb	2
Macclsfld	H	9	3			8			10	11	1												5			4		6	7	2
Halifax	A	9	3			8			10	11	1	sb											5			4		6	7	2
Northwch	A		3			8			10	11	1	9						sb					5			4		6	7	2
Farnboro	H	sb	3			8			10	11	1	9						sb					5			4		6	7	2
Woking	A		3	9		8				11	1		10					sb					5			4		6	7	2
Stevenge	H	9	3			8			10	11	1						6	sb					5			4			7	2
Hednsfrd	A	9				8			10	11	1						6			3			5			4			7	2
Welling	H	9				8			10	11	1						6			3	7		5	sb		4			sb	2
Kiddrmns	A			7		8			10	11	1	sb	sb				6			3		sb	5	4					9	2
Gateshd	H	9	3	6		8			10	11	1		sb				sb				7		5	4					sb	2
Southport	A	9				8			10		1		sb			4	7			3	sb	11	5					6	sb	2
Dover	H	9				8			10		1		3			4	7				sb	11	5					6		2
Morecmb	A			9		8			10		1	sb	11			4	7				sb		5				3	6	sb	2
Bath	H					8	7		10	sb	1		11			4							5	6			3		9	2
Telford	A	sb				8			10	7	1		11		2	4						sb	5	6			3		9	
Brmsgrve	H	11	5			8			10	7	1	sb			2		sb					4		6			3		9	
Kiddrmns	H	11	3			8			10	7	1		sb		2	4							5	6						
Stalybrge	A	11	3			8				7	1		sb		2	4	sb						5	6			10			
Farnboro	A	11	3			8			9	7	1				2				10				5		6	4				
Morecmb	H	11	3		1	8			9	7					2				10				5		6	4				
Hednsfrd	H	11	3		1	8	6		9	7					2				10				5			4				
Macclsfld	A	11	3				8		9	7	1		sb		2				10				5			4	6		sb	
Gateshd	A	sb	3			8	11		9	7	1				2				10				5		6					
Slough	H	9				8	7		sb	sb	1		3		2				10			11	5			6				
Kettering	A	9				8	7		sb	3	1		11		2				10			4	5		sb	6				
Brmsgrve	A	9		sb		8	7			3	1		11		2		sb		10			4	5			6				
Kettering	H	9				8	7			3	1		11		2		sb		10			4	5		sb	6				
Telford	H	9				8	7	1		3			11						10			4	5		2	6				
Welling	A	9				8	7	1		3			11						10			4	5		2	6				
Dover	A	9				8	7	1	sb	3			11		2		sb		10			4	5			6				
Hayes	H	sb				8		1	9	3			11		2		7		10			4	5			6			sb	
Southport	H	9				8		1	7	3			11		2				10			4	5			6				
Bath	A	9				8		1	10	3			11		2		7					4	5		sb	6				
Stevenge	A	9				8		1	7	3			11		2				10			4	5			6				
Halifax	H	9				8		1	7	3			11		2				10			4	5			6				
Woking	H	9				8		1	7	3		sb	11		2		sb		10			4	5			6				
Altrinchm	H	9				8		1	7	3		sb	11		2		sb		10			4	5			6				

Ayorinde - 9 Kidderminster H; 9 Stalybridge A. *Crossley* - 4 Gateshead A; 4 Slough H.
Allardyce - sb Altrincham H.

1996-1997 Teams

		Alford	Ashby	Bailey	Benstead	Butterworth	Capone	Collins	Crammans	Davies	Furnell	Hackett	Hannigan	Hodson	Holden	King	Kirkup	Lilwall	Morrison	Peaks	Rodwell	Smith	Stott	Tucker	Wilson	Wilkin	Wooding
FA Cup																											
Westfields	A		3			8		10	11	1	9	sb					sb			sb	5		4		6	7	2
Gresley Rovers	H	9	3			8		10	11	1						6	sb			sb	5		4		sb	7	2
Bilston Town	H			sb		8		10	11	1						7		3			5	6	4			9	2
Bognor Regis	H	9		sb		8		10		1		sb			4	7		3		6	5				11		2
Boreham Wood	A	9		sb		8		10		1		11			4	7					5			3	6	sb	2
Boreham Wood	H			sb		8	sb	10		1	sb	11			4	7					5	6		3		9	2
FA Trophy																											
Farnborough	H	11				8	9	10	7	1				2	4	sb					5		6	3		sb	
Spalding Cup																											
Dover Athletic	A					8		10	11	1						6		3	7		5	sb	4			9	2
Stevenage	H			8				10		1		11			4	7			9		5			3	6	sb	2
Kidderminster H	A	11	3	sb		8		10	7	1	sb				4							6		5		9	2
SL Championship																											
Nuneaton Boro	H	sb			1	8		10	7			11	4				sb	3		2			5		6	9	sb
Hillier Cup																											
Kettering Town	A	9				8		10		1		3			4	7			sb	11	5				6		2

1996-1997 Appearances

	Start						Substitute						Total					
	L	C	T	LC	CC	Ttl	L	C	T	LC	CC	Ttl	L	C	T	LC	CC	Ttl
Carl ALFORD	32	3	1	1	1	**38**	4			1		5	36	3	1	2	1	**43**
Craig ALLARDYCE						**0**	1					1	1					**1**
Nick ASHBY	20	2		1		**23**						0	20	2		1		**23**
Sammy AYORINDE	2					**2**						0	2					**2**
Richard BAILEY	4			1		**5**	1	4		1		6	5	4		2		**11**
Graham BENSTEAD	6			1		**7**						0	6			1		**7**
Garry BUTTERWORTH	41	6	1	3	1	**52**						0	41	6	1	3	1	**52**
Julian CAPONE	11		1			**12**		1				1	11	1	1			**13**
Steve CHERRY	10					**10**						0	10					**10**
Darren COLLINS	33	6	1	4	1	**45**	3					3	36	6	1	4	1	**48**
Kenny CRAMMAN	37	3	1	3		**44**	2					2	39	3	1	3		**46**
Matt CROSSLEY	2					**2**						0	2					**2**
Martin DAVIES	26	6	1	3	1	**37**						0	26	6	1	3	1	**37**
Andy FURNELL	2	1				**3**	6	1		1		8	8	2		1		**11**
Brendan HACKETT	23	2		2	1	**28**	7	2				9	30	4		2	1	**37**
Al James HANNIGAN	2			1		**3**						0	2			1		**3**
Simeon HODSON	21		1			**22**						0	21		1			**22**
Steven HOLDEN	7	3	1	2	1	**14**						0	7	3	1	2	1	**14**
Ian KING	11	5		2	1	**19**	10		1			11	21	5	1	2	1	**30**
Andy KIRKUP						**0**	7	2		1		10	7	2		1		**10**
David LEWORTHY	18					**18**						0	18					**18**
Steve LILWALL	4	2		2		**8**						0	4	21		2		**8**
David MORRISON	2			2		**4**	3				1	4	5			2	1	**8**
Andy PEAKS	19	1		1	1	**22**	2	2				4	21	3		1	1	**26**
Jim RODWELL	41	6	1	2	1	**51**						0	41	6	1	2	1	**51**
Neil SMITH	7	2		1		**10**	1			1		2	8	2		2		**12**
Simon STAPLETON	5					**5**	3					3	8					**8**
Steve STOTT	31	3	1	2		**37**						0	31	3	1	2		**37**
Mark TUCKER	6	2	1	2		**11**						0	6	2	1	2		**11**
Terry WILSON	9	3		2	1	**15**		1				1	9	4		2	1	**16**
Kevin WILKIN	13	4		3		**20**	8	1	1	1		11	21	5	1	4		**31**
Tim WOODING	17	6		3	1	**27**	1			1		2	18	6		4	1	**29**
MAXIMUM	42	6	1	4	1	**54**							42	6	1	4	1	**54**

Goalscorers

	L	C	T	LC	CC	Total
Carl ALFORD	13	2		1		16
Darren COLLINS	8	5		3		16
Kevin WILKIN	4	2	1	2		9
David LEWORTHY	8					8
Kenny CRAMMAN	6			1		7
Jim RODWELL	4					4
Brendan HACKETT	3	1				4
Julian CAPONE	3					3
Ian KING	2	1				3

	L	C	T	LC	CC	Total
Andy FURNELL		3				3
Garry BUTTERWORTH	2					2
Simon STAPLETON	2					2
Steve STOTT	2					2
Richard BAILEY	1					1
Terry WILSON	1					1
Steven HOLDEN					1	1
own goal	2					2
TOTAL	61	14	1	7	1	84

1996-97 Playing Record

HOME	P	W	D	L	F	A	Pts
League	21	8	8	5	30	25	32
FA Cup	4	3	0	1	9	3	
FA Trophy	1	0	0	1	1	2	
League Cup	2	2	0	0	4	0	
County Cup	-	-	-	-	-	-	
TOTAL	28	13	8	7	44	30	
AWAY							
League	21	6	3	12	31	38	21
FA Cup	2	1	1	0	5	1	
FA Trophy	-	-	-	-	-	-	
League Cup	2	1	0	1	3	3	
County Cup	1	0	0	1	1	2	
TOTAL	26	8	4	14	40	44	
TOTAL							
League	42	14	11	17	61	63	53
FA Cup	6	4	1	1	14	4	
FA Trophy	1	0	0	1	1	2	
League Cup	4	3	0	1	7	3	
County Cup	1	0	0	1	1	2	
TOTAL	**54**	**21**	**12**	**21**	**84**	**74**	

Attendance Summary

HOME	Total	Ave	High		Low	
League	52800	2514	5170	Kettering	1853	Bath
FA Cup	7943	1986	2619	Boreham Wood	1605	Bilston
FA Trophy	1759	1759	1759	Farnborough	1759	Farnborough
League Cup	2283	1142	1210	Nuneaton	1073	Stevenage
County Cup	-	-	-	-	-	
TOTAL	64785	2314	5170	Kettering	1073	Stevenage
AWAY						
League	30546	1455	4628	Kettering	632	Gateshead
FA Cup	2085	1043	1567	Boreham Wood	518	Westfields
FA Trophy	-	-	-	-	-	-
League Cup	1534	767	811	Kidderminster	723	Dover
County Cup	1862	1862	1862	Kettering	1862	Kettering
TOTAL	36027	1386	4628	Kettering	518	Westfields
TOTAL						
League	83346	1984	5170	Kettering H	632	Gateshead A
FA Cup	10028	1671	2619	Boreham Wd H	518	Westfields A
FA Trophy	1759	1759	1759	Farnborough H	1759	Farnborough H
League Cup	3817	954	1210	Nuneaton H	723	Dover A
County Cup	1862	1862	1862	Kettering A	1862	Kettering A
TOTAL	**100812**	**1867**	**5170**	Kettering H	**518**	Westfields A

MEN OF YOUTH

The man most associated with the reserve and youth teams has been Kenny Mist (left), a colleague of Roger Ashby in Kettering's reserve team in the sixties, who ran Rushden Town's reserve team for several seasons before spending five and a half years at Nene Park in a similar capacity. When the Football for Life scheme was introduced in 1997, Cyril Lea (centre), capped twice for Wales in 1965 and a former Leyton Orient and Ipswich Town wing half was appointed to take charge. More recently Jeff Vetere (right), previously at Charlton Athletic, has been appointed full time youth coach. The youth programme at Rushden & Diamonds now features teams at several age groups.

PHYSIOS THREE

The first Rushden & Diamonds physio (or trainer as the more elderly remember them) was Adrian 'Tish' Felton (left). *During the rise through the Beazer Premier and into the Conference, Pete Brown* (centre) *took over the increasingly complex responsibilities of the role. When it became a full-time role, he was succeeded by Simon Parsell* (right).

SEASON SIX

1997 - 98

" From Hell, Hull and Halifax
Good Lord deliver us "

16th century proverb

Back (l to r): Brian Talbot, Darren Collins, Chris Whyte, Jim Rodwell, Mark Smith, Darren Watts, Tim Wooding, Michael Mison, Danny O'Shea, Simon Parsell.

Front (l to r): Paul Underwood, Julian Capone, Adrian Foster, Kenny Cramman, Garry Butterworth, Darren Bradshaw, Mark Cooper, Warren Kelly, John Hamsher.

Following the impressive run-in to the previous campaign, hopes were high at the start of the new season. Whilst the most optimistic would only have made Diamonds outsiders for the championship, the majority believed, even expected, a challenge for a place in the top six was a realistic aim. Few could have foreseen there would be a repeat of the previous season's dreadful start, a beginning that blighted what might otherwise have been a sustained championship challenge.

The close season departures went to two principal destinations. Midlands based players Richard Bailey, Ian King and Kevin Wilkin joined Nuneaton Borough under the managership of Brendan Phillips. Southern based Graham Benstead and David Leworthy moved to Kingstonian who were gearing up for a major assault on gaining a Conference place, having enticed manager Geoff Chapple away from Woking. Other close season moves saw Craig Allardyce off to Chorley, Nick Ashby sign for Burton Albion, Steve Holden link up with Stevenage Borough, Steve Lilwall rejoin Kidderminster Harriers, Neil Smith make a brief attempt to overcome his injury problems at Hednesford Town and Mark Tucker remain in the county, transferring his allegiance to Kettering Town. Loan players Sammy Ayorinde and Matt Crossley joined Dover Athletic and Kingstonian respectively.

During the summer two players were bought for substantial fees. Paul Underwood, a left sided wing-back or midfield player was signed from ICIS League side, Enfield. His career had been spent entirely in the Isthmian League (which would change its sponsor from ICIS to Ryman early in the season), his other clubs being Kingstonian, Sutton United and Carshalton Athletic, though he had been beyond the M25 when he was selected for the Middlesex Wanderers trip to Vietnam. The other big money buy was striker Adrian Foster who had played for Brian Talbot at West Bromwich Albion. A successful spell at Torquay United (24 goals in 75 appearances) preceded a big money move to Gillingham. A loan spell at Exeter City was followed by a move to Hereford United where he played 43 Division Three matches in 1996-97 and was, by a long way, the leading scorer with sixteen goals.

The most notable signing was probably that of Danny O'Shea. The thirty-four year old Londoner, once of Arsenal, Charlton Athletic, Exeter City, Southend United and Cambridge United, had been assistant to Ian Atkins at Northampton Town. He had appeared in 35 of the Cobblers' Division Three matches the previous season but had missed the glory of Wembley; his nine first team appearances for Arsenal were all in 1982-83 and all in the company of Brian Talbot. With over 450 League appearances to his name he was expected to bring this vast experience to the back line, tightening a defence that had been consistently over-generous. Another, but much younger, Londoner who arrived on a free transfer was Michael Mison. Twenty-two years old and well over six foot, the midfielder had made over fifty appearances for Fulham before ending the previous season on loan at Stevenage Borough.

There was no significant change to the scenery at Nene Park, though work continued throughout the season on the re-modelled North Stand. Thought by many to have been ambitiously overlarge when constructed in 1993, it had actually been found to be too small and possess too few facilities.

The first pre-season friendly was a low-key affair against Peter Morris's King's Lynn at the Walks and was followed by further outings against Enfield, Aylesbury United, First Division Ipswich Town and Third Division Leyton Orient which not only allowed Brian Talbot to run the rule over trialists like Kevin Noteman and Worrell Sterling but to experiment with different formations prior to the opening Conference fixture against Northwich Victoria at Nene Park on August 16th.

In the event only Michael Mison and Paul Underwood of the new signings were included in the Diamonds side. Among the absentees were the injured O'Shea and Foster and, significantly, Garry Butterworth, whose indiscretion in the final minutes of the last game of the previous campaign had resulted in a three match suspension. Also out for three matches was Brendan Hackett as a consequence of his red card at Stevenage. Enthusiasts of coincidental trivia will notice that for the fourth time in five seasons the first home match was refereed by Keith Hill who, at the end of the season, was promoted to the Nationwide League.

Rushden & Diamonds (0) 0			**Northwich Victoria (0) 1**		
1	Steve Cherry		1	Dean Greygoose	
2	Simeon Hodson		2	Dominic Crookes	
3	Paul Underwood	(sub: Stott)	3	Peter Billing	
4	Michael Mison		4	Wayne Fairclough	
5	Jim Rodwell		5	Wes Simpson	
6	Andy Peaks		6	Eddie Bishop	
7	Darren Collins		7	Mark Ward	(sub D Ward)
8	Simon Stapleton		8	Steve Walters	
9	Julian Capone	(sub: Sterling)	9	Paul Tait	
10	Carl Alford		10	John Stannard	(sub: Carroll)
11	Kenny Cramman		11	Darren Vicary	(sub: Hussain)
12	Steve Stott		12	Derek Ward	
14	Worrell Sterling		14	Tony Carroll	
15	Andy Chapman		15	Eddie Hussain	

Referee: KD Hill (Royston)

Goal: Bishop (68, **0-1**)
Booked: Hodson, Rodwell, Bishop

A reasonably large crowd of 2,302 saw their expectations dashed as they watched the Diamonds get off to a dismal start. Despite achieving overall superiority the team's failure to convert chances into goals, the brilliance of visiting keeper Dean Greygoose, and a simple, fateful error from a Northwich free-kick conspired to present the Vics with all three points. In the absence of Foster, Brian Talbot elected to play Julian Capone in a central attacking position to avoid radical disruption of his line-up, but despite promising performances by Simon Stapleton, Jim Rodwell and the efficient Andy Peaks (becoming the first Rushden & Diamonds player to make 200 appearances) the side lacked cohesion. Even the introduction of winger Worrell Sterling, once Peterborough United's most expensive player and with over 400 League appearances behind him, failed to spark a recovery and the game petered out to a disappointing conclusion.

Worse was to follow. Four days later the side travelled to Farnborough and were well beaten 2-0. The Head Coach kept faith with the eleven that had started against Northwich. Trialist Jamie Ndah, formerly with Torquay United and Barnet, joined Steve Stott and Andy Chapman on the substitutes bench, Worrell Sterling having been discarded after his fleeting appearance. (He was later spotted on a wet evening in Yaxley plying his trade down Spalding United's left wing). However, it is doubtful if even the omnipotent George Best could have inspired the Diamonds to success against a Farnborough side that was simply too strong on the day. Worryingly the two goals resulted from similar defensive errors to those that characterised the poor start to the 1996-97 season. Diamonds were already a goal down when Michael Mison was sent off after being shown his second yellow card. Disciplinary problems blighted Mison's season, frequent suspensions meant that his longest run of consecutive League games was nine. Farnborough's clincher, five minutes from time, was scored by the same man who had scored Bath City's winner against Rushden towards the end of the previous season, David Mehew.

Newly promoted Leek Town were the next to profit from Diamonds' generosity, the Staffordshire side coasting to a 2-0 victory, courtesy of an early goal from Dean Trott - who, just as at Stalybridge a few months earlier, had run the defence ragged, and a late strike from Steve Soley. The Diamonds were unable to string more than two passes together for much of the game and the continued absence of Garry Butterworth deprived the side of much needed steel and drive in midfield. Steve Stott, in his first full game of the season, seemed ill at ease and several heroes of the 'revival' were decidedly off-colour, most notably Simeon Hodson, the Leek game proving to be his last Conference appearance until mid-November. This game provided a memorable baptism for two substitutes, youth team product Adam Cann who flickered briefly in the second half in his only first team appearance and former Fulham junior, John Hamsher. Hamsher had arrived at Nene Park during the summer in the joint role of utility player and chauffeur to his former Craven Cottage colleague, Michael Mison, and would fully justify Brian Talbot's faith in his versatility, filling a number of positions with credit during the coming months. But it was a depressing afternoon for supporters from east Northamptonshire. Some may have enjoyed the moorland scenery, many may have delighted in England's victory over Australia at the Oval, but was it a Freudian slip that caused one returning driver to miss his turn on the outskirts of Derby and find himself heading for Burton-on-Trent, home of Albion of the Dr Martens League?

The seriousness of the club's predicament - three defeats, five goals conceded and none scored - prompted the introduction of the familiar and the fleetingly famous for the home game with Hednesford. 2,468 faithful fans had anticipated the return of Garry Butterworth and Brendan Hackett - both after three match suspensions - but the inclusion of former Nottingham Forest winger Gary Crosby was more of a surprise. Many remembered the TV goal of yesteryear with which he had embarrassed Manchester City custodian Andy Dibble, but he proved less than convincing in his new role as supplier-in-chief to goal-starved strikers, Darren Collins and Jamie Ndah. Although Collins at last opened his, and the Diamonds', account to earn the season's first point the side still lacked balance. The equaliser, Diamonds' first goal of the season was a controversial close range effort after keeper Scott Cooksey had dropped a cross. It came three minutes after the game had resumed following an eighteen minute break caused by floodlight failure. Hednesford were one of the favourites for the title - they had invested heavily during the summer - and although the ability of Robbie Dennison, capped eighteen times by Northern Ireland, was obvious in midfield, manager John Baldwin must have been disappointed that they did not build on Joe O'Connor's tenth minute goal. Hednesford's cause was not helped by the second half dismissal for violent conduct of Micky Norbury.

One point became four after the next game against Gateshead. The north-eastern side had done the double over the Diamonds in 1996-97 but their performance at Nene Park on August 30th suggested that they were destined for a long, hard season. Goals from Michael Mison, Jamie Ndah and Darren Collins propelled Diamonds to a three goal lead ten minutes before the break. But that was as good as it got. Steve Bowey and Graham Robinson scored late goals for the Tynesiders which made the score look more respectable from their point of view but there was never any serious danger of an equaliser despite Rushden continuing to look complacent even after the introduction of substitutes Carl Alford and Paul Underwood. It was Andy Peaks' last Conference appearance in a long and distinguished Diamonds career.

The trip to Slough was again an early season Tuesday evening fixture. The previous season it had produced the most humiliating defeat of the campaign but on this occasion it was avenged with a 2-1 victory. Brian Talbot gave a Conference debut to Glen Fuff who took over from Andy Peaks but the Head Coach demonstrated his disappointment with the ineffective Ndah and Crosby by withdrawing both before either had time to draw a second wind. Diamonds fell behind to a third minute long range free kick from Lee Randall. Early in the second half Darren Collins equalised and the winner came a quarter of an hour from the end from the foot of Michael Mison. The evening of celebration was then blighted by Carl Alford managing to get himself two yellow cards in the final five minutes of the game.

At the end of a week which brought an unprecedented national outpouring of grief Diamonds fans had an additional reason for dismay following their Sunday afternoon excursion to Whaddon Road, Cheltenham. It was perhaps inevitable that 'old boy' Dale Watkins would play a significant part in the downfall of his previous club, but the Diamonds hardly helped their own cause. Gary Crosby paid the price for his indiscretion, which had led to Jason Eaton's 4th minute opener, by being substituted at half time and never appeared for Rushden and Diamonds again. Another missing after half-time was the less experienced Glen Fuff, dismissed shortly before the break by referee Wendy Toms for a 'professional' foul. Highly rated reserve team player, Andy 'Boris' Chapman, entered the fray but it was an inauspicious Conference debut, culminating in the foul which gave the Robins their second goal. In truth there was probably little the else the youngster could have done to stop a marvellous run by the effervescent Watkins who converted the spot kick himself to make the points safe. Steve Stott played his last game for the club, deputising for the suspended Mison. Adrian Foster made his debut, replacing Carl Alford ten minutes into the second half. It would be a long time before Alford would again appear in the first team.

The return fixture with Farnborough on Saturday September 13th produced the freak scoreline of 5-5. Never in front, Farnborough twice came back from two down to equalise. 3-5 down with ten minutes to go, they then scored twice in the space of sixty seconds. Adrian Foster *(left)* appeared in the starting line-up for the first time and celebrated the occasion by hitting four goals without being in a winning team. Surprisingly, as impressive as Foster's goals had been - and he had certainly looked razor sharp in the box - it was the visitors' fifth that proved the most significant feature of an afternoon of almost surreal entertainment. Isolated on the left touchline David Mehew appeared to have few options until Steve Cherry elected to race out of his area in a bid to block the anticipated cross. It was an unwise decision, both in the context of the game and for the goalkeeper's future at the club. As Diamonds fans watched in stunned disbelief and grudging admiration, Mehew chipped exquisitely over the stranded Cherry from the most acute of angles to level the scores. The match report might easily have been lifted from the pages of the long-departed 'Hotspur' or 'Wizard', but it's certain Brian Talbot found little to smile about when contemplating his club's league position after the first eight games had brought exactly eight points.

		Home					Away					
	P	W	D	L	F	A	W	D	L	F	A	Pts
16 Rushden & Diamonds	8	1	2	1	9	9	1	0	3	2	7	**8**
17 Telford United	8	1	1	2	5	8	1	1	2	5	9	**8**
18 Stalybridge Celtic	7	2	1	1	9	4	0	0	3	0	3	**7**
19 Leek Town	8	1	2	1	4	3	0	2	2	4	11	**7**
20 Gateshead	7	1	1	2	6	8	0	2	1	7	8	**6**
21 Kidderminster Harriers	7	1	2	1	4	5	0	1	2	2	5	**6**
22 Kettering Town	8	0	1	2	4	7	0	3	2	4	6	**4**

There were big changes and some new faces seven days later when the side ran out for the club's first appearance at Yeovil's Huish Park. There were two new signings, one reserve player making his debut, Tim Wooding making his first appearance of the season, and goalkeeper Darren Watts *(left)* playing only his second first team game for the club.

At the centre of the defence was the imposing figure of Chris Whyte, a League Championship winner with Leeds United in 1992, the last season before the formation of the FA Premier League. Brought up in Highbury, Whyte had spent seven years with Arsenal and had also played for West Bromwich Albion, Birmingham City, Charlton Athletic and Oxford United as well as a number of American teams. Defender Warren Kelly *(left)*, named as a substitute at Yeovil, was, at twenty-nine, nearly seven years younger than Whyte and with a very different history. Born in Watford, his experience had been restricted to the Isthmian League with Hemel Hempstead, St Albans City and Hayes until he was a leading light in the team which brought the ICIS championship and a Conference place to Hayes. At the end of Hayes' inaugural season in the Conference he moved to Stevenage but soon fell out of favour and took the opportunity to move to Nene Park on a month's loan - an arrangement which was soon made permanent. Young Mark Rawle, a recent arrival from Leicester YMCA, was another substitute and Darren Watts took over in goal. Watts had been understudy to Kevin Fox at Rushden Town and played just one game for Rushden &

Diamonds, deputising for the suspended Kevin Shoemake, against Evesham in November 1992. He spent a couple of seasons with Cogenhoe United before returning to Nene Park in the summer of 1995.

Fans who braved the narrow Somerset lanes, heavily populated with slurry carts, en-route to the modernistic Huish Park (though presumably not all travelling supporters needed to use the Jetwash facility at the garage in Curry Mallett to remove a liberal and rapidly-solidifying coat of bovine and porcine excrement from their wife's cherished Fiesta) will savour memories of a stirring Diamonds victory. Nothing seemed less likely at half-time, however, as they trailed an impressive Yeovil side, including former Diamonds Al James Hannigan and debutant (and captain) Steve Stott, by a goal to nil. The central defensive trio of Michael Mison, Jim Rodwell and Chris Whyte lacked collective pace and were frequently exposed by the fast moving home attack. Owen Pickard's twenty-ninth minute opener might well have heralded a goal rush. Shortly before the break Steve Parmenter's fierce drive struck the crossbar with Watts beaten and minutes later Matt Hayfield showed a crucial lack of accuracy when well placed. Brian Talbot made a vital tactical switch at the interval, a switch which not only changed the pattern of the game but also gave a new direction to the season. Warren Kelly was brought on in a sweeper role behind Rodwell and Whyte, releasing Mison into his more favoured midfield position. The Diamonds were already beginning to take control of the game when Hannigan was dismissed for a second bookable offence and within minutes the uncompromising defender was sorely missed as first Darren Collins and then Brendan Hackett rose unchallenged to convert crosses from the right. Mark Rawle, who made a late appearance replacing the limping Adrian Foster, gave glimpses of his electrifying pace but Warren Kelly's calm authority and the team's overall commitment and discipline were the outstanding features of a deserved victory against a side that had a second man sent off two minutes from time.

The journey to Haig Avenue, Southport, the affluent end of Merseyside proved fruitless for the second successive season. Adrian Foster gave his side the perfect start, capitalising upon hesitation by veteran player-manager Paul Futcher who seemed strangely out of sorts at the heart of the home defence. Futcher's lethargy proved illusory, however, and as his side grew in confidence he became an increasingly influential figure. The defensive formation which had seemed so secure in the second half at Yeovil failed to gel and it was no surprise when Southport levelled, going on to establish an unassailable 3-1 lead. Although substitute Mark Rawle leapt prodigiously to head the Diamonds back into contention the Sandgrounders weathered the late storm with considerable ease.

The side returned to winning ways at Nene Park the following Saturday defeating John McGovern's Woking 2-1. The former Derby County and Nottingham Forest star had replaced the highly successful Geoff Chapple on the latter's surprise defection to Kingstonian. Whilst his team, now without Clive Walker, was still in a state of transformation, the Diamonds victory was both fully deserved and welcome as it lifted the side towards mid-table respectability. The first half had followed a familiar Nene Park pattern. The Diamonds took an early lead through Michael Mison after seventeen minutes when the Woking defence failed to clear a Paul Underwood free kick, failed to consolidate and gifted the visitors an equaliser six minutes later when the impressive Grant Payne was allowed to turn on the edge of the area and fire past Darren Watts. Although Diamonds dominated the remainder of the game the winning goal did not arrive until the last minute - and what a goal it was. Substitute Mark Rawle collected the ball on the halfway line, skipped past a couple of tackles and delivered the perfect through pass to Adrian Foster who volleyed the ball past Laurence Batty's despairing dive from fully twenty yards.

Although the side beat a hasty exit from the Spalding Cup, losing 0-2 at Hayes in what proved to be Andy Peaks's final first team game, it kept up its winning league momentum in its next match by defeating Hereford United at Nene Park. Another large crowd, swelled by a sizeable contingent of visiting fans, saw the game decided by a single goal, Darren Collins making the vital strike following a rare error by loan keeper Mark Gayle. For Gayle, at the time on the books of Crewe Alexandra, being on loan was not a novel experience; he had also been at Birmingham City and Liverpool under such an agreement. Playing against a Rushden side was no new experience either as he had played at Hayden Road for Worcester City. Once again Diamonds' victory was due to a good team performance and there were signs that the side was beginning to achieve the cohesion that had been strangely absent at the beginning of the season. The midfield trio of Garry Butterworth, Michael Mison and Kenny Cramman, ably supported by wing backs Paul Underwood and Brendan Hackett, proved the springboard for sustained attacks which could, indeed should, have brought greater reward than the single goal advantage. It was difficult not to sympathise with chief offender, Adrian Foster. The former Hereford striker was the butt of incessant abuse from a section of visiting fans whose selective memory conveniently ignored his major contribution to their side's goalscoring tally in their relegation season. Sadly he frittered several good opportunities to silence their boorish chants in the most effective manner. If the visitor's loanee had blotted his copybook there was no such blemish on the performance of Guy Branston, the Diamonds' latest recruit. The Leicester City trainee enjoyed an impressive debut in the first game of what became a maximum three month loan period alongside the majestic Chris Whyte in the centre of defence. One source of worry for the team management was that referee Keith Hill (yes, back at Nene Park yet again) booked six Diamonds players.

The thirteenth Conference game of the season resulted in victory at Kidderminster Harriers and it elevated the side to a lofty ninth place, the highest position the club had achieved in the Conference to date, goals from Michael Mison and Kenny Cramman securing the points. The introduction of former Nottingham Forest, Crewe Alexandra and Walsall keeper Mark Smith, a twenty-three year old native of Birmingham, and a late substitute appearance by youth team player Malcolm Ndekwe brought the total number of players used in the thirteen league games played to thirty. Significantly only four who had played in the opening game against Northwich, Darren Collins, Kenny Cramman, Michael Mison and Paul Underwood appeared at Aggborough.

The run of good form augured well for the FA Cup campaign which began, coincidentally, with a home Fourth Qualifying Round tie against Boreham Wood - the Ryman League (as the Isthmian had become after its dispute with previous sponsor ICIS) side that had brought the Diamonds' cup hopes to an inglorious end in 1996. There was just one change from the side that had played so well at Kidderminster. Jim Rodwell was reinstated to the back line in place of the ineligible Guy Branston. The performance, however, could hardly have been more different. Garry Butterworth gave his side the perfect start, scoring after eighteen minutes with a spectacular left foot strike from twenty five yards. But that was as good as it got. Chances were squandered, possession conceded, and when Darren Collins missed a clear one-on-one with the keeper shortly after half-time the odds swung firmly in favour of a shock result. Minutes later Boreham Wood were level, the impressive Tony Samuels pouncing upon a poor Mark Smith clearance. The Hertfordshire side might easily have gone through at the first attempt had veteran Terry Robbins' shot struck the back of the net rather than the upright. Only the determined Butterworth and a cool Warren Kelly emerged from an unsatisfactory display with reputations intact. The replay meant that the scheduled home fixture with Kettering Town had to be postponed.

Brian Talbot gave the same eleven that had started the first game a chance to redeem themselves in the replay. If, like the fans who travelled hopefully down the A1, he believed they could hardly play so badly again he was sadly misguided. On a firm, lightly frosted surface the underdogs showed a greater appetite for the game, defending deep and frustrating their opponents by tight marking and breaking quickly from the back, Tony Samuels again posing the greatest threat. The Diamonds hardly mustered a attack of note and were further hampered by the loss of Adrian Foster with yet another recurrence of the foot injury that had blighted his season. Boreham Wood snatched a deserved winning goal minutes from the end of extra-time earning the right to meet another Conference side, Hayes, in the First Round Proper. There was hardly time for their celebrated substitute, Kerry Dixon, to tread the turf let alone sample the action before the curtain came down on another disappointing Diamonds FA Cup campaign.

The Head Coach made no secret of the fact that further changes were necessary if the side was to meet the standards he demanded. For the next league game at home to Slough Town he introduced two more new faces to the side. Darren Bradshaw stepped in to replace the injured Garry Butterworth and loan player Jamie Barnwell-Edinboro was among the substitutes. Bradshaw's younger brother Carl played most of his football near his Sheffield home (apart from his time at Norwich City), but Darren had travelled more widely, numbering Newcastle United and Plymouth Argyle amongst his former clubs. Chesterfield, York City, Peterborough United and Blackpool had been the other ports of call for the thirty-year old who had experienced the world of non-League football at Matlock Town in his younger days. Hull born Barnwell-Edinboro was on loan from Cambridge United for whom he had made 40 Division Three appearances the previous season, scoring six times. He had begun his career at Coventry City, making just one Premiership appearance - at Middlesbrough's Cellnet Riverside Stadium, and played on loan for Swansea City and Wigan Athletic before signing for Cambridge. Bradshaw *(right)* would become arguably the most impressive signing since Garry Butterworth and Darren Collins joined the club back in 1994 but his debut performance, in midfield, was nowhere near as impressive as what soon became the norm. Indeed it was overshadowed by the second home defeat of the season, Paul Hardyman's goal on the stroke of half-time gaining Slough revenge for their defeat at Wexham Park back in September. It could easily have been 2-0 but Gary Abbott's twice-taken late penalty was twice saved by Mark Smith *(below)*.

The prospect of a trip to Welling, always a difficult place to eke out a result, was less than enticing. In the previous season the Diamonds had returned with three points courtesy of David Leworthy's late goal but it had been a real struggle. When Paul Underwood scored a fine opener within minutes of the start it seemed that there was little chance of a nail biting encounter. The home defence was continuously in disarray relying on an outstanding performance by keeper Sasa Ilic to keep their side in the game. Ilic, observed in the second half by two grey squirrels sitting on the perimeter fence, was watched by much larger crowds later in the season. Once of Partizan Belgrade, he had found St Leonards Stamcroft a much safer place to play his football, helping them to the Premier Division of the Dr Martens League. He then signed for Charlton Athletic, from whom he was on loan. When recalled to the Valley he played a vital role in the Nationwide First Division club's progress to the play-offs and ended his season in the slightly more salubrious setting of Wembley Stadium. There he made the vital penalty shoot out save from Sunderland's Michael Gray which took Charlton into the Premier League. Boosted by the confidence that comes with playing with a reliable keeper, Welling fought back with their pacy attack often troubling the heart of the Diamonds defence. Warren Kelly was yet to consistently reproduce his early form and Chris Whyte, although impressive in possession, was often exposed. It required a number of last ditch tackles by the promising Branston, some wayward finishing and two fortuitous rebounds from the woodwork to safeguard the three points.

Brian Talbot described the first forty-five minutes of the 4-1 victory over Kidderminster Harriers as the best performance since he had taken charge of the side. Loanee striker Jamie Barnwell-Edinboro *(right)*, who had been largely peripheral in the previous game at Welling, opened the scoring after eleven minutes, skilfully converting Michael Mison's perfect right wing cross. Playing football which at times was of breathtaking quality the Diamonds missed numerous opportunities to increase their single goal advantage before the interval. It was the visitors, however, who scored next, the dangerous Neil Doherty equalising from Deakin's teasing cross. Just as it seemed that the Diamonds would pay a heavy price for their first half profligacy they compiled the most fluent move of the game. Garry Butterworth, back to his bustling best, found Mison, the ball was switched to Darren Collins whose precise pass sent Barnwell through to restore the lead. He completed his hat-trick on seventy-one minutes, cutting in from the left and placing his shot past the advancing keeper. Collins completed the scoring three minutes later, forcing home Mison's perfect pull back to end a recent barren spell. Just to complete a thoroughly entertaining afternoon, Mark Smith produced a remarkable save from Doherty's penalty kick and a round up of Vauxhall Conference results showed that the Diamonds now occupied a dizzy sixth place in the table.

			Home					Away					
		P	W	D	L	F	A	W	D	L	F	A	Pts
1	Halifax Town	15	7	0	0	21	4	4	3	1	10	8	**36**
2	Hednesford Town	17	7	2	0	14	5	3	3	2	15	15	**35**
3	Cheltenham Town	15	5	2	0	16	7	4	2	2	12	10	**31**
4	Woking	17	5	2	1	17	8	3	4	2	11	9	**30**
5	Morecambe	15	3	3	2	15	16	5	2	0	18	5	**29**
6	Rushden & Diamonds	16	4	2	2	16	12	4	0	4	9	12	**26**

Collins gave further evidence of his return to goalscoring form three days later hitting a hat-trick in the 3-1 Hillier Senior Cup victory at Brackley Town. The game, played on a quagmire of a pitch which tested the stamina of the youngest members of the side, saw Head Coach Brian Talbot (making his first and, so far, only first team appearance) lead by example from the middle of the park while Andy Furnell made his first and final first team appearance of the season before his eventual departure for Nuneaton Borough. Brackley, newcomers to the Dr Martens Midland Division, were a much better side than the one that provided the opposition for Rushden & Diamonds first ever Senior Cup tie in 1992. But Diamonds had also got a little better since then and, despite Phil Mason's equaliser just before the break, there was never any real prospect of an upset.

The fixture list for Saturday November 22nd 1997 sent Diamonds to Morecambe just as the fixture list for Saturday November 23rd 1996 had done. Both matches resulted in two goal defeats but other similarities were few. The weather was certainly different; ebony clouds were replaced by wall-to-wall sunshine and the Isle of Man was visible from the promenade. As in 1996 Morecambe were the better side, but this time the Diamonds did make a bit of a fight of it, even though they were two down at the interval. Defensive changes did not help: Simeon Hodson *(right)* was drafted in for his last appearance before joining Telford United and Danny O'Shea played his only forty-five minutes of Conference football. It was substitute Julian Capone who gave the travelling supporters who had battled through the M6 jams or investigated the time-keeping of Mr Branston's Virgin Trains a glimmer of hope with a stunning long-range goal ten minutes from time. But Morecambe clinched the points the midfield domination of Brian Healy and Stuart Drummond deserved with a third goal five minutes later. Architect of that clincher was Andy Milner who was making his debut after signing from Chester City; three weeks earlier Milner had played at Morecambe while on loan to Hereford and had scored a hat-trick.

The following Tuesday evening was the rearranged date for the big one: Kettering Town at Nene Park. A measure of the difference just a few months can make in football is immediately apparent on comparing Conference tables from March and November 1997. In what amounted to almost complete role reversal it was the Poppies who now languished just one place off the bottom while the Diamonds sat proudly in sixth place. On this occasion, however, the underdogs were unable to record a much needed victory, denied by those triple impostors so familiar to struggling sides - poor finishing, excellent goalkeeping and rank bad luck. Just as in the previous season the only goal of the game came at the visiting supporters end of the ground just before the break, Darren Collins delighting the home fans. The increasingly influential Darren Bradshaw was the pick of the outfield players while Mark Smith earned most plaudits with several matchwinning saves most notably from the dangerous, but profligate, Chris Pearson. Kettering's central defender Mark Tucker would have been delighted with his own commanding performance but desperately disappointed that his return to Nene Park had ended without a point.

Darren Bradshaw has it all under control. The Kettering player at the extreme left is Mark Tucker.

It had not been an impressive display against Kettering but fans will forgive virtually anything if the result is right. The next performance, at home to Hayes, was indisputably poor and did not have the right result. Many fans were highly critical, an indication of how expectations had changed since the abysmal start to the season had been followed by the rapid rise to the top six. One criticism was the rapid turnover of players. Against Hayes it was hello and good-bye to Leo Cotterell, a wing back who had played League football for Ipswich Town and Bournemouth. The Cambridge born England schools international played the first half and no more. The thirty-seventh man to appear in the first team so far this season was Colin West, signed on a month's loan from Leyton Orient. Just past his thirty-fifth birthday, the Geordie had made his debut for Sunderland in the old First Division in 1981-82. It was into April before he secured a regular first team place, taking over from Ally McCoist. Six goals in the final eleven games made him the club's second highest scorer for the season and enabled Sunderland to finish one place above the relegated trio with two points more than Leeds United. Subsequent moves took him to Leyton via Watford, Rangers, Sheffield Wednesday, West Bromwich Albion, Port Vale and Swansea City. He replaced Jamie Barnwell-Edinboro whose loan period had ended but was unable to make much of an impression on his debut as some inept defending gave Hayes a fifth minute goal, a lead which they had extended to three before Diamonds managed a consolation three minutes from time. Even that was an own goal.

Colin West

If that performance had merited the scorn that many fans heaped on the team, the following week's exhilarating showing deserved exactly the opposite reaction. In a scintillating display of attacking football, Vics were pulverised to their first home defeat of the season. The 4-2 scoreline was a little flattering to the Cheshire side who would probably have suffered a bigger battering if keeper Dean Greygoose had been shown a red rather than yellow card after handling ouside the area just before the break. The victory at Yeovil had been a significant turning point when new players and a new defensive formation provided new hope. The Northwich game was an equally important turning point. It marked a return to 4-4-2 and it was the start of a run of fine form, good results and entertaining football. It also marked the end of wholesale changes to the side; thirty-seven players had been used in the first seventeen fixtures - only twenty-three were used in the final twenty-five.

The following Saturday, December 13th, provided an unlucky return to Nene Park for Martin Davies. Released shortly after the start of the season, Davies had joined Dover Athletic but his new side were thoroughly dispirited by the end of an uneven contest in which Colin West gave a masterful display of front running. The experienced striker led the line with strength, good movement off the ball and clinical finishing and fully deserved his brace of goals in the 4-1 win. Darren Collins, back to his predatory best, netted the other two, his second equalling Dale Watkins' club scoring record of 98 goals. Dover's consolation came from former Diamond Sammy Ayorinde whom nearly everybody saw control the ball with his hand before firing past Mark Smith. A local radio reporter told his audience back in Kent, *"What a waste of a dodgy goal. How much better it would have been had it been a last minute winner against Welling!"*

How high could the Diamonds go? The last match before Christmas, away to Hayes, would answer a few questions. Just three weeks earlier, Hayes, one of the Conference's top battlers, had made monkeys of Rushden at Nene Park. A point from west London would be more than useful but would also be necessary to show that the team had the qualities required to overcome such opposition. Diamonds passed the test with flying colours. Trailing to a goal from Mark Hall, Darren Collins levelled things in the final minute of the first half and the winner came early in the second period, Brendan Hackett's shot from outside the area grazing the inside of the post. Three consecutive victories, flair at Northwich, opposition blown away at Nene Park, grit at Hayes. Result: fifth place in the table.

		Home					Away					
	P	W	D	L	F	A	W	D	L	F	A	Pts
1 Halifax Town	21	10	1	0	32	8	4	4	2	12	12	**47**
2 Cheltenham Town	19	7	2	0	20	8	5	3	2	14	11	**41**
3 Hednesford Town	21	8	2	0	16	6	3	5	3	18	19	**40**
4 Morecambe	20	5	3	3	21	20	6	2	1	22	8	**38**
5 Rushden & Diamonds	22	6	2	3	22	16	6	0	5	16	18	**38**
6 Woking	21	6	3	1	22	10	4	4	3	14	11	**37**

Stevenage Borough would become familiar with controversy early in 1998; as a sample there was some manufactured for the two holiday games against Rushden & Diamonds. On Boxing Day at Nene Park it was more farce (although pantomime would be more seasonally appropriate) than controversy as Stevenage undressed more often than Brian Rix. After a few minutes the referee realised that Stevenage's white and pale blue shirts were far too similar to Diamonds' white. Stevenage retreated to the touchline and changed into a Diamonds away strip. Amazingly Stevenage appeared for the second half in their first choice white and red shirts which they had not used, presumably because it was realised they clashed with Rushden's. So, before the second half could start it was back to the touchline to change back into the Diamonds strip they had worn in the first half. This shambles took the attention off a hardworking Diamonds performance that extended the winning run to four. Simon Stapleton returned to Nene Park in an unaccustomed full back role and was tormented throughout the first half by former team mate Brendan Hackett who beat him almost at will and it seemed just a matter of time before the Diamonds' superiority brought that all important opening goal. After the extended break it was obvious that Borough's defensive frailty of the first period had been firmly addressed by manager Fairclough and with Diamonds keeper Mark Smith restricted by injury it required another impeccable display by Darren Bradshaw to keep the home goal intact. Bradshaw was becoming a regular recipient of the 'Man of the Match' award with his cool, no-nonsense style of play and it is inconceivable that he would have made the sort of mistake that turned the game the Diamonds way. When Robin Trott over-played on the edge of his own penalty area he was quickly dispossessed by Darren Collins, who unselfishly squared for Colin West to put his side ahead with an expert finish. The record goalscorer turned provider once more in the final minute when his clever one-two set up Julian Capone to beat Gallagher and make the game safe.

The controversy surrounding the return game at Broadhall Way on New Year's Day was whether the game should have taken place on that day. Two days later Stevenage were due to play Swindon Town in the Third Round of the FA Cup and wanted the game postponed. Brian Talbot insisted on playing. Perhaps that incited Stevenage to their victory but looking at the situation from a distance it is very difficult to argue that Talbot was wrong. It is necessary to ask whether the Conference's status is so lowly that matches can be postponed to allow clubs a longer period of preparation for an FA Cup tie. The match became a milestone in Darren Collins's Diamonds career, his eighth minute opening goal of the game taking his tally to one hundred. It was his 187th appearance - a remarkable record and a graphic reminder of his immense value to the club since his arrival back in 1994. Stevenage hit back in the second half, winning 2-1 with goals from Dean Wordsworth and the man who scored Wembley's goal at Nene Park in the FA Trophy in October 1994, Guiliano Grazioli. Two days later one was left to wonder what damage this fixture did to Stevenage's FA Cup prospects. It had been an ideal warm-up some reckoned, as Borough came from behind to beat Swindon 2-1 and set up those clashes with Newcastle United.

If the Boreham Wood FA Cup repeat was just a coincidence, fatalists might point knowingly to the FA Trophy First Round draw which, for the third season in four, paired Rushden & Diamonds with Farnborough Town. The Diamonds cleared the hurdle this time but it was a close run thing, goals from Darren Collins once more deciding the outcome. Both sides were depleted through injury, suspension or ineligibility. Brian Talbot drafted in Kenny Cramman at full back for his first game for over a month, the versatile John Hamsher moved into midfield but it was up front where the Head Coach sprang his greatest surprise. Transfer listed Carl Alford, who had made his last first team appearance at Cheltenham on September 7th, was selected to take the place of Colin West, who, being a loan signing, could not play. All three produced creditable performances. Cramman equalised Barry Miller's opener with one of his trade mark free kicks, Hamsher gave Garry Butterworth good support in the middle of the park and Alford's commitment was commendable until he tired through lack of match practice. Despite this, and another faultless contribution from Darren Bradshaw, Farnborough went 2-1 up with just eight minutes remaining, a rare error by Mark Smith gifting Jamie Laidlaw the simplest of goals. Enter Darren Collins. The leading scorer had been decidedly out of sorts, earlier squandering an easy chance from Brendan Hackett's pin point centre, but he quickly reverted to type levelling the scores from a right wing cross and then, in the final minute, pouncing upon Chris Whyte's knock-down to stroke home the winner. It was the first win in the Trophy since the unforgettable Semi-Final victory over Woking three years earlier.

Yet another Darren Collins goal gained three hard won Conference points against Southport in the next game. Carl Alford was on the bench, but unused, as Brian Talbot brought Colin West back into the side. With visiting goalkeeper Billy Stewart in inspired form it required a goal of consummate skill two minutes before half-time to beat the former Cobbler. Brendan Hackett's measured cross-field ball found Hamsher and he slipped a perfect pass to the unmarked Collins who scored from an acute angle. Collins' goalscoring run had brought nine goals in six games;

he was in second place in the Conference scoring charts with fourteen goals, just ahead of Cheltenham's Jason Eaton and Farnborough's David Mehew but nine goals adrift of Halifax's Geoff Horsfield.

Suspension, however, meant that Collins would miss the next two matches beginning with the Conference trip to Dover, a side unbeaten in its last eight games. His absence allowed Carl Alford a second start in a fortnight. The prodigal striker gave a reminder of the goalscoring flair that had prompted Roger Ashby to pay a non-league record fee for his services by hitting two splendid goals after Paul Underwood had headed the Diamonds in front. The 3-0 victory was just reward for a fine team performance as Martin Davies and Sammy Ayorinde again failed to enjoy success against their former club.

Raunds Town visited Nene Park three days later in the Hillier Senior Cup, seven days earlier than originally planned. It was to Raunds' advantage because it meant there would be no Darren Collins to face. It also meant that Collins had now served his suspension and would be available for Saturday's FA Trophy Second Round at Cheltenham. Visiting manager Keith Burt's side included former Rushden

& Diamonds men John Flower, David Johnson, Darrell Page and Paul York in the starting line-up but it was another ex-Diamond, substitute Kevin Slinn, who scored the only goal of the game in the final minute to take the Dr Martens Midland Division side into the final at Rockingham Road. It was not the most auspicious of debuts for Mark Cooper *(left)*, a new signing from Leyton Orient. A month past his thirtieth birthday, Cooper, the son of former Leeds United favourite Terry, included spells at Bristol City, Exeter City, Southend United, Birmingham City, Fulham, Huddersfield Town, Wycombe Wanderers, Exeter City (again) and Hartlepool United on his curriculum vitae.

A bigger prize was at stake at Whaddon Road, Cheltenham on January 31st. The Robins had prepared for the game with a trip to Portugal - the players' reward for their FA Cup exploits which had culminated in a narrow Third Round replay defeat at Reading. Darren Collins was partnered by Carl Alford who played because of Colin West's ineligibility. Alford was substituted after an hour; it was the last time he played in a Rushden & Diamonds shirt. It was a low-key ending to his Nene Park career which, if it were required to be encapsulated in one word, could be termed 'inconsistent'. Alford spent the rest of the season on loan to Dover Athletic. John Hamsher, deputed to curb the influence of the evergreen ex Woking veteran Clive Walker, came so close to giving his side a third minute lead when his shot clipped the top of the Cheltenham crossbar but the eventual outcome was virtually decided in a two minute spell midway through the first half. First Jason Eaton pounced on a poor clearance to put the Robins ahead and then

Dale Watkins (who else?) unleashed a venomous drive from fully thirty yards which Mark Smith could barely have seen. Cheltenham did not extend their lead until twenty minutes from time when Watkins notched his second. It could have been an embarrassing scoreline: Watkins spurned the opportunity of a hat trick when his weakly struck penalty was saved by Smith and a Walker pile driver rebounded from the crossbar with the keeper well beaten. A late Darren Collins goal did little more than provide the final scoreline with some respectability but it brought Diamonds fans scant consolation. Their side had measured itself against one of the Conference front runners and had been found wanting.

Disappointment at exiting the Trophy is always assuaged by the belief that it provides the advantage of being able to concentrate on the league. And there could hardly have been a game more likely to concentrate the mind than the next fixture, the visit of runaway leaders, Halifax Town. And so Saturday February 7th 1998 joined the lengthening list of key dates in the club's brief history. 3,675 were at Nene Park to watch the clash with George Mulhall's Shaymen, beaten only twice in 26 league outings and conceding less than a goal per game.

			Home					Away					
		P	W	D	L	F	A	W	D	L	F	A	Pts
1	Halifax Town	26	12	1	0	35	8	5	6	2	17	16	**58**
2	Morecambe	25	7	3	4	24	22	7	3	1	27	10	**48**
3	Cheltenham Town	24	9	3	0	24	9	5	3	4	16	16	**48**
4	Rushden & Diamonds	26	8	2	3	25	16	7	0	6	20	20	**47**
5	Hednesford Town	26	10	3	0	21	9	3	5	5	19	22	**47**
6	Woking	25	8	3	1	27	10	5	4	4	17	14	**46**

The Diamonds couldn't have ordered a better start. Just twenty-eight seconds had elapsed when Paul Underwood crossed from the left, Halifax failed to clear and Darren Collins swept the ball past second choice keeper Andy Woods. With the visiting defence, in particular giant centre half Brian Kilcline, an FA Cup winner in 1987, looking anything but secure it was only a matter of time before one became two. Garry Butterworth's left foot strike after thirty-two minutes would have graced any game but the exquisite build-up involving Mison and West added to its quality. With Conference leading scorer Geoff Horsfield effectively shackled by Chris Whyte and Darren Bradshaw the visitors first serious threat came when a Michael Midwood header was well saved by Mark Smith shortly after the interval. Halifax were consistently outplayed in every department and it was no surprise when, with an hour gone, Collins took his league tally to sixteen, forcing home the loose ball after John Hamsher's fine shot had struck the woodwork. The introduction of the combative Mark Cooper in midfield kept the pressure on the visitors and with their discipline evaporated and their much vaunted defence once more in complete disarray Paul Underwood ghosted in to head Kenny Cramman's perfect cross beyond the hapless Woods. The 4-0 final scoreline barely reflected the extent of the Diamonds' superiority in what must be rated as the outstanding display in the club's history. With Halifax's lead cut to eight points, fifteen games remaining, and the two sides due to meet at the Shay on March 21st optimistic Diamonds fans dared to think the 'p' word if not actually utter it aloud.

Saturday February 7th, 1998

Rushden & Diamonds (2) **4** — **Halifax Town** (0) **0**

Rushden & Diamonds			Halifax Town		
1	Mark Smith		1	Andy Woods	
2	Tim Wooding		2	Andy Thackeray	
3	Darren Bradshaw		3	Mark Bradshaw	
4	Michael Mison	(sub: Cooper)	4	Jamie Murphy	
5	Kenny Cramman		5	Brian Kilcline	
6	Chris Whyte		6	Paul Stoneman	
7	John Hamsher		7	Jamie Paterson	(sub: Lyons)
8	Garry Butterworth		8	Kevin Hulme	
9	Colin West	(sub: C Smith)	9	Michael Midwood	
10	Darren Collins	(sub: Capone)	10	Geoff Horsfield	
11	Paul Underwood		11	Kieran O'Regan	
12	Julian Capone		12	Darren Lyons	
14	Craig Smith		14	Gary Brook	
15	Mark Cooper		15	Noel Horner	

Referee: JR Hubbard (Leicester)

Goals: Collins (1, **1-0**); Butterworth (32, **2-0**); Collins (59, **3-0**); Underwood (65, **4-0**)

Booked: West, Collins, Hulme, Thackeray, M Bradshaw, O'Regan, Paterson, Midwood.

Sent off: Stoneman

However, promotion was the last word on supporters lips just seven days later at the International Stadium when bottom of the table Gateshead defeated their high-flying visitors 2-1 to record only their third win of the season. Young trialist Craig Smith, who had substituted for the injured Colin West late in the Halifax match, took the veteran's place in the starting line-up and was given an object lesson in finishing when Darren Collins opened the scoring after twelve minutes. Indeed Collins should have doubled his tally after dispossessing the over-indulgent Kenny Lowe only to side-foot over from close range. However, the overworked Gateshead defence survived and, shortly after half-time, uncharacteristic hesitation by Darren Bradshaw allowed Paul Proudlock to beat Mark Smith with a clever lob to level the scores. The introduction of Adrian Foster, back after a successful operation on his previously misdiagnosed broken toe, for the luckless Craig Smith brought additional flair up front but the Diamonds continued to fritter chances, another glaring defensive error contributing to Gateshead's last gasp winner. Mark Smith's mistimed punch fell to the onrushing Nick Peverell whose shot rebounded into the net off the helpless Bradshaw. Unfortunately the game had provided a poor advertisement for Conference football for the viewers watching on national cable television - if only they had chosen the match at Nene Park the previous Saturday! The result, which had severely dented hopes of sustaining a credible title challenge, was worsened by injury to Garry Butterworth who was stretchered off five minutes from time. Craig Smith, on loan from Derby County, did not play for Diamonds again, deciding to give up football and pursue an alternative career.

Mark Cooper replaced Butterworth for his first Conference start in the next match - the derby game against Kettering Town at Rockingham Road. The Poppies had lifted themselves out of the relegation places with some stirring performances since the sides had met at Nene Park in November but were destined to suffer another heavy home defeat as Diamonds made it four out of four in the Conference meetings of the county rivals. From the moment Michael Mison *(right)* headed Kenny Cramman's perfect cross past Chris Taylor after nineteen minutes the Diamonds were in total control. Paul Underwood capitalised on poor defending by Ian Ridgway to increase the lead shortly before half-time; two goals by Colin West completed a convincing 4-0 final scoreline. There was a hint of arrogance about West's first as he coolly rounded Taylor before walking the ball into an empty goal. The second owed more to good fortune and the innate positional sense that marks the natural striker as the ball found the back of the net via his chest. Despite referee French entering ten names into his notebook (Kettering Town 4 Rushden & Diamonds 6) the game lacked the passion expected of such occasions, although Diamonds fans weren't complaining. In the national context victory took their side into second place in the table, albeit eleven points adrift of the leaders.

Struggling Stalybridge Celtic were easily despatched 3-0 with goals from Michael Mison, Darren Collins and half-time substitute Adrian Foster highlighting a competent and efficient performance. Julian Capone, recently restored to the starting line-up after a series of appearances as substitute, gave a splendid performance especially in the first half. It was, however, an unhappy return to Nene Park for Steve Cherry (still connected with the club in a coaching role) who gave a thoroughly professional display in the visiting goal but stood little chance with any of the goals. Halifax remained eleven points clear, but who were their nearest challengers, second placed Rushden & Diamonds or Cheltenham Town, games in hand but still involved in the FA Trophy?

			Home					Away					
	P	W	D	L	F	A	W	D	L	F	A	Pts
1 Halifax Town	30	13	1	0	36	8	7	6	3	19	20	**67**
2 Rushden & Diamonds	30	10	2	3	32	16	8	0	7	25	22	**56**
3 Woking	29	9	3	2	30	12	6	5	4	19	15	**53**
4 Cheltenham Town	26	9	4	0	25	10	6	3	4	17	16	**52**
5 Morecambe	29	8	3	5	27	25	7	3	3	28	14	**51**
6 Hednesford Town	30	11	3	1	22	10	3	6	6	24	28	**51**

The soccer loving poet T S Eliot once described April as '*the cruellest month*' but a glance at the Diamonds fixture list for March might have caused him to rewrite his line. The five matches scheduled for the month were against the other five clubs in the top six. And first on the agenda was the visit from Cheltenham Town on March 7th. Cheltenham's own title aspirations were constrained by a long backlog of fixtures - the price of FA Cup and Trophy success - and their hopes of taking the runners-up spot were dealt a heavy blow as the Diamonds recorded a fine 4-1 victory. In truth the Robins contributed to their own downfall conceding an unnecessary penalty, for which perpetrator Keith Knight was dismissed, and then losing Mark Freeman after the uncompromising defender had foolishly repeated a clumsy challenge on the canny Adrian Foster. The penalty, the first awarded to the Diamonds since December 21st 1996, was coolly converted by Cramman after thirty-two minutes but the eleven men were unable to make their numerical advantage count again before half-time. Reduced to nine, Cheltenham continued to hold out until the sixty-sixth minute when Capone and Underwood combined to set up Darren Collins for the elusive second. Even then the visitors might have forced their way back into the game, wing back Jamie Victory carrying the ball unchallenged into the Diamonds penalty area and beating Mark Smith with a fine shot. Within a minute, however, Adrian Foster had restored the two goal lead and Mark Cooper sealed the win with a measured forty yard shot after Robins keeper, Steve Book, had injudiciously lost possession outside his area. It was not as scintillating a performance as the one against Halifax but the Diamonds had again demonstrated that when the going gets tough, the side that loses its discipline loses the game.

Halifax's home draw with Dover meant that the gap at the top had closed to nine points and the next stern test of the Diamonds title credentials was the trip to Woking's Kingfield. Diamonds strengthened their squad by signing Farnborough's leading scorer, David Mehew. Bristol-based but Surrey-born, Mehew had been a thorn in the Diamonds side when with Bath and Farnborough. Prior to that he had made over two hundred Football League appearances, scoring over seventy goals, with Bristol Rovers and Walsall. Whilst the recent victory over the league leaders had been achieved with style and flair, the 2-0 defeat of Woking owed more to a determined, battling performance to which every team member, from Mark Smith to newcomer David Mehew *(right)*, made an immense contribution. Michael Mison, returning after a one match suspension, gave his side the perfect start with a perfect goal. Just four minutes had passed when Paul Underwood set out on a mazy crossfield run. As he approached the edge of the penalty area he released the ball to Mison who had timed his run to the far post with perfection. With Woking keeper Laurence Batty stranded, the imposing midfielder crashed the ball into the net with obvious delight. As Woking strove to get back into the match the backline of Tim Wooding, Chris Whyte, Darren Bradshaw and Kenny Cramman defended resolutely and the arrival of substitute John Hamsher early in the second half stiffened the midfield challenge. The second decisive moment of the game came in the final minute when the impressive Kevin Betsy spurned a golden opportunity to level the scores. Within seconds the ball was in the back of the Woking net. Coincidentally it was the same combination that had conspired to undo John McGovern's side back in October that created this goal. Substitute Mark Rawle's through pass found Adrian Foster who unleashed an unstoppable twenty yard strike past the helpless Batty. News of Halifax's goalless draw at Hednesford widened Brian Talbot's smile at the final whistle. Although the leaders won in midweek to widen the gap, victory at the Shay on March 21st would reduce the deficit to a mere seven points, the Diamonds having a game in hand.

			Home					Away					
		P	W	D	L	F	A	W	D	L	F	A	Pts
1	Halifax Town	33	14	2	0	42	10	7	7	3	19	20	**72**
2	Rushden & Diamonds	32	11	2	3	36	17	9	0	7	27	24	**62**
3	Woking	32	10	3	3	33	15	7	5	4	22	16	**59**
4	Cheltenham Town	28	10	4	0	26	10	6	3	5	18	20	**55**

In the context of the season to date the result at Halifax was entirely predictable. Brian Talbot's side had lost ten games, seven away from home. Halifax had lost just three and were undefeated at the Shay. Yet there was a palpable air of disappointment among the travelling Diamonds contingent as their side crashed to a 0-2 defeat. Stung by their capitulation at Nene Park six weeks earlier Halifax played like champions from the first whistle with the diminutive Jamie Paterson pulling all the midfield strings. The suspended Darren Collins was sorely missed as the Diamonds front pairing of Adrian Foster and Colin West posed little threat to a confident Halifax backline for whom Brian Kilcline was a towering presence. Yet despite their superiority the leaders failed to break the deadlock before half-time. David Mehew replaced West shortly after the interval but could do little better than his predecessor as Halifax poured relentlessly forward. With Chris Whyte in commanding form and Mark Smith at his brilliant best it seemed the Diamonds might even salvage a point as fortune continued to favour the visitors. However, shortly after Kevin Hulme had struck the Diamonds bar, a free-kick from Paterson was headed on by Kilcline and with the ever dangerous Geoff Horsfield lurking in attendance, an unfortunate Tim Wooding sliced his attempted clearance into his own net. In an unusual move Mark Rawle replaced substitute David Mehew but the final word went to Halifax and 'Man of the Match' Paterson who raced on to Mark Bradshaw's raking through pass, rounded Smith and scored with considerable aplomb. No one could deny that the Shaymen were worthy winners.

Close encounters of a hairy kind at the Shay; Paul Underwood meets Brian Kilcline.

After such a dismal result it was important that the Diamonds rediscovered their form for the Monday evening trip to Hednesford. Hednesford themselves had dropped out of the title race but had only been beaten once at home, so it was a tough task that confronted Assistant Head Coach Billy Jeffrey, deputising for the indisposed Brian Talbot. Jeffrey explained the mood of the players before the game, *"After Saturday it would have been all too easy to let the season slip away, but to a man they insisted they didn't want to waste all the good work that had gone on before."*

That resolve was amply demonstrated by the manner in which they defended a marvellous fourteenth minute strike from John Hamsher *(right)* to secure a first ever victory over the Pitmen. Mark Smith made several spectacular saves to preserve the lead but it was the tireless running of midfielder Mark Cooper, deputising for the injured Butterworth, that epitomised the Diamonds abundant spirit. Hednesford were without their injured striker Joe O'Connor which meant that defender Kevin Collins was the only man from either side who had played in Rushden & Diamonds' first ever FA Cup defeat back in September 1992.

If, after witnessing that performance, anyone had predicted that the side would win just two of its remaining eight games it's doubtful if they would have been taken seriously. After all there were still twenty-four points at stake and Halifax might just possibly falter. Yet five days later at Nene Park the Diamonds frittered an apparently unassailable lead in much the same fashion as they had way back in September against Farnborough Town. For the opening thirty-five minutes visitors Morecambe were run ragged as Julian Capone, Kenny Cramman and Paul Underwood cut through the visiting defence like a knife through polyunsaturated spread. The quality of attacking football was remarkable and on this occasion was rewarded with the goals it deserved. Darren Collins took his Conference haul to twenty-one with two goals in the first fifteen minutes, Paul Underwood adding a third twenty minutes later. Morecambe, understandably, looked a well beaten side. But then inexplicably the whole game changed. Within sixty seconds Stuart Drummond was allowed time and space to set up Andy Milner for the easiest of side foot finishes. Two minutes later wing-back Paul Burns cut in from the right and beat Mark Smith at his near post. Diamonds hung on until half-time but the equaliser, Mark Shirley robbing Tim Wooding some thirty yards out and beating the keeper with a fierce drive, came midway through a half dominated by the visitors for whom midfield duo Drummond and Brian Healy were outstanding, just as they had been at Morecambe before Christmas. Now Rushden seemed in serious danger of jeopardising the coveted runners-up spot.

More action from the Shay, this time featuring the less hirsute Chris Whyte.

There was further disappointment on April 4th when the side suffered an ignominious defeat at lowly Telford United. Diamonds were out of sorts both physically and mentally and were unable to deal with the Shropshire side's changes in tactics. When a storm from Wales swept in across the Wrekin half an hour before the start, Telford retreated indoors to complete their preparation. They began the game dry and, seemingly, on fire. Micky Norbury, who had never failed to disappoint against the Diamonds, whether it was with Stafford, Halifax or Hednesford, had a magnificent game pulling the visiting defence all over the place. Playing just behind the front two, Gez Murphy, a recent signing from Gresley, and Michael Moore, who had appeared for Stafford at Nene Park when they conceded six pulled the Rushden defence out of shape with their purposeful running. At the back, Simeon Hodson, sweeping behind the two conventional central defenders, played impressively and hugely enjoyed his first encounter with his former colleagues. After ex West Bromwich Albion midfielder Craig Shakespeare had volleyed Telford in front, Murphy tapped in a second and the twenty minute mark had not yet been reached. Over-elaboration in the Diamonds defence created the opportunity for Moore to extend the lead to three in the second half. Telford then withdrew Moore and introduced an extra defender, a move which worked in Diamonds' favour. Telford's defence was not their strong point and with fifteen minutes left, Darren Collins took advantage of a basic goalkeeping error to give Rushden a glimmer of hope. Immediately Jim Rodwell joined the fray instead of Julian Capone but the move did not work. Telford countered by putting on the extra pace of Brian Gray and he broke clear to set up Murphy's second and Telford's fourth. There was just time for Mark Cooper to make the score a little more respectable and get himself booked. Cooper scored directly from a free-kick - or so he thought. Referee Mark Warren, soon to be promoted to the Nationwide League and who, three months later ran the line at the World Cup Final, said he had taken it too quickly and produced the yellow card. Cooper replaced the ball, waited for the whistle, and again fired into the net.

Yet again Diamonds bounced back from a dismal display with a much improved performance thought they had to wait longer than expected for the opportunity. Heavy - to put it lightly - rain caused the Nene to flood and on Easter Saturday morning the car parks at Nene Park were under several inches of water. The pitch itself was just about playable but as it was impossible to cater adequately and safely for spectators the game against Leek Town was called off. Instead Diamonds were able to redeem themselves at Stalybridge Celtic on Easter Monday. Celtic were effectively relegated, though it was not yet mathematically certain. Striker Lee Trundle did his best to make it so, receiving a red card for elbowing Tim Wooding with only seven minutes played. The ten men actually took the lead through Brendan Burke but Darren Collins equalised before the break and Mark Cooper put Diamonds in front shortly after. In total control, Collins completed the fourth hat-trick of his Nene Park career before Celtic secured an injury time consolation. Paul Underwood came on for the final quarter of an hour, but an injury meant that this was his last appearance of the season. With Garry Butterworth and Michael Mison also ruled out for the remainder of the season, midfield was going to cause some interesting selection problems for the Head Coach for the remaining five games.

The visit of relegation threatened Leek Town, with an horrendous back log of fixtures, was rescheduled for the following Saturday, just one week after its postponement, thanks to some astute fixture juggling by the Conference. With so many midfield players absent Brian Talbot included Jim Rodwell for his first Conference start since September 27th. But Leek, sensing an escape route under caretaker manager Mike Pejic, were the major contributors to the script. Ahead in the twenty-eighth minute through Hugh McAuley's splendid goal they successfully defended the lead to the end despite half-time substitutions which brought on David Mehew and Warren Kelly (his first appearance of 1998) for the unimpressive Foster and Rodwell. Supporters' disappointment was compounded by post match news that Halifax had beaten Kidderminster Harriers to take the Conference title, not that anyone could have been remotely surprised.

With so much fixture congestion caused by the April rains, one was forced to wonder why the Conference visit of Yeovil Town had always been scheduled for Tuesday April 21st. Surely it would be more sensible to keep midweeks at this time of the year blank to cater for late postponements? It would certainly have been better for Rushden & Diamonds had this fixture been scheduled for earlier in the season, not least because it would undoubtedly have attracted considerably more than the lowest Nene Park Conference gate, 1784. Those who attended saw plenty of entertainment, even though most of it was at the vacant east end of the ground. It was another Hyde and Jekyll performance, highly reminiscent of the Morecambe encounter. This time the Diamonds dominated the opening forty-five minutes and established a two goal lead. Darren Collins opened the scoring after ten minutes as Rushden threatened to over-run the west country side but it was a further half hour before the second goal arrived. It was well worth the wait. When David Mehew collected the ball wide on the left he appeared to have limited options. Few, least of all Yeovil keeper Tony Pennock, expected him to turn and chip into the far corner of the net from the narrowest of angles. However, those with memories of his remarkable late equaliser in the early season 5-5 draw with Farnborough could correct anyone ignorant enough to shout *'fluke!'* There was also nothing lucky about the unstoppable shot with which the precocious Ben Smith reduced the arrears seven minutes into the second half. By now Steve Stott, relishing his return to Nene Park, and Steve Thompson had imposed a stranglehold in midfield and, with Lee Archer donated hectares of space, it was no surprise when sustained Yeovil pressure brought a sixty-first minute equaliser. Smith turned provider this time, conjuring a goal for Sam Winston. Like fellow ex-Diamond Stott, Al-James Hannigan could derive considerable pleasure both from his own performance and the eventual result.

There was a carnival atmosphere amongst a crowd of 3,055 at Edgar Street, Hereford to see the home side wind up its first home Conference programme. Many had turned up because there was still the prospect of financially troubled United being wound-up in court, though, as usual in these cases, the threat was averted and this wasn't their last home match. It was another game of two distinctly different halves as the Diamonds improved on a poor first half display to salvage a point with a late goal from Darren Collins. Mark Smith was beaten as early as the third minute by a speculative shot by veteran Tony Agana and with good football very much at a premium on a hard, bumpy surface the Diamonds played second fiddle to their former Football League opponents for much of the first period. In another bold half time substitution Colin West and Julian Capone replaced David Mehew and Mark Cooper and, with the wind at their backs, the visitors gradually forced their way into game. Adrian Foster, a sixty-fifth minute substitute for Brendan Hackett and again the target for the Hereford boo boys, missed a good opportunity, miskicking Capone's cross in front of a gaping goal. It was Darren Collins who earned the deserved point hooking home Colin West's fortuitous pass four minutes from the end of a generally dour encounter. Meanwhile, Woking's victory at Northwich dropped the Diamonds to third place.

There were echoes of the early season struggle in the penultimate game against Welling United on April 28th as the visitors snatched victory through a Ritchie Hanlon header in the final minute. Brian Talbot included three strikers, Collins, Mehew and West, but a combination of poor service from midfield and slipshod finishing failed to breach a determined Welling defence. Other than the goal, scored by a man who within a month had signed for the Diamonds, there was little of significance for a new record low Conference crowd of Nene Park, just 1459. This match, like the fixture at Hereford, was controlled by a Nationwide League referee. In neither game was a player booked; in the other forty games at least one man was shown the yellow card. Significant or a coincidence?

For the second successive season relegation hung like a dark cloud over the visitors to Nene Park for the last game of the season. This time though the visitors still had a chance of escaping. It was likely that only a victory would save Telford United's Conference place, though it also depended on how Farnborough and Leek fared. The three clubs were battling to avoid the one remaining relegation spot - Gateshead and Stalybridge Celtic had booked the other two. It was an afternoon of tremendous drama and tremendous emotion - if you were a Telford fan. Diamonds fans were able to sit back and enjoy the spectacle, knowing that there was little at stake for their team, acknowledging that they would probably finish fourth now that Cheltenham had won their games in hand and moved up to second place. The Telford supporters arrived in a wide variety of fancy dress, determined to enjoy the day, even if it turned out to be their last in the Conference. Their club boasted a proud record of longevity in non-League fooball's elite. Founder members of the Conference in 1979, they were one of only three of those twenty clubs who had maintained continuous membership. Prior to 1979 they had been members of the Southern League Premier Division since its inception in 1959. For thirty-nine seasons they had avoided relegation, although once it took a technicality, Wimbledon's election to the Football League, to keep that record. At various times during the afternoon all three threatened clubs - Farnborough, Leek and Telford - occupied the third relegation spot, as the scores and fortunes changed. In fact Telford were out of the bottom three after fewer than four minutes, scorer Gez Murphy again proving to be a major problem for the Diamonds defence. Darren Collins equalised before the interval and early in the second half visiting fans became agitated as scores elsewhere moved them back to the dreaded twentieth place. But the wigs were thrown in the air again in the sixty-third minute when Murphy restored United's lead and propelled them two places up the table. With just under twenty minutes left the nerves of the fancy-dressed approached breaking point as Colin West equalised. Two minutes later it was total despair in the Airwair Stand as referee Jordan, bidding farewell to the Conference on his promotion to the Nationwide, pointed to the penalty spot at the Peter DeBanke end. Darren Collins converted, Diamonds were in front and Telford fans didn't need confirmation of other scores to know they were definitely down. The postscript is that the agony and depression that Telford supporters suffered was unnecessary. At the Conference's AGM, there was such doubt about the ability of unrepresented Slough Town to continue in business that they were expelled. Telford United were invited back; their run continues.

For once at Nene Park it had been Rushden & Diamonds who had been given the minor role in the proceedings but they responded with a determined performance in which there were a number of landmarks. Darren Collins took his Conference goals to twenty-nine to finish second in the chart behind Halifax's Horsfield and there were final appearances for Warren Kelly and Brendan Hackett. Hackett could look back on his Nene Park career with considerable pride. He had, in the match at Telford, become the thirteenth player to make a century of appearances for Rushden & Diamonds but he was unwilling to go full-time and soon signed for Burton Albion.

There was disappointment at the time that Halifax could not be caught but they had a formidable record and they finished a long way ahead of the rest. A final position of fourth, having genuinely challenged for the title, will, in the fullness of time, be regarded as a considerable achievement. Six short years previously there had been no Rushden and Diamonds Football Club. 1998-99 begins with a full complement of full-time players. Expectations will be higher than ever.

Vauxhall Conference 1997-1998

			Home					Away					
		P	W	D	L	F	A	W	D	L	F	A	Pts
1	Halifax Town (19)	42	17	4	0	51	15	8	8	5	23	28	**87**
2	Cheltenham Town (-)	42	15	4	2	39	15	8	5	8	24	28	**78**
3	Woking (5)	42	14	3	4	47	22	8	5	8	25	24	**74**
4	Rushden & Diamonds (12)	42	12	4	5	44	26	11	1	9	35	31	**74**
5	Morecambe (4)	42	11	4	6	35	30	10	6	5	42	34	**73**
6	Hereford United (-)	42	11	7	3	30	19	7	6	8	26	30	**67**
7	Hednesford Town (8)	42	14	4	3	28	12	4	8	9	31	38	**66**
8	Slough Town (16)	42	10	6	5	34	21	8	4	9	24	28	**64**
9	Northwich Victoria (6)	42	8	9	4	34	24	7	6	8	29	35	**60**
10	Welling United (18)	42	11	5	5	39	27	6	4	11	25	35	**60**
11	Yeovil Town (-)	42	14	3	4	45	24	3	5	13	28	39	**59**
12	Hayes (15)	42	10	4	7	36	25	6	6	9	26	27	**58**
13	Dover Athletic (17)	42	10	4	7	34	29	5	6	10	26	41	**55**
14	Kettering Town (14)	42	8	6	7	29	29	5	7	9	24	31	**52**
15	Stevenage Borough (3)	42	8	8	5	35	27	5	4	12	24	36	**51**
16	Southport (11)	42	9	5	7	32	26	4	6	11	24	32	**50**
17	Kidderminster Harriers (2)	42	6	8	7	32	31	5	6	10	24	32	**47**
18	Farnborough Town (7)	42	10	3	8	37	27	2	5	14	19	43	**44**
19	Leek Town (-)	42	8	8	5	34	26	2	6	13	18	41	**44**
20	Telford United (9)	42	6	7	8	25	31	4	5	12	28	45	**42**
21	Gateshead (10)	42	7	6	8	32	35	1	5	15	19	52	**35**
22	Stalybridge Celtic (13)	42	6	5	10	33	38	1	3	17	15	55	**29**

Figures in brackets are 1996-97 positions.

- Halifax Town were promoted to Nationwide Division Three.
- Relegated to the Conference from Division Three were Doncaster Rovers.
- Promoted from the Unibond League were champions Barrow, from the Ryman League champions Kingstonian and from the Dr Martens League champions Forest Green Rovers.
- Gateshead and Stalybridge Celtic were relegated to the Unibond League and Telford United were relegated to the Dr Martens League. To maintain the correct numbers, Boston United transferred from the Unibond to the Dr Martens and Hastings Town transferred from the Dr Martens to the Ryman. However at the Conference's AGM, the non-attendance of Slough Town and the club's inability to provide any assurances about its future caused Slough to be expelled and Telford reinstated.
- The Dr Martens League lost Hastings Town (transferred to the ICIS), Dudley Town (resigned before the start of the 97-98 season), Waterlooville (merged with Havant Town) and Trowbridge Town (resigned). They were replaced by Andover, Bloxwich Town, Folkestone Invicta and Stamford.

1997-1998 Results

Vauxhall Conference

Aug	16	Northwich Victoria	H	0	1		2302
Aug	20	Farnborough Town	A	0	2		905
Aug	23	Leek Town	A	0	2		809
Aug	25	Hednesford Town	H	1	1	Collins	2468
Aug	30	Gateshead	H	3	2	Mison, Ndah, Collins	2211
Sep	2	Slough Town	A	2	1	Collins, Mison	872
Sep	7	Cheltenham Town	A	0	2		1614
Sep	13	Farnborough Town	H	5	5	Foster 4, Underwood	2051
Sep	20	Yeovil Town	A	2	1	Collins, Hackett	2317
Sep	27	Southport	A	2	3	Foster, Rawle	1116
Oct	4	Woking	H	2	1	Mison, Foster	2837
Oct	11	Hereford United	H	1	0	Collins	2728
Oct	18	Kidderminster Harriers	A	2	1	Mison, Cramman	2210
Nov	1	Slough Town	H	0	1		2193
Nov	8	Welling United	A	1	0	Underwood	833
Nov	15	Kidderminster Harriers	H	4	1	Barnwell 3, Collins	2234
Nov	22	Morecambe	A	1	3	Capone	1449
Nov	25	Kettering Town	H	1	0	Collins	3866
Nov	29	Hayes	H	1	3	own goal	2158
Dec	6	Northwich Victoria	A	4	2	own goal, Capone, Collins 2	932
Dec	13	Dover Athletic	H	4	1	Collins 2, West 2	2284
Dec	20	Hayes	A	2	1	Collins, Hackett	679
Dec	26	Stevenage Borough	H	2	0	West, Capone	3527
Jan	1	Stevenage Borough	A	1	2	Collins	3107
Jan	17	Southport	H	1	0	Collins	2477
Jan	24	Dover Athletic	A	3	0	Underwood, Alford 2	1280
Feb	7	Halifax Town	H	4	0	Collins 2, Butterworth, Underwood	3675
Feb	14	Gateshead	A	1	2	Collins	616
Feb	21	Kettering Town	A	4	0	Mison, Underwood, West 2	4016
Feb	28	Stalybridge Celtic	H	3	0	Mison, Collins, Foster	2470
Mar	7	Cheltenham Town	H	4	1	Cramman (p), Collins, Foster, Cooper	3857
Mar	14	Woking	A	2	0	Mison, Foster	3930
Mar	21	Halifax Town	A	0	2		3951
Mar	23	Hednesford Town	A	1	0	Hamsher	1342
Mar	28	Morecambe	H	3	3	Collins 2, Underwood	2758
Apr	4	Telford United	A	2	4	Collins, Cooper	893
Apr	13	Stalybridge Celtic	A	4	2	Collins 3, Cooper	952
Apr	18	Leek Town	H	0	1		2064
Apr	21	Yeovil Town	H	2	2	Collins, Mehew	1784
Apr	25	Hereford United	A	1	1	Collins	3055
Apr	28	Welling United	H	0	1		1459
May	2	Telford United	H	3	2	Collins 2 (1 pen), West	2197

1997-1998 Results

FA Cup

Oct 25	4Q	Boreham Wood	H	1	1	Butterworth	2107
Oct 28	4QR	Boreham Wood	A	0	1		704

FA Trophy

Jan 10	1	Farnborough Town	H	3	2	Cramman, Collins 2	2154
Jan 31	2	Cheltenham Town	A	1	3	Collins	2058

Spalding Cup

Oct 7	1	Hayes	A	0	2		438

NFA Hillier Senior Cup

Nov 18	QF	Brackley Town	A	3	1	Collins 3	235
Jan 27	SF	Raunds Town	H	0	1		868

- The FA Cup was won by Arsenal who beat Newcastle United 2-0 in the final. Four non League sides reached the Third Round proper: Cheltenham Town drew at home with Reading but lost the replay 1-2, Emley lost 1-2 at West Ham United, Hereford United lost at home to Tranmere Rovers and Stevenage Borough beat First Division Swindon Town 2-1 at Swindon. In the Fourth Round Stevenage drew 1-1 with Newcastle United at home but lost the replay 1-2 at St. James's Park. The four non-League sides that qualified for the Third Round all beat Football League opposition: Emley (Lincoln City), Hednesford Town (Hull City), Hereford United (Brighton & Hove Albion and Colchester United) and Stevenage Borough (Cambridge United and Swindon Town)

- In the FA Trophy final, Cheltenham Town beat Southport 1-0. Dale Watkins gained a winners medal. The beaten semi-finalists were Dover Athletic and Slough Town.

- In the Spalding Cup Morecambe beat Woking in the two-legged final.

- The Hillier Senior Cup was won by Kettering Town who beat Raunds Town in the final.

1997-1998 Teams   Vauxhall Conference

(see next page for Conference appearances not included in this table)

		Alford	Barnwell-Ed	Bradshaw	Branston	Butterworth	Capone	Cherry	Collins	Cooper	Cramman	Foster	Fuff	Hackett	Hamsher	Hodson	Kelly	Mehew	Mison	Ndah	Peaks	Rawle	Rodwell	MSmith	Stott	Underwoods	Watts	West	Whyte	Wooding
Northwich	H	10					9	1	7		11					2			4		6		5		sb	3				
Farnboro	A	10					7	1	9		11					2			4	sb	6		5		sb	3				
Leek	A						7	1	10		11				sb	2			4	9	6		5		8	3				
Hednesford	H					8		1	10		3			11	2	2			4	9	6		5							
Gateshead	H	sb				8		1	10		3			11	2				4	9	6		5			sb				
Slough	A	sb				8		1	10		3		6	11	2				4	9			5			sb				
Cheltenham	A	9				8		1	10		3	sb	6	11	2								5		4	sb				
Farnboro	H					8		1	10		3	9	6	7	2				4				5			11				
Yeovil	A					8			10		3	9		7	sb		sb		4			sb	5			11	1		6	2
Southport	A					8			10		sb	9		7	sb		3		4			sb	5			11	1		6	2
Woking	H					8			10		3	9	5	2			7		4			sb				11	1		6	
Hereford	H				5	8			10		3	9		2			7		4							11	1		6	
Kiddrmnstr	A				5	8			10		3	9					7		4					1		11			6	2
Slough	H		sb	8	5		sb		10		3	9		sb			7		4					1		11			6	2
Welling	A		9	8	5		sb		10		3			2			7		4					1		11			6	
Kiddrmnstr	H		9	7	5	8			10		3			sb					4					1		11			6	2
Morecambe	A		9	7	5	8	sb		10		3			sb		2								1		11			6	
Kettering	H		9	4	5	8	sb		10		3			2			7						sb	1		11			6	
Hayes	H			4	5	8	sb		10		3			11			7					sb		1				9	6	
Northwich	A			3	5	8	7		10					11					4					1				9	6	2
Dover	H			3	5	8	7		10					11	sb		sb		4					1				9	6	2
Hayes	A			3		8	7		10					11	5				4					1				9	6	2
Stevenage	H			3		8	7		10					11	5				4					1				9	6	2
Stevenage	A			3	sb	8	7		10					11	5				4			sb		1				9	6	2
Southport	H			3		8	sb		10		4			7	5									1		11		9	6	2
Dover	A	10		3		8	sb				5				7				4					1		11		9	6	2
Halifax	H			3		8	sb		10	sb	5				7				4					1		11		9	6	2
Gateshead	A			3		8	sb		10	sb	5	sb			7				4					1		11			6	2
Kettering	A			3		8	7		10	8	5	sb		sb					4					1		11		9	6	2
Stalybridge	H			3		8	7		10	sb	5	sb			sb				4					1		11		9	6	2
Cheltenham	H			3		8	7		10	4	5	9			sb								sb	1		11			6	2
Woking	A			3		8	7				5	9			sb			10	4			sb		1		11			6	2
Halifax	A			3		8	sb				5	10			7			sb	4			sb		1		11		9	6	2
Hednesford	A			3					10	8	5	9			7			sb	4					1		11			6	2
Morecambe	H			3			7		10	8	5	9		sb	sb			sb	4					1		11			6	2
Telford	A			3		8	7		10	4	5	sb		sb	11			9					sb	1					6	2
Stalybridge	A			3			7		10	8	5	9		11	4									1		sb			6	2
Leek	H			3			7		10		5	9		11	4		sb	sb				sb	8	1					6	2
Yeovil	H			3			7		10	8	5			11	4		sb	9						1					6	2
Hereford	A						sb		10	8	5	sb		11	4		7	9					3	1				sb	6	2
Welling	H			3			sb		10	8	5				4		11	7						1				9	6	2
Telford	H			3			7		10	sb	5			11	4		8	sb						1				9	6	2

1997-1998 Additional Conference appearances:

Cann- sb Leek A. *Chapman*- sb Cheltenham A; sb Hayes H. *Cotterell*- 2 Hayes H.
Crosby- 7 Hednesford H; 7 Gateshead H; 7 Slough A; 7 Cheltenham A.
Ndekwe- sb Kidderminster A; sb Dover H. *O'Shea*- 4 Morecambe A.
C Smith- sb Halifax H; 9 Gateshead A.
Stapleton- 8 Northwich H; 8 Farnborough A. *Sterling*- sb Northwich H.

1997-1998 Teams Cup competitions

		Alford	Bradshaw	Branston	Butterworth	Capone	Collins	Cooper	Cramman	Foster	Fuff	Furnell	Hackett	Hamsher	Kelly	Mison	Ndekwe	Peaks	Rawle	Rodwell	M Smith	Talbot	Underwood	Watts	Whyte	Wooding
FA Cup																										
Boreham W	H				8	sb	10		3	9					7	4			sb	5	1		11		6	2
Boreham W	A				8	sb	10		3	9			sb		7	4			sb	5	1		11		6	2
FA Trophy																										
Farnboro	H	9	3		8	7	10		4				11	5							1		sb		6	2
Cheltenham	A	9	3		8	sb	10	sb	5					7		4	sb				1		11		6	2
Spalding Cup																										
Hayes	A				8		10		3	9	5		7	sb		4		2	sb				11	1	6	sb
Hillier Cup																										
Brackley	A			5		3	10				6	9		sb		4	sb			7		8	11	1		2
Raunds	H	9	3		8	sb		10	5				11	7		4	sb			6				1		2

Goalscorers

	L	C	T	LC	CC	Total
Darren COLLINS	29		3		3	35
Adrian FOSTER	9					9
Michael MISON	7					7
Paul UNDERWOOD	6					6
Colin WEST	6					6
Jamie BARNWELL-EDINBORO	3					3
Julian CAPONE	3					3
Mark COOPER	3					3
Kenny CRAMMAN	2		1			3
Carl ALFORD	2					2
Brendan HACKETT	2					2
Garry BUTTERWORTH	1	1				2
John HAMSHER	1					1
David MEHEW	1					1
Jamie NDAH	1					1
Mark RAWLE	1					1
own goal	2					2
TOTAL	79	1	4	0	3	87

1997-1998 Appearances

	Start						Substitute						Total					
	L	C	T	LC	CC	Tot	L	C	T	LC	CC	Tot	L	C	T	LC	CC	Tot
Carl ALFORD	4		2		1	**7**	2					**2**	6		2		1	**9**
Jamie BARNWELL-ED	4					**4**	1					**1**	5					**5**
Darren BRADSHAW	28		2		1	**31**						**0**	28		2		1	**31**
Guy BRANSTON	10				1	**11**	1					**1**	11				1	**12**
Garry BUTTERWORTH	28	2	2	1	1	**34**						**0**	28	2	2	1	1	**34**
Adam CANN						**0**	1					**1**	1					**1**
Julian CAPONE	18		1		1	**20**	12	2	1		1	**16**	30	2	2		2	**36**
Andy CHAPMAN						**0**	2					**2**	2					**2**
Steve CHERRY	8					**8**						**0**	8					**8**
Darren COLLINS	39	2	2	1	1	**45**						**0**	39	2	2	1	1	**45**
Mark COOPER	9				1	**10**	4		1			**5**	13		1		1	**15**
Leo COTTERELL	1					**1**						**0**	1					**1**
Kenny CRAMMAN	36	2	2	1	1	**42**	1					**1**	37	2	2	1	1	**43**
Gary CROSBY	4					**4**						**0**	4					**4**
Adrian FOSTER	14	2		1		**17**	6					**6**	20	2		1		**23**
Glen FUFF	4			1	1	**6**						**0**	4			1	1	**6**
Andy FURNELL					1	**1**						**0**					1	**1**
Brendan HACKETT	23		1	1	1	**26**	6	1				**7**	29	1	1	1	1	**33**
John HAMSHER	21		2		1	**24**	8			1	1	**10**	29		2	1	2	**34**
Simeon HODSON	4					**4**						**0**	4					**4**
Warren KELLY	11	2				**13**	4					**4**	15	2				**17**
David MEHEW	5					**5**	5					**5**	10					**10**
Michael MISON	29	2	1	1	2	**35**						**0**	29	2	1	1	2	**35**
Jamie NDAH	4					**4**	1					**1**	5					**5**
Malcolm NDEKWE						**0**	2		1		2	**5**	2		1		2	**5**
Andy PEAKS	5			1		**6**						**0**	5			1		**6**
Mark RAWLE						**0**	8	2		1		**11**	8	2		1		**11**
Jim RODWELL	12	2			2	**16**	3					**3**	15	2			2	**19**
Craig SMITH	1					**1**	1					**1**	2					**2**
Mark SMITH	30	2	2			**34**						**0**	30	2	2			**34**
Simon STAPLETON	2					**2**						**0**	2					**2**
Worrell STERLING						**0**	1					**1**	1					**1**
Steve STOTT	2					**2**	2					**2**	4					**4**
Danny O'SHEA	1					**1**					1	**1**	1				1	**2**
Brian TALBOT					1	**1**						**0**					1	**1**
Paul UNDERWOOD	25	2	1	1	1	**30**	4		1			**5**	29	2	2	1	1	**35**
Darren WATTS	4			1	2	**7**						**0**	4			1	2	**7**
Colin WEST	14					**14**	1					**1**	15					**15**
Chris WHYTE	34	2	2	1		**39**						**0**	34	2	2	1		**39**
Tim WOODING	28	2	2		2	**34**				1		**1**	28	2	2	1	2	**35**
MAXIMUM	42	2	2	1	2	49							42	2	2	1	2	49

1997-98 Playing Record

	P	W	D	L	F	A	Pts
HOME							
League	21	12	4	5	44	26	40
FA Cup	1	0	1	0	1	1	
FA Trophy	1	1	0	0	3	2	
League Cup	-	-	-	-	-	-	
County Cup	1	0	0	1	0	1	
TOTAL	24	13	5	6	48	30	
AWAY							
League	21	11	1	9	35	31	34
FA Cup	1	0	0	1	0	1	
FA Trophy	1	0	0	1	1	3	
League Cup	1	0	0	1	0	2	
County Cup	1	1	0	0	3	1	
TOTAL	25	12	1	12	39	38	
TOTAL							
League	42	23	5	14	79	57	74
FA Cup	2	0	1	1	1	2	
FA Trophy	2	1	0	1	4	5	
League Cup	1	0	0	1	0	2	
County Cup	2	1	0	1	3	2	
TOTAL	**49**	**25**	**6**	**18**	**87**	**68**	

Attendance Summary

	Total	Ave	High		Low	
HOME						
League	53600	2552	3866	Kettering	1459	Welling
FA Cup	2107	2107	2107	Boreham Wood	2107	Boreham Wood
FA Trophy	2154	2154	2154	Farnborough	2154	Farnborough
League Cup	-	-	-		-	
County Cup	868	868	868	Raunds	868	Raunds
TOTAL	58729	2447	3866	Kettering	868	Raunds
AWAY						
League	36878	1756	4016	Kettering	616	Gateshead
FA Cup	704	704	704	Boreham Wood	704	Boreham Wood
FA Trophy	2058	2058	2058	Cheltenham	2058	Cheltenham
League Cup	438	438	438	Hayes	438	Hayes
County Cup	235	235	235	Brackley	235	Brackley
TOTAL	40313	1613	4016	Kettering	235	Brackley
TOTAL						
League	90478	2154	4016	Kettering A	616	Gatreshead A
FA Cup	2811	1406	2107	Boreham Wd H	704	Boreham Wd A
FA Trophy	4212	2106	2154	Farnboro H	2058	Cheltenham A
League Cup	438	438	438	Hayes A	438	Hayes A
County Cup	1103	552	868	Raunds H	235	Brackley A
TOTAL	**99042**	**2021**	**4016**	Kettering A	**235**	Brackley A

THE MANAGEMENT

***Roger Ashby**'s playing career was inextricably linked to Kettering Town for whom he made over 600 first team appearances between 1967 and 1981, including the FA Trophy final in 1979. His first managerial post was with Irthlingborough Diamonds whom he took to the United Counties championship in 1983 before moving to Wolverton Town of the Isthmian League. Within a season Wolverton were transformed from a bottom of the table team into one which won promotion. His next move was to Rushden Town, winning promotion from the Beazer Homes Midland Division as runners-up to Halesowen Town in 1991.*

***Billy Jeffrey** began his professional career at Oxford United making his debut at home to Fulham in 1973 and becoming Oxford's youngest ever first team player. In 1981, after making over 300 appearances for Oxford, he joined Blackpool for a brief spell before signing for Northampton Town for just over a season. From there he moved to Kettering Town and, after a year in Australia, Rushden Town.*

***Brian Talbot** began his professional career at his home town club, Ipswich Town, making his debut in February 1974 in a 1-0 win at Burnley which moved Ipswich up to third place in Division One (or the Premiership as it would now be). He made debut for England in the Home Championship at Windsor Park in May 1977, coming on to replace Ray Wilkins. A week later he made his first start for England, at Wembley against Scotland. He then played in all three matches of England's tour of South America against Brazil, Argentina and Uruguay. At the end of the following season he won an FA Cup winners medal when Ipswich beat Arsenal 1-0 and three weeks later won his sixth cap against Australia in Sydney. In January 1979 he was sold by Ipswich to Arsenal for £450,000, just under the then English record figure of £480,000. At the end of the season he won his second FA Cup winners medal in one of the most dramatic finals of all time when Arsenal beat Manchester United 3-2, with Talbot scoring the first goal. A year later, though, he was on the losing side as Trevor Brooking scored the only goal for West Ham. Managerially he has been at West Bromwich Albion, Aldershot and Maltese club Hibernian.*

STATISTICAL SUMMARY

The final section lists aggregate statistics for appearances, goalscorers, playing record and attendances for the first six seasons of Rushden & Diamonds Football Club.

Goalscorers Aug 1992 - May 1998

This table shows the total number of goals scored during the first six seasons of Rushden & Diamonds FC. The order is determined by (i) the total number of goals; (ii) the total number of league goals; (iii) alphabetic order of surname.

	L	C	T	LC	CC	Totl
Darren COLLINS	84	12	11	7	5	**119**
Dale WATKINS	74	5	5	6	8	**98**
Mickey NUTTELL	44	3	2	3	11	**63**
Andy KIRKUP	36	1	2	4	5	**48**
Adie MANN	26	4	5	7	2	**44**
Kevin WILKIN	29	8	1	2	3	**43**
Glen DONEGAL	12	1	5	6	2	**26**
Carl ALFORD	22	2		1		**25**
Ollie KEARNS	10			3	3	**16**
John FLOWER	11		1	2	1	**15**
Ian KING	9	1	2	2	1	**15**
Richard BAILEY	11			1		**12**
Brendan HACKETT	11	1				**12**
Glen BEECH	8				3	**11**
Tim WOODING	6		1	2	2	**11**
Kenny CRAMMAN	8		1	1		**10**
Adrian FOSTER	9					**9**
David LEWORTHY	8					**8**
Dougie KEAST	5		1	1	1	**8**
Paul YORK	5		1	2		**8**
Michael MISON	7					**7**
Garry BUTTERWORTH	6	1				**7**
Julian CAPONE	6				1	**7**
Frank BELFON	4	1		1	1	**7**
Dave JOHNSON	6					**6**
Paul UNDERWOOD	6					**6**
Colin WEST	6					**6**

	L	C	T	LC	CC	Totl
Barrington LESLIE	5				1	**6**
Colin WAITE	5				1	**6**
Paul RICHARDSON	4	1			1	**5**
Al James HANNIGAN	3	2				**5**
Nick ASHBY	4					**4**
Paul COE	4					**4**
Jim RODWELL	4					**4**
Jamie BARNWELL-E	3					**3**
Mark COOPER	3					**3**
Shaun DIVER	3					**3**
Steve STOTT	3					**3**
Steve SPOONER	2		1			**3**
Andy FURNELL		3				**3**
Simon STAPLETON	2					**2**
Junior WILSON	2					**2**
John COE	1					**1**
John HAMSHER	1					**1**
Mark JAMESON	1					**1**
David MEHEW	1					**1**
Jamie NDAH	1					**1**
Mark RAWLE	1					**1**
Neil SMITH	1					**1**
Terry WILSON	1					**1**
Steve HOLDEN					1	**1**
Alan KURILA				1		**1**
Simon MASON					1	**1**
own goal	8				1	**9**
TOTAL	532	46	40	52	54	724

Appearances Aug 1992 - May 1998

This table shows the total number of appearances made during the first six seasons of Rushden & Diamonds FC. The order is determined by (i) the total number of appearances; (ii) the total number of starting appearances; (iii) the total number of league appearances; (iv) alphabetic order of surname.

	Start						Substitute						Total					
	L	C	T	LC	CC	Totl	L	C	T	LC	CC	Ttl	L	C	T	LC	CC	Totl
Andy PEAKS	143	12	14	15	12	**196**	3	4		2		9	146	16	14	17	12	**205**
Darren COLLINS	146	15	15	13	10	**199**	3			1	1	5	149	15	15	14	11	**204**
Garry BUTTERWORTH	152	14	14	11	10	**201**						0	152	14	14	11	10	**201**
Tim WOODING	118	15	12	11	11	**167**	3			2		5	121	15	12	13	11	**172**
Andy KIRKUP	86	12	5	13	9	**125**	23	4	3	6	5	41	109	16	8	19	14	**166**
Dale WATKINS	98	10	8	13	9	**138**	20	1	1		2	24	118	11	9	13	11	**162**
Dave JOHNSON	107	10	17	15	9	**158**						0	107	10	17	15	9	**158**
Paul YORK	93	10	9	15	7	**134**	10		5	1	1	17	103	10	14	16	8	**151**
John FLOWER	93	8	10	14	10	**135**	1		1			2	94	8	11	14	10	**137**
Adie MANN	74	9	8	13	8	**112**	10		5	1	2	18	84	9	13	14	10	**130**
Mickey NUTTELL	68	9	10	11	9	**107**	5	1	1	1		8	73	10	11	12	9	**115**
Darrell PAGE	80	8	6	11	8	**113**		1				1	80	9	6	11	8	**114**
Brendan HACKETT	76	2	2	5	4	**89**	13	3				16	89	5	2	5	4	**105**
Kevin FOX	72	2	7	7	11	**99**						0	72	2	7	7	11	**99**
Kevin WILKIN	46	10	1	4	5	**66**	23	1	1	3	1	29	69	11	2	7	6	**95**
Kenny CRAMMAN	73	5	3	4	1	**86**	3					3	76	5	3	4	1	**89**
Nick ASHBY	60	8	1	3	3	**75**						0	60	8	1	3	3	**75**
Dougie KEAST	48	1	10	8	6	**73**	2					2	50	1	10	8	6	**75**
Ian KING	38	5	8	6	2	**59**	14		1		1	16	52	5	9	6	3	**75**
Jim RODWELL	53	8	1	2	3	**67**	3					3	56	8	1	2	3	**70**
Richard BAILEY	18		4	5	1	**28**	26	7	1	5	3	42	44	7	5	10	4	**70**
Glen BEECH	50	2		4	5	**61**	3	1	2		2	8	53	3	2	4	7	**69**
Carl ALFORD	46	3	3	1	2	**55**	6			1		7	52	3	3	2	2	**62**
Martin DAVIES	44	6	5	5	1	**61**						0	44	6	5	5	1	**61**
Steve STOTT	50	3	2	2		**57**	4					4	54	3	2	2		**61**
Julian CAPONE	30		2		1	**33**	16	4	1	2	4	27	46	4	3	2	5	**60**
Graham BENSTEAD	45	6	1	2	4	**58**						0	45	6	1	2	4	**58**
Neil SMITH	39	8	1	3	5	**56**	1			1		2	40	8	1	4	5	**58**
Steve SPOONER	27		7	5	6	**45**	10	2		1		13	37	2	7	6	6	**58**
Paul RICHARDSON	37	6	1	6	2	**52**	1					1	38	6	1	6	2	**53**
Glen DONEGAL	33	2	5	6	4	**50**	2					2	35	2	5	6	4	**52**
Kevin SHOEMAKE	28	7	5	9	1	**50**						0	28	7	5	9	1	**50**
Colin WAITE	31	2	4	5	3	**45**	2				1	3	33	2	4	5	4	**48**
Al James HANNIGAN	31	5	1	2	4	**43**	2					2	33	5	1	2	4	**45**
Chris WHYTE	34	2	2	1		**39**						0	34	2	2	1		**39**
Ollie KEARNS	15	1	2	3	2	**23**	11			1	1	13	26	1	2	4	3	**36**
Michael MISON	29	2	1	1	2	**35**						0	29	2	1	1	2	**35**
Paul UNDERWOOD	25	2	1	1	1	**30**	4		1			5	29	2	2	1	1	**35**
Mark SMITH	30	2	2			**34**						0	30	2	2			**34**
John HAMSHER	21		2		1	**24**	8			1	1	10	29		2	1	2	**34**
Junior WILSON	16	1		3	3	**23**	9		1	1		11	25	1	1	4	3	**34**
Darren BRADSHAW	28		2		1	**31**						0	28		2		1	**31**
Alan KURILA	18	4		5	1	**28**	2				1	3	20	4		5	2	**31**
Mark BUSHELL	21	2	3	3	1	**30**						0	21	2	3	3	1	**30**
Steve HOLDEN	21	3	1	2	1	**28**	1					1	22	3	1	2	1	**29**
Paul COE	23				2	**25**	4					4	27				2	**29**

Appearances Aug 1992 - May 1998

	Start						Substitute						Total					
	L	C	T	LC	CC	Totl	L	C	T	LC	CC	Ttl	L	C	T	LC	CC	Totl
Barrington LESLIE	15		2	3	2	**22**	4			1		5	19		2	4	2	**27**
Simeon HODSON	25		1			**26**						0	25		1			**26**
Adrian FOSTER	14	2		1		**17**	6					6	20	2		1		**23**
Frankie BELFON	10	3	3	1		**17**	2		1		1	4	12	3	4	1	1	**21**
Steve LILWALL	8	4		4	1	**17**	3					3	11	4		4	1	**20**
Steve CHERRY	18					**18**						0	18					**18**
David LEWORTHY	18					**18**						0	18					**18**
Warren KELLY	11	2				**13**	4					4	15	2				**17**
Terry WILSON	9	3		2	1	**15**		1				1	9	4		2	1	**16**
Colin WEST	14					**14**	1					1	15					**15**
Mark COOPER	9				1	**10**	4		1			5	13		1		1	**15**
Shaun DIVER	2			1	2	**5**	5	1	1	2		9	7	1	1	3	2	**14**
Glyn CREASER	9	1		2	1	**13**						0	9	1		2	1	**13**
John COE	7	1	1	2	2	**13**						0	7	1	1	2	2	**13**
Guy BRANSTON	10				1	**11**	1					1	11				1	**12**
Andy FURNELL	2	1			1	**4**	6	1		1		8	8	2		1	1	**12**
Mark TUCKER	6	2	1	2		**11**						0	6	2	1	2		**11**
Mark RAWLE						**0**	8	2		1		11	8	2		1		**11**
Simon STAPLETON	7					**7**	3					3	10					**10**
David MEHEW	5					**5**	5					5	10					**10**
Andy LOMAS	6			1	1	**8**	1					1	7			1	1	**9**
Darren WATTS	5			1	2	**8**						0	5			1	2	**8**
David MORRISON	2			2		**4**	3				1	4	5			2	1	**8**
Darren HILLIER	1	1	1	2	1	**6**	1					1	2	1	1	2	1	**7**
Simon MASON	2		2	1		**5**	1				1	2	3		2	1	1	**7**
Glen FUFF	4			1	1	**6**						0	4			1	1	**6**
Chris McKENZIE	3		1	2		**6**						0	3		1	2		**6**
Kenny WEBSTER	3		1	1	1	**6**						0	3		1	1	1	**6**
Jamie BARNWELL-ED	4					**4**	1					1	5					**5**
Jamie NDAH	4					**4**	1					1	5					**5**
Malcolm NDEKWE						**0**	2		1		2	5	2		1		2	**5**
Gary CROSBY	4					**4**						0	4					**4**
Graham REED	4					**4**						0	4					**4**
Steve TAYLOR	4					**4**						0	4					**4**
Peter GREEN						**0**	3	1				4	3	1				**4**
Sammy AYORINDE	2					**2**						0	2					**2**
Matt CROSSLEY	2					**2**						0	2					**2**
Kevin SLINN	2					**2**						0	2					**2**
Lee CRANE	1	1				**2**						0	1	1				**2**
Mark JAMESON	1	1				**2**						0	1	1				**2**
Steven HEARD	1					**1**	1					1	2					**2**
David HOLMES	1					**1**	1					1	2					**2**
Craig SMITH	1					**1**	1					1	2					**2**
Danny O'SHEA	1					**1**					1	1	1				1	**2**
Andy CHAPMAN						**0**	2					2	2					**2**
Leo COTTERELL	1					**1**						0	1					**1**
Brian TALBOT					1	**1**						0					1	**1**
Craig ALLARDYCE						**0**	1					1	1					**1**
Adam CANN						**0**	1					1	1					**1**
Worrell STERLING						**0**	1					1	1					**1**
Simon RICHMOND						**0**					1	1					1	**1**
Maximum	252	24	21	27	20	**344**							252	24	21	27	20	**344**

Playing Record August 1992 - May 1998

HOME	P	W	D	L	F	A	Pts
League	126	79	27	20	306	134	264
FA Cup	14	9	2	3	29	13	
FA Trophy	14	8	3	3	30	20	
League Cup	15	12	2	1	38	14	
County Cup	12	10	1	1	41	9	
TOTAL	181	118	35	28	444	190	
AWAY							
League	126	60	28	38	226	170	208
FA Cup	10	5	2	3	17	9	
FA Trophy	7	3	1	3	10	10	
League Cup	12	4	3	5	14	20	
County Cup	8	4	1	3	13	8	
TOTAL	163	76	35	52	280	217	
TOTAL							
League	252	139	55	58	532	304	472
FA Cup	24	14	4	6	46	22	
FA Trophy	21	11	4	6	40	30	
League Cup	27	16	5	6	52	34	
County Cup	20	14	2	4	54	17	
TOTAL	**344**	**194**	**70**	**80**	**724**	**407**	

Attendance Summary August 1992 - May 1998

HOME	Total	Ave	High		Low	
League	210807	1673	5170	Kettering	201	Grantham
FA Cup	24996	1785	4214	Cardiff	301	Desborough
FA Trophy	22490	1606	4375	Woking	242	Anstey
League Cup	9256	617	1098	King's Lynn	162	Atherstone
County Cup	11423	952	2352	Kettering	113	Stewarts & Lloyds
TOTAL	278972	1541	5170	Kettering	113	Stewarts & Lloyds
AWAY						
League	113339	900	4628	Kettering	109	Forest Green
FA Cup	5884	588	1567	Boreham Wd	105	Long Buckby
FA Trophy	10119	1446	4643	Woking	123	Halesowen Harriers
League Cup	4593	383	811	Kidderminster	120	Atherstone
County Cup	5868	734	1862	Kettering	165	Long Buckby
TOTAL	139803	858	4643	Woking	105	Long Buckby
TOTAL						
League	324146	1286	5170	Kettering H	109	Forest Green A
FA Cup	30880	1287	4214	Cardiff H	105	Long Buckby A
FA Trophy	32609	1553	4643	Woking A	123	Halesowen Harrs A
League Cup	13849	513	1098	Stevenage H	120	Atherstone A
County Cup	17291	865	2352	Kettering H	113	Stewart & Lloyds H
TOTAL	**418775**	**1217**	**5170**	Kettering H	105	Long Buckby A